Amy Signs

Amy Signs

A Mother, Her Deaf Daughter, and Their Stories

Rebecca Willman Gernon and

Amy Willman

GALLAUDET UNIVERSITY PRESS
Washington, DC

Gallaudet University Press
Washington, DC 20002
http://gupress.gallaudet.edu

Library of Congress Cataloging-in-Publication Data

Gernon, Rebecca Willman.
    Amy signs : a mother, her deaf daughter, and their stories / Rebecca Willman
Gernon and Amy Willman.
        p. cm.
    ISBN 978-1-56368-537-8 (pbk. : alk. paper) — ISBN 1-56368-537-X (pbk. : alk. paper)
— ISBN 978-1-56368-538-5 (e-book) — ISBN 1-56368-538-8 (e-book)
    1. Deaf children.   2. Child rearing.   3. Mother and child.   4. Parenting.
I. Willman, Amy.   II. Title.
    HV2391.G47   2012
    362.4'20922—dc23
    [B]   2012022375

Rebecca Ruth and Amy Ruth
dedicate Amy Signs *in memory of*
Ruth Schmierer,
Mother and Grandmother

Contents

Acknowledgments   ix
Preface   xi
 1. December 1969 / *Rebecca*   1
 2. Day Two and Beyond: Waiting / *Rebecca*   9
 3. Date with Destiny / *Rebecca*   17
 4. Stunned and Numb / *Rebecca*   26
 5. Stomaching the Diagnosis / *Rebecca*   35
 6. The Mechanical Tyrant / *Rebecca*   42
 7. Starting the Climb / *Rebecca*   50
 8. Twenty Minutes of Torture / *Rebecca*   56
 9. Gibberish / *Rebecca*   61
10. Pavlov's Daughter / *Rebecca*   65
11. Hard Lessons / *Rebecca*   69
12. Gain and Loss / *Rebecca*   71
13. The Scarlet Letter / *Rebecca*   79
14. Blessings and Fellow Travelers / *Rebecca*   83
15. Terrible Twos / *Rebecca*   92
16. Miles and Moments / *Rebecca*   95
17. Respite and Renewal / *Rebecca*   104
18. On the Road Again / *Rebecca*   110
19. Ready, Aim . . . / *Rebecca*   116
20. Dreams and Reality / *Rebecca*   123
21. Pets and Playmates / *Amy*   133
22. Hearing in a Deaf World / *Rebecca*   137
23. Summer Workshop Times Two / *Rebecca*   147
24. Emptying the Nest / *Rebecca*   164
25. The Year with Few Memories / *Rebecca*   171

26. Residential Life in the Primary Dorm / *Amy*   174
27. Smooth Roads / *Rebecca*   182
28. Education, the Primary Years / *Amy*   192
29. Moving into Deaf Culture / *Rebecca and Amy*   197
30. Caution, Speed Bumps Ahead / *Rebecca*   202
31. Mainstreaming, Not for Me / *Amy*   207
32. The Decision / *Rebecca*   209
33. Deaf Child in a Hearing World / *Amy*   214
34. Tossed and Blown by Life / *Rebecca*   219
35. Middle School / *Amy*   225
36. Gaining Independence / *Rebecca*   230
37. Do You Sign? / *Amy*   236
38. Driving Miss Daisy Crazy / *Rebecca and Amy*   243
39. More Audism / *Rebecca and Amy*   252
40. Stateside Travel / *Rebecca and Amy*   255
41. Plans in Turmoil / *Rebecca and Amy*   260
42. Europe and Beyond / *Rebecca and Amy*   265
43. Making Memories, High School / *Amy*   269
44. Last Chances / *Rebecca*   274
45. The Big Question / *Rebecca and Amy*   277
46. Graduation and College Bound / *Rebecca and Amy*   281
47. Gallaudet, New Horizons / *Amy*   287
48. No Choice, Mainstreamed in 1994 / *Amy*   291
49. Deaf in the Hearing World / *Amy*   295
50. Deaf or deaf, Does It Matter? / *Amy*   300
51. Adapting to Live in Two Worlds: Hearing and Deaf / *Amy* 303
52. My Eyes Are My Ears / *Amy*   311
53. Concluding Thoughts / *Amy and Rebecca*   314

Acknowledgments

When I asked Amy if she wanted to thank anyone on our acknowledgment page she said, "No, I did all the work myself. No one helped me." Even so, she owes a debt of gratitude to her godmother Marge Beatty who was her excellent preschool Deaf educator and spiritual guide. In addition, all of the staff at the Nebraska School for the Deaf encouraged Amy to excel; they should be as proud of her accomplishments as I am. Gallaudet University did more than present Amy with a diploma after she finished her studies. Her years of involvement with the Deaf community and a variety of organizations on campus prepared her to a proud Deaf leader.

As for me, I give credit and thanks to my friend Cindy Mangers Johnson who suggested Amy and I should collaborate on a book. Her encouragement throughout this lengthy process has been a blessing. To all my fellow writers, especially Nancy Richard, Judy Creekmore, Teena Myers, the members of the Southern Christian Writers Guild, and of Realms of Fiction, led by Randy Roussell, your thoughtful critiques improved my writing. Our author photos are a product of my talented sister, Margaret Walthers.

Words can't convey my excitement when Ivey Pittle Wallace, Assistant Director, Editorial at Gallaudet University Press requested a copy of our manuscript in 2009. Her belief in the merit of our book and the editing skill of Deirdre Mullervy, Gallaudet University Managing Editor, and her staff, has made *Amy Signs* a promise fulfilled. To all my friends and family who have followed my writing progress, thank you for your support. A special thanks to my loving husband, Walt, who has the dubious honor of living with an author.

Preface

Thirty-seven years ago, after reading a book about one family's struggle with their deaf son, a story that seemed unrealistic and sugarcoated, I vowed to write a truthful book about raising a deaf child. The book would be filled with disappointment and pain, as well as hope and triumph. *Amy Signs* is that book.

Our story begins in December of 1969, years before most states required neonatal hearing tests on infants within a few days of their birth. Before 1990, most doctors relied on parents to determine if their child could hear. Even the most observant parents might not realize their child had a hearing loss until the child's lack of speech was noted at age two or three. By then, several years of crucial pre-school speech and language training were lost.

Parents who have a deaf child now should have an easier journey than we did. Neonatal testing should be conducted within a month of a child's birth. Early detection of deafness or any disability allows the parents to begin educating themselves, so the best decisions can be made for their child before school age.

But, regardless of when parents discover their child has a disability, most are overwhelmed with feelings of shock, loss, anger, sadness, guilt, and frustration. In addition, most babies with birth defects are born to parents with no obvious health problems or risk factors (www.kidshealth.org). About 90 percent of children with congenital hearing loss are born to hearing parents (www.marchofdimes.org), so deciding how best to raise and educate the child is difficult. Professionals offer suggestions based on years of clinical experience, but ultimately the parents must decide what is best for their child.

When Amy was first diagnosed as profoundly deaf, an audiologist told us that our only option was to send her to a residential school for the deaf. Several years into her education at a deaf school, Congress passed the Education for All Handicapped Children Act, which mandated that public schools make accommodations for all disabled students, including deaf students. As a result of this act, today many residential schools for deaf children, including Amy's school, the Nebraska School for the Deaf, have closed their doors. The majority of deaf and hard of hearing students now attend public schools, for better or worse.

Parents of deaf children must decide how to communicate with their child. They have two choices, which are at opposite ends of the spectrum. The first is oral communication. The deaf child wears hearing aids and is taught to lipread and speak by relying on the child's residual hearing. Oral communicators avoid the use of sign language. Advances in medical technology, particularly the cochlear implant, give parents another option: surgery. This permanent surgery may restore partial hearing to child making oral communication easier.

The second option is manual communication. Educators have devised several methods of implementing American Sign Language (ASL) into the classroom. Amy's school endorsed Total Communication; the teachers and students signed but the students also received speech training and wore hearing aids to maximize their language skills.

Before making any decisions about the education of your deaf child, parents may need to revise *their* dreams for this child. Having unrealistic expectations will frustrate you and your child. Families will still suffer heartache when the words, "your child does not hear" are spoken, but the Internet puts a world of information just a click away. Support groups and educational services can easily be located. The age of technology allows the Deaf to be fully integrated into the hearing society via captioned TV, video relay telephone systems, texting, and Skype. A variety of lighted alerting devices keep Deaf people aware of their surroundings. I would encourage any parent of a Deaf child to think long and hard before expending value time and money to make your child "normal." (Whatever that means.) Deaf people are not abnormal; they just use a different means of communication.

Amy Signs is primarily Amy's story, but as in any family, each person's life has an effect on the other members. The journey my husband Jack, son John, and Amy and I took had its ups and downs, but the overall progression was forward, even though many days it was against a stiff wind. My journey was made easier by my faith in God.

John, I'm sure, became a sensitive, caring individual because of, not in spite of, having Amy for his sister. He bonded with Amy the day she came home from the hospital. Her deafness was never an issue in their relationship. Their close bond remains even now in their adult lives. As for Amy, she's accomplished more than I ever imagined, earning not one but two college degrees. Her stubborn attitude and independence often worry me when she embarks on another adventure, but I'm her mother—that's the best excuse I can offer for my concern.

Readers will note that Amy and I have distinctly different writing styles. Mine is more emotional, while Amy's is more didactic and straightforward. Our personalities are much the same. I react to stressful situations by tensing up, gnawing my fingernails, or feeling overwhelmed. Amy, on the other hand, considers the situation and decides: "That's not my problem," or makes a decision and charges ahead.

For example, when I asked Amy to expand some sections of her writing, she sent me this e-mail: "Not everybody can write long book . . . some people write short book. What you wrote is yours and what I wrote is my kind of style."

Amy's writing style is also different from mine because English is her second language. ASL, her primary means of communication, is very expressive, but emotions are conveyed through facial gestures more so than by words. Never having heard a spoken language, converting the visual actions of ASL to written English was a challenge for both of us.

This book was an emotional experience for me because of the painful events I had to recall. Some of my memories were as fresh as if they had occurred yesterday. The choices I had to make were neither simple nor exact. I learned about deafness, Deaf culture, hearing aids, and speech therapy. I talked to other parents to help me decide which methods of communication and education were best for Amy and my family. But I always worried that I might have failed her.

During the book-writing process, I often e-mailed Amy with questions, comments, and suggestions about her writing. Her busy schedule generally kept me waiting weeks for a reply, as it did in January of 2007, when I asked: "Amy, do you feel you have missed out on a lot of life because you can't hear?" Two months later I received her response:

> Well, I never hear or understand what sound means, so it does not matter to me. Compared to people who have heard, maybe they would want to hear again, but I am just fine, so I am happy. Maybe not all deaf people are happy, but for me, I am happy. I have a job, home, friends, et cetera. The Deaf same as hearing people, some are happy, some are not. So hearing does not matter.

I believe my decisions were the best for Amy. Instead of wanting her to be hearing, I embraced her Deafness. Were my decisions right? I've hoped so for years. While writing this book with her, I gained a better understanding of her Deaf world. Knowing she is happy and content, with no reservations about my decisions, has been my greatest reward.

1

December 1969

Rebecca

An anxious sigh escapes my lips. In the cold December air, my warm breath is a small cloud that soon vanishes; my concerns do not. I remove my daughter, Amy, from her car seat, position her on my left hip and trudge through ankle-deep snow toward the doctor's office. The wind is cold and raw; so are my thoughts.

"Come on, John." I extend my right hand to my almost three-year-old son. Lugging my purse, he runs to catch up with me.

Pushing the door open with my body, we enter an unfamiliar waiting room packed with adults. Heads turn toward us. I scan the room for a vacant seat. An old man seated between two empty chairs nods at me and moves over to make room for us. I smile my thanks.

"Sit down there, John." I motion to the empty chairs and walk to the receptionist's desk.

John climbs onto a chair and squirms to the back of the deep seat. The toes of his rubber boots jut toward the ceiling. He is a compliant child, happy to do what I ask without question. In public he is quiet, almost to the point of shyness, but at home he talks and talks.

The warmth of the office is stifling. While holding Amy, I loosen my wool scarf and unbutton my coat. "I'm Rebecca Willman. Amy's here to see Dr. James Proffitt." The receptionist nods and hands me a clipboard. I add my name to the long list and retreat to the vacant chair.

I place Amy in the chair to remove her snowsuit. When I pull off her knit cap, static electricity sends her wispy blonde hair skyward. I smooth the flyaway hair and pull her floral tee shirt over the top of her pink slacks. I help John unzip his jacket while scanning the room for a coat rack; there isn't one.

"Scoot forward a bit, John."

He uses the wooden armrests to pull himself to the edge of the seat, dislodging clumps of snow from his boots. I shove his jacket and Amy's snowsuit behind him, and then I sit holding Amy on my lap. She squirms to be free, but I do not release her to crawl on a floor covered with snowy footprints and muddy smudges.

The old man beside me tickles Amy under her chin. "What's his name? How old is he?"

"*Her* name is Amy, and *she's* eleven months old." My exasperated voice tells him he is not the first person to mistake Amy for a boy. Most people pay no attention to her lace trimmed shirts, but instead focus on her short hair, which has never been cut, and assume she's a boy. Amy inherited my fine thin hair, with one difference. I'm a brunette; she's a blonde, so she appears bald.

"Sorry." He picks up a worn magazine.

"That's okay. A lot of people think she's a boy."

A woman in a starched white uniform appears in the waiting room. She runs her finger down the list of people on the sign-in sheet. "Mrs. Carstens. Mr. Beckman."

Two people stand, gather their belongings, and disappear down the hall. The nurse scans the room until our eyes meet. She consults the list again. "Rebecca Willman."

I rise, grab my purse and Amy's small diaper bag. "John, get the coats, please."

I stare at the nurse's back as she leads us to a small examination room. "The doctor will be with you in a minute." She exits, pulling the door shut.

Today my worries, not my claustrophobia, press upon me. The tiny room has two chairs, an examination table, a desk, and a metal tray on a stand. The desk is lined with glass jars of tongue depressors, cotton balls, and swabs. An odd assortment of metallic instruments lies on the metal tray.

John sits on the edge of a chair and swings his boots. The swaying boots distracts me momentarily from peering at the metal tools. As I rise to look at the unfamiliar medical equipment, the door springs open.

"Hello," Dr. Proffitt says. The nurse who ushered us to this room stands behind him.

Dr. Proffitt is Grand Island, Nebraska's, only ophthalmologist and ENT doctor. If he wore a red velvet suit with plenty of padding, he could pass for Santa Claus. Under his snow-white hair, black-rimmed glasses perch on his nose. His voice is soft; his gaze filled with solemn concern. He and my mother- and father-in-laws are friends, but I have never met him. He looks over the top of his glasses at Amy, cups her chin in his hand, and tips her face toward him. He pats John's legs and says, "You look just like your Daddy."

"Yes, he does," I reply.

"Well. What can I do for you today?" He asks.

I take a breath and blurt, "I don't think Amy hears, I took her to Dr. Anderson, he's our family doctor, and he said he wasn't qualified to determine if Amy has a hearing problem or not, and he said I should have you examine her, so I made an appointment and here we are."

"Okay, put Amy on the exam table so I can take a look in her ears."

As he examines Amy's ears with various tools, my nervous chatter fills the room. Dr. Proffitt nods and says "Uh huh." When I gasp for breath, he asks about Amy's birth and medical history. I rattle off the requested information.

CLANG! "Sorry." The nurse grabs the heavy metal tuning fork she dropped on the metal tray and nestles it into a foam slot in a wooden box. She moves to the door.

"I don't see anything physically wrong with Amy's inner and outer ears," Dr. Proffitt says, "but, *she does not hear.*"

On December 12, 1969 at 10:15 a.m. those four words ring louder than the dropped tuning fork. Moments ago my voice filled the room, now my tongue cleaves to the roof of my mouth.

While Dr. Proffitt explains his examination, I recall the countless times Amy moved her lips in silent imitation to my chatter or was unresponsive to loud noises. *What kind of mother am I? I should have known she didn't hear after the Fourth of July.* Cherry bombs and whistling rockets exploded near us and Amy slept through the entire fireworks display. People around us couldn't believe she didn't wake up. *That was my wake-up call and I missed it.* Stories my mother told me about visiting the Chicago School for the Deaf when she was a child emerge from my subconscious. "Deaf children don't speak because they can't hear their language," she told me. *I'm an idiot. I should have known this months ago.*

"Rebecca." Dr. Proffitt jars me from my self-persecuting reverie to the stark reality of the examination room. "You should have my diagnosis confirmed by an audiologist."

Confirmed? Isn't hearing bad news once enough?

"Do you want me to send a letter to the university's audiology department requesting an appointment for a hearing test?"

Usually ready with a quick response, in this moment I'm locked in a slow-motion world, speechless. The nurse's pen is poised to write my response on Amy's chart. John has added thumb sucking to his boot swinging behavior. Dr. Proffitt removes a small flashlight from his shirt pocket and flicks the light off and on. Amy reaches for the light, and he gives it to her. My answer will set the room in motion. Seconds pass. I force my dry, paralyzed tongue to move.

"Yes."

"Good." Dr. Proffitt nods to his nurse. She scribbles something on Amy's chart. He lifts Amy from the exam table and hands her to me, taking the flashlight in the process. Before exiting he says, "Tell J.W. and Esther 'Hello' from me the next time you see them."

"I will." J.W. and Esther are my husband Jack's parents. I could pass Dr. Proffitt's greeting to them fifteen minutes from now if I stopped at Willman's Grocery on my way home, but I've no desire to utter "she does not hear" in a busy store.

Outside I suck cold air into my lungs. An hour ago the sun shone; now the sky is sullen and grey. A light snow is falling, covering the dirty, two-week-old snow with a pristine blanket. *This could be a sign. Don't give up hope, Rebecca. Dr. Proffitt could be wrong.*

On the short drive home I change my mind and decide to stop at Willman's grocery store, to pick up a few items, and tell Jack about the examination, but my mind is numb, bogged down with processing Amy's diagnosis. Lost in thought, I drive past the grocery and arrive home, wondering how many stop signs and red lights I ignored.

Once inside our duplex, I contemplate calling Jack, but he is usually too busy to take phone calls. The news won't change. I'll tell him when he comes home. Before I fix the children lunch, I pull a baby gate across the open stairwell to the basement. I spoon mounds of Spaghetti-Os on two plates and warm jars of baby food. John enjoys his lunch; mine slips down my throat, untasted. The meal finished, I wipe a cherry cobbler smile off Amy's face and remove her from the high chair. She crawls toward the baby gate.

I turn her on the polished linoleum floor so she now crawls toward the living room. The gate is attached to sheet rock. If she pushed her twenty pounds against it, it could give way, allowing her to tumble onto the landing two steps below, or God forbid, down the entire flight of stairs to the concrete basement floor. I move her high chair in front of the gate, forming a second line of defense.

"Can I watch *Sesame Street?*" John wipes his hands on a kitchen towel.

"Sure. It's on channel twelve." I stack the dishes on the counter. I consider leaving them there until I wash dishes tonight, but my compulsion for neatness won't allow this. I fill the sink with water and squirt in Ivory liquid.

As Amy crawls to the living room, the knees of her pink slacks collect food particles off the kitchen floor. She crawls to where John is seated on the floor sucking his thumb and clutching his blanket and stuffed dog. With a soft pop, he removes his thumb and says, "Look, Amy, it's the Cookie Monster."

Amy shifts from her knees onto her butt beside John and grabs his stuffed dog.

"No! It's mine." Ever the diplomat, he extends a corner of his blanket. She pushes it away and reaches for the dog again. John rises, keeping a firm grasp on his dog and blanket and finds her pink cat pillow. "Here, take this. It's yours."

Amy grabs the pillow and stuffs her index and middle fingers in her mouth. John giggles at the antics of Cookie Monster. He leans over Amy, shakes his body and growls. "Cookie." Even with two fingers in her mouth, Amy smiles.

I wash the dishes, stack them in the cupboard, align the silverware in the drawer, close the cupboard doors, wipe down the counters, sweep the floor, and join John and Amy. Oscar the Grouch is grumbling on TV. I'm a silent zombie on the couch.

The rest of the afternoon, Dr. Proffitt's diagnosis whirls in my brain. At last, Jack arrives home. I spew the result of Amy's examination as he removes his coat and stuffs his gloves in the pocket. I speak the words, "Dr. Proffitt says Amy does not hear," to the back of his head, not to his freckled face.

He tosses his coat on the couch and turns. His brow is wrinkled, his brown eyes filled with confusion. He stares as if I have spoken gibberish, and then picks up the newspaper and sits in our recliner.

"We have to take Amy to the University of Nebraska in Lincoln so an audiologist can test her hearing." I set a tossed salad and several bottles of dressing on the table.

Jack looks up from the paper, astonished. "I can't take a day off from work to do that." He buries his head in the sports page.

Why not? This is your daughter! You work for your parents. I don't see why you can't take a day off to do this. It's important! I don't speak my thoughts. Three years of marriage has taught me begging a workaholic not to work is pointless.

I remove a pizza from the oven. "Supper's ready."

Jack puts the paper down. "Good. I'm hungry."

Jack and I watch the ten o'clock news in silence, propped against pillows in bed. The TV gives the room an eerie blue glow. After the sports report, Jack snaps off the TV. The streetlight filters through the curtains casting muted shadows. The space between us is narrow, but that gap keeps our thoughts and feelings separate, unspoken. Jack curls onto his side, facing the wall. He sleeps this way most nights, but tonight I see his back as an impenetrable wall. I want to tell him about the doctor's visit again, hoping that this time the story will have a different ending. I stare at his back, angry and envious. After standing on his feet ten hours preparing produce, lifting heavy boxes, and dealing with customers at a large grocery store, sleep comes easy for Jack; tonight is no exception. *It's not fair. I'm a nervous wreck, and you're sleeping like you haven't a care in the world!*

I rise and shuffle to the bedroom John and Amy share. Our duplex has two large bedrooms. There is plenty of room for a crib, twin bed, dresser, rocking chair, and boxes of toys in their room that I painted a bright yellow. Circus-print curtains cover the windows. A nightlight illuminates the room. John has kicked off his blankets and is sprawled across his twin bed. His feet, encased in Winnie-the-Pooh pajamas, dangle off the edge. I scoot him to the center of his bed, dislodging his thumb from his mouth. I pull a blanket over him and brush his dark curls from his brow. He rolls onto his side and puts his thumb into his mouth; the rhythmic sucking lulls him into a deeper sleep.

On the other side of the room, Amy sleeps in her crib. I smooth her hair and wonder if she will ever have hair as thick as John's. Amy and my younger sister, Susan, were both born on January 23, but nineteen years apart. Amy and her aunt share more than a birthday. Each opted to suck the first and second fingers of their right hand, with one disgusting difference: Amy shoves her ring finger up her nose. I reach to remove the offending nose-picking finger as I have done countless times. For an instant life seems normal, and then Dr. Proffitt's words, *She does not hear,* pierce my memory. Instead of pulling the finger from my daughter's nose, I sink into the rocking chair beside her crib. The rocker squeaks my internal plea to God: *Why? Why? Why?* God is silent.

I drift back to my junior year in college, five short years ago. My girlfriends and I were discussing our dreams of marriage and children. We had idealistic views of fidelity and child rearing. Someone broached the subject of having a handicapped child. I remember my comment as clearly as if I had said it five minutes ago. "I could deal with any kind of handicap but mental retardation. Everything else can be overcome." The old adage, "Be careful what you wish for," springs to mind. *Oh no! I brought this on myself by my own words.* The rocker squeaks: *Why? Why? Why?*

I am afraid to ask God, "Why me?" I fear He's punishing me and if I press Him for answers, He'll remind me of sins I want to forget.

If this is my cross to bear, take it away. I don't want it. I want the life I had yesterday, the one I had before the visit to Dr. Proffitt.

I drift into a groggy sleep. In my dreams, monsters chase me, snapping at my heels, bent on devouring me. I jerk awake, disappointed I wasn't eaten. I look at Amy. Her cheeks are rosy. The fingers on her right hand droop away from her lips; a trickle of saliva shines in the dim light. I lift her blanket and touch her chubby feet that extend beyond the hem of her pink nightgown. She appears perfect. How can she be deaf? What am I going to do? Who can I talk to? I don't know anyone who can't hear.

I return to the rocker. It chants. *Why? Why? Why?* I slip into fitful slumber.

Three hours later, I am betrayed by the sun. December 13 dawns bright and sunny. The words *she does not hear* did not destroy the world; only my existence is in turmoil. I rise and stare in the mirror. The face resembles me, but sorrow and worry have altered my youthful face. The vacant eyes in the mirror blink; I must still be alive.

"Mommy, I'm hungry."

I know it's John. Amy doesn't make any noise except to cry or laugh. *She does not hear* is my first conscious thought. I squeeze my eyes shut and plug my ears with nail-bitten fingers to banish the words. A tug on my nightgown breaks my concentration.

"When are we going to eat?" John asks.

"Right now, John." I shuffle to the kitchen, pour milk into a bowl of Cap'n Crunch and set it before him. I hold the box of cereal, confused, unable to decide if I should place it in the cupboard or leave it on the counter.

"Juice, Mommy. I want juice now, please." John's plea interrupts my ruminations.

I pull a container of orange juice from the refrigerator and set a glass before him. "Be careful. Don't spill it."

2

Day Two and Beyond: Waiting
Rebecca

"Can I have more Cap'n Crunch?" John extends his bowl. The milk splashes onto the floor.

"Sure." I ignore the spilled milk, jerk open the lazy-susan cupboard door and spin the shelf. Cheerios. Froot Loops. Oatmeal. No Cap'n Crunch. *Where's the Cap'n Crunch? I just had it.* I run my hand through my uncombed hair and spin the shelf again. *It's not here.* The counters in our kitchen are uncluttered, the way my perfectionism demands. A mixer and toaster oven are the only items in sight. *What in the world did I do with it?* "How about Froot Loops instead?"

"Good, Mommy. I like them. The purple ones are my favorite." His hazel eyes watch as I fill his bowl.

As I replace the cereal box on the lazy-susan shelf, I hear the rhythmic sound of Amy shaking her crib rail in an effort to release the locked side of the crib. "Amy's awake. Keep eating while I get your sister dressed." I shuffle toward their bedroom.

"Wait, Mommy. I need milk on my cereal."

"Sorry, John. I forgot." I open the refrigerator and am greeted by a box of Cap'n Crunch. *Geez, I'm losing my mind.*

An hour later, Amy has been fed, I've vacuumed the living room, swept the bathroom, bedroom, and kitchen floors, and am ready to start the laundry or dusting. Never one to waste time, I decide to toss a load of clothes in the washer and dust while the clothes wash.

John and Amy are occupied playing with giant Legos in the living room, but I can't leave Amy there while I take the laundry to the basement because of the flimsy baby gate. "Come here, Amy." I sit on the couch and extend my arms. She crawls to me; her white leotards bunch around her knees. "Stand up, come on. You can do it." I pat the cushion on the couch to encourage her. She pulls herself upright by grasping the edge of the couch and bounces on her chubby legs. Her blue-flowered dress, which matches her eyes, sways. She smiles her six-toothed grin. I lift her onto my lap and squeeze her in a bear-hug. Her hands push against me. I loosen my grasp, carry her to the bedroom, and put her in the crib. She howls as I pull up the crib rail and latch it. "I'll be back soon. I have to put clothes in the washer." Before I leave the room she is shaking the rail, anxious to be free.

I take a deep breath, grab the diaper pail and an armful of dirty clothes, and walk toward the basement stairs. Amy's cries follow me. "John, go play in your bedroom to keep Amy company until I come up from the basement." John stops what he is doing without question and runs to entertain Amy. As I pull open the baby gate, I hear his soothing chatter; the shaking of the crib rail ceases.

As I sort the clothes in our unfinished basement, I remember the day I brought Amy home from the hospital; John was almost two. I'd heard stories about older siblings mistreating younger ones and feared John might hurt Amy, so I bought a playpen. When I arrived home, I sat on the couch and laid Amy across my thighs so I could supervise John's first encounter with her. When I pulled back the blanket, he leaned over her tiny, squirming body and exclaimed, "My sister. My sister." His face beamed as he stroked her hand. John soon became Amy's guardian and defender. The playpen was used once and then sold at a garage sale.

I shove clothes in the washer, add detergent, and stare through the basement window above the washer. Snow is drifting against the glass. I don't have a dryer. I'll have to hang the clothes in the basement. They'd freeze in the clothes-basket before I could get them hung on the lines outside.

I trudge upstairs, spring Amy from her crib prison, and begin the household chore I hate the most: dusting. I lift the lamp from the end table, and swish my dust cloth over the table. *She does not hear,* accompanies flying dust. I raise the cover over the piano keys. The black and white keys play octaves of *she does not hear.* The ashes from Jack's ashtray flutter into the wastebasket along with *she does not hear.* I snap the lid of the wastebasket closed; the ashes stay inside, but *she does not hear* seeps out.

Jack will not be home for lunch until one o'clock today, but John and Amy's active bodies are hungry long before then. At noon, I set John's lunch on the table and put Amy in her high chair. I thrust a spoonful of creamed chicken and rice from a baby food jar into her mouth. She spits the offending lumps on her tray. I wipe the mess from the tray, but *she does not hear* remains.

The meal finished, John and Amy return to the living room. I wash their dishes, leaving the sink full of water for Jack's lunch dishes. Amy watches as John builds a block tower. Once completed, he kicks the tower. As it falls, he and Amy roll on the floor with laughter. The storm door opens.

"Daddy!" John runs to greet his father.

"What have you and your sister been doing?" He tosses his coat on a chair.

"Playing with blocks. I rode my tricycle downstairs. Mommy hung up clothes and Amy crawled on the basement floor and got her knees all dirty." He follows Jack into the kitchen.

"Good. How did you do on the trike?" Jack sits at the table, tilting his chair against the wall. I set his lunch before him. He drops the chair legs to the floor.

"Good. I can go faster now." John stands beside his father. "Wanna see?"

"No, I have to go back to work after I eat. Maybe I can see you ride it tonight." He grabs a paper napkin from the holder. "Did you eat, Rebecca?"

"No." I set my lunch on the table. "John, *Sesame Street* is on. You and Amy watch it while Daddy and I talk, okay?"

Jack and I say grace while John and Amy enjoy Bert and Ernie. Weeks ago we decided not to alarm our friends and family with our suspicion that Amy didn't hear until we had her examined, but we agreed our parents should be informed. Jack's head is bent over his plate. "Well?" I say to his brown hair.

"Well, what?" He mumbles through a mouthful of a toasted cheese sandwich.

"Did you tell your mom and dad about Amy's examination?"

"Yeah." He reaches for his soup spoon.

I wait. Silence. "What did they say?"

Jack stirs his soup. A spiral of steam follows his spoon. "You know my dad, he never says much, but he seemed worried. Mom said to get a second opinion. She thinks we're overreacting. She said . . ." He blows on a spoon of tomato soup and shoves it in his mouth. He swallows and exhales. "Wow! The soup's hot."

"What else did your mom say?" I lean forward, anxious for a full report.

Jack bites into his sandwich. "She said just because Amy doesn't talk yet that doesn't mean anything. Amy's only eleven months old. Maybe she's a late bloomer."

I sit upright. "Maybe, but Amy doesn't even babble. John spoke several words when he was her age." I rise and grab the saucepan from the stove. "Do you want any more soup?"

Jack nods. I pour the remaining soup in his bowl and wash the pan. I shake water from my hands before grabbing the metal saucepan lid from the stove. Even so, it slips from my wet hand and clatters to floor, rolling on its rim several times filling our small kitchen with its metallic rings.

John turns toward the kitchen and shouts, "What was that?"

Amy, whose back is to the kitchen, does not even twitch a muscle.

"A lid, John. I dropped a lid. It's nothing."

"It was a big noise." He returns to *Sesame Street*.

"You see what I mean, Jack?" I toss the lid into the sink. Water splashes across the counter. I wipe it off with a paper towel and toss it into the trash.

Less than a month ago I'd written my mother a letter detailing my concern about Amy's hearing. Mother's response surprised me. She wrote, "Rebecca, you know I never tell you how to raise your family, but now I must. If you think there is something wrong with Amy, don't sit around and do nothing. Take her to a doctor now. Better safe than sorry."

"I think my mother was right." I sit facing Jack. "I'd rather be branded a worrywart by your mom than kick myself later."

Jack shrugs. "Do what you want to do." He pushes away from the table. "I have to leave." He clumps across the kitchen floor and stoops to kiss the top of Amy's head. She looks up, surprised, unaware he had approached her. He tousles John's hair and grabs his coat. "I'll be home late tonight. It's my night to close the store."

Cold air rushes into the house as he opens the door. "Bye, Daddy."

"Bye, John." The storm door shuts, sweeping a skiff of snow onto the doorsill. John presses his nose against the storm door glass melting a small hole in the frost.

"Shut the door, John. It's cold." I carry Amy to their bedroom. "Come on, John. Nap time." As if programmed, John pops his thumb in his mouth and drags his blanket toward the bedroom.

As I put Amy in her crib, John asks, "Will you play music?" I wind his music box and Brahms *Lullaby* fills the room. I pull the door closed as I leave.

She does not hear urges me to call my mother. My voice quivers when I tell her Jack won't go to the audiologist appointment in Lincoln with me.

"Are you sure?" Her disbelief is apparent.

"Yes. I asked him a couple of times. He had all kinds of reasons. Monday and Friday he has to unload the truck from the warehouse. Tuesday he designs the newspaper advertisement. Wednesday and Thursday he stocks the shelves. I'll go by myself, it's no big deal." *So what else is new?* I love being a mother, and until today, the fact that raising John and Amy has been solely my responsibility hasn't bothered me, but now I need Jack's support.

"Rebecca, I don't think you should go there alone. I could go with you." Although a statement, Mother's voice is questioning, asking if I would like her company.

"That would be nice, but . . ." My voice fades as I ponder the logistics. Mother doesn't drive. My parents live in Beatrice, forty miles south of the university; we live one hundred miles west. Including her would add eighty miles to the trip.

Sensing my dilemma, Mother says, "Why don't you stay here the night before Amy's appointment? We'd love to have you visit. The next day I could go to Lincoln with you and keep John entertained while you and Amy talk to the doctor."

I agree. "Dr. Proffitt's sending a letter to the university today. As soon as I know when Amy's appointment is, I'll let you know."

We quickly change the subject. Christmas is less than two weeks away, but even a conversation about that usually happy subject is difficult. While Mother tells me about a new cookie recipe she plans to try, I interrupt with, "I need to go. I have laundry to fold."

"Give John and Amy a hug from me." Her voice cracks.

Her sorrow grieves me. I hold the receiver until the dial tone stirs me to hang up.

December 22; a week has passed. Each afternoon while John and Amy nap, I pace in front of our picture window, watching for the postman. When he approaches, I rush outside without my coat and stand shivering by our curbside mailbox. Today he hands me a stack of envelopes: Christmas cards, junk mail, and the electric bill. Nothing from the university.

Yesterday I borrowed all the books our public library had on deafness. There wasn't much. The medical information was more than ten years old. I'm thwarted in my quest for information. Now I'm reading a biography of Helen Keller. I thank God that Amy is not blind and deaf.

December slips off the calendar into oblivion. This was Amy's first Christmas, but I have no recollection of what we ate for dinner or what gifts we exchanged. The New Year arrives, crisp and cold. Ten days into the new year I still have not received a letter from the university. During the day, for fleeting moments when I am occupied with chores, I forget *she does not hear*, but at night *she does not hear* keeps me awake. In two weeks, Amy will celebrate her first birthday. John walked at nine months; Amy crawls and makes a few attempts to stand. I add her inability to walk to my list of worries.

After her nap, I encourage Amy to walk by standing her upright and holding my arms out to her. She plops on her diapered behind each time. The telephone rings. Amy drops to her knees and crawls across the room to play with John.

"Hello."

"Rebecca, how are you doing?" My neighbor Kathy asks.

"Fine," I lie. "How was your Christmas?"

I twirl the phone cord around my fingers as Kathy relates a lengthy story about Christmas with their two young sons at her parents. I gnaw a ragged cuticle while she details the toys she and her husband gave the boys.

"That's nice." I've lost track of what she's saying. I hope my comment is appropriate.

"Rebecca, you don't know how *lucky* you are to have a son and *a daughter*. We don't plan to have more children and I hoped our second child would be a girl. You are so lucky to have a daughter. You don't know how lucky you are."

Lucky, lucky, lucky! My brain mocks me. I long to scream, "Shut up! You're the lucky one! You have two, normal, healthy children. You have all the luck!" Instead, I listen as Kathy drones on about having two sons. I seethe in silence. At last the conversation ends.

Rebecca, if you're this upset before you're even sure Amy is deaf, what will you be like if the audiologist confirms she's deaf? Then I recall Dr. Proffitt's nurse dropping the tuning fork on the metal tray. She wasn't clumsy. That was a test, and Amy failed. Amy paid no attention to the noise. *Stop kidding yourself. You knew right then and there Amy didn't hear. When will you accept it? The trip to the audiologist will only confirm what you have known for months.*

Unable to wait any longer, I use my shaking fingers to dial the Audiology Department at the university. A female answers. When I ask about Amy's appointment, she replies with disinterest, "We're in the middle of semester break. Call back in two weeks."

I can't wait another two weeks for an appointment. I refrain from screaming, "How can you do this to me? This is my daughter you're talking about here! Don't you understand I'm going nuts?"

I squelch my anger and frustration, and say as sweetly as possible, "Perhaps you could make an exception this time? I need to hire a babysitter for my son, and it's hard to find one on short notice." I pray that God will forgive me for this lie. She says nothing. "I'd really appreciate it." Silence. "Are you a student at the university?" I ask.

"Yes." Her response is filled with caution.

"I was a student at the university four years ago. My husband too. His fraternity is a block from your office, Beta Sigma Psi. Are you familiar with it?"

"No. I don't have much to do with frat rats and sorority girls. I'm a GDI." Her tone is relaxed, but guarded.

"I was one of those dang independents also. I lived in Selleck Quad. My folks never would have paid for me to join a sorority, and I probably wouldn't have fit in anyway."

"I know what you mean." Her tone is sympathetic.

"So, how about giving a former GDI a break?" I scan my fingernails, deciding which one to bite.

"All right, I'll make an exception. But don't tell anyone." I hear pages being flipped. "What about February 23 and 24?"

"We have to be there for two days?" I jerk my little finger from my lip; a drop of blood oozes near the cuticle.

"Yes. Dr. Zimmer likes to test young children on two consecutive days to be sure the results are accurate." Her voice is once again businesslike.

I take the appointment and thank her. Next, I inform both sets of grandparents. My parents react with concern and comfort, Jack's with disbelief and denial.

Seven weeks to wait.

3

Date with Destiny

Rebecca

Packing the paraphernalia that two toddlers require for a trip demands organization, a skill I possess, and patience, a skill I don't have this morning. I want this trip to be perfect. I must do everything right, because everything about the visit to Dr. Zimmer seems so wrong. Underwear. I need underwear. I jerk open a dresser drawer with such force it comes off its track, tipping its contents on the floor. "Just what I need." I fling underwear into my suitcase, and jostle the drawer onto its track and slam it shut. "Ouch!" I suck my index finger for an instant to lessen the pain.

In the next room, Amy shakes her crib rail. John is to be keeping her company, but her behavior indicates he's not with her. "John, where are you?" I stuff my cosmetic bag into the suitcase and struggle to secure the clasps.

"Right here," John replies.

"Where?" John's response is muffled by my grunt of frustration. One lock snaps shut, the other is obstinate. I lean on the suitcase. It surrenders under my weight and clicks shut. With the suitcase in one hand and the high chair under my other arm, I shuffle toward the front door. As I enter the hall, the tray falls off the high chair, nicking the wall before clattering to the floor. John, bundled in his winter coat and hat, is standing by the front door, holding his blanket and Pooh bear.

"What are you doing there, John? Get out of my way." My voice is sharp, full of tension, fueled by tomorrow's worries.

"I'm ready to go see Granmere and Grandpa." My scowl does not dislodge his smile.

"I told you to entertain your sister. Now go play with her." I nudge the storm door open with my shoulder. A blast of frigid air whips around me. Patches of hard-packed snow on the steps crunch as I tread on them, breaking into smaller pieces, like miniature icebergs calving off a glacier. I hurry along the shoveled sidewalk to the car, anxious to unload my burden and return to the warm house.

Minutes later, after a quick scan of the house for forgotten items, I strap John and Amy into their identical car seats and back out of the driveway. I check my watch. Nine o'clock. Right on schedule. The winter sun glares off the snowy landscape. I slip on my sunglasses as I approach the on-ramp to eastbound Interstate 80. In less than three hours, I'll arrive at my parents' home, just in time for lunch.

The Nebraska landscape in January is bleak, barren, and brown. A tumbleweed escapes the grasp of a snow fence, rolls across the highway, and bounces out of sight. We whiz past miles of corn stubble where fat cattle nose away the snow, searching for corn husks to supplement their diet of hay. On several hills, the wind has blown away the snow, exposing a green mat of winter wheat to the harsh elements. I promised to call Jack tomorrow night after Amy's first day of tests, but perhaps I'll call him tonight, to let him know we arrived. *No, he knows where we are. Besides he won't be home until late, and I'll be asleep by then since we have an early appointment tomorrow in Lincoln.* I'm kidding myself about sleeping; insomnia has plagued me for weeks. *On no! The high chair tray. I left it in the hall. Well, too bad. I'm not going back for it.*

The conversation I had several weeks ago with Esther, my mother-in-law, surfaces. "You're overreacting," she said as I stacked plates from Amy's birthday celebration in the sink. "There's nothing wrong with Amy."

"Maybe," I countered, "but normal children say a word or two before they are a year old. John said 'dada,' 'cookie,' and several other words by his first birthday. Amy never makes a sound, except to cry or laugh."

"You shouldn't compare Amy to John. Children develop at their own pace. Amy's fine." Esther picked up a dishtowel. "She'll be talking soon enough. All three of my boys developed at different rates. Don't worry." Esther smiled. I was not comforted or convinced.

I remind her about the noisy Fourth of July celebration. "Amy slept through the entire display."

"That doesn't mean anything. She's just a sound sleeper. You worry too much."

"Yesterday I dropped a skillet. She was less than two feet from me and didn't turn —"

"Where do these plates go?" Esther asked.

"In that cupboard." Esther turned to put the plates away; I shook my head. We've had similar conversation in the past few weeks, all with the same results.

How will Amy's hearing problem affect her life and ours? I don't know. I've had no exposure to people with a hearing loss. Two months ago I was not prepared to hear Dr. Proffitt say, "She does not hear." I didn't ask any pertinent questions. I will not sit like a stone tomorrow. *Let's see. Tomorrow, we'll see the doctor. He'll run some tests, and then he'll say . . .* My imagination is stumped, dumbfounded, unable to picture what the audiologist will say or how I will react.

Nine o'clock, February 23. The Temple Building, a massive maroon brick structure, looms in front of us, a monolith on the corner. Huge concrete pillars soar upward past two floors of windows, dwarfing the entrance, a set of double doors at the top of steep stairs.

I carry Amy, and Mother assists John by holding his hand. After opening the heavy wooden door, I discover we're on the second floor. Bare fluorescent light bulbs flickering high above glare upon the worn wooden floor and illuminate scuffed walls. A framed directory indicates the Speech and Hearing Department waiting room is to our right.

We walk past closed doors. Voices within tell me students are listening to lectures. The waiting room is empty. Sunlight streaming through the windows makes the room inviting compared to the shabby hall. John selects a chair near the huge windows and climbs to his knees to watch the traffic outside. Mother sits beside him, her arm ready to catch him should he lean backwards. I sit on the opposite side of the room near the door holding Amy. I feel dwarf-like under the high ceiling.

I scan the room for something to count, a behavior that calms my racing mind. I look up. No ceiling tiles. A cramp seizes my neck and shoots down my spine. I hunch my shoulders, inhale, and hold my breath a few seconds before exhaling, but I'm unable to relax. Six windows. Fourteen chairs. The olive vinyl on three of the seats is split. Two tables. Amy squirms on my lap; I rub her back, a gesture that relaxes her. Floor tiles! Tan and brown squares checkerboard the floor. I caution myself not to cheat by counting the number of squares in one row and multiplying it by the tiles in the opposite direction. I decide to count the tan tiles first. *One, two, three.*

My tongue is swollen and dry, swallowing is difficult. *Eleven, twelve, thirteen.* Maybe there is a water fountain in the hall. *Don't move, Rebecca. If you leave this spot, you'll miss the appointment. Thirty-six, thirty-se—what's that?* I lean forward. It's a white tile where a tan one should be. It could be a sign of hope.

Fifty-one, Fifty-two. I wipe my sweaty palms on my slacks. *Sixty-five.* A large table obscures several tiles. I debate if I should guess how many tiles are under the table or skip that area. *Sixty-five.* The wrong choice could result in a bizarre cosmic curse on me and Amy. *Sixty-five. What should I do? Sixty-five. Six—*

"Mrs. Willman?" A voice spares me a fateful decision.

"Yes." A young graduate student introduces herself and beckons me to follow. I stand and realize I have already forgotten her name.

"Where are you going?" John asks. Mother's arm snaps to attention.

"Taking Amy to see the doctor. You stay here with Granmere."

John accepts my answer without protest, but to ensure he does not run after me, Mother says, "Look what I have, John." She opens her purse and retrieves a small bag filled with miniature plastic farm animals. She nods to me, a comforting gesture to indicate John will be fine.

I follow the grad student to the basement. Its decor is like the second floor, dismal and depressing, except the ceiling is low. My claustrophobia is aroused. She leads us to a small, windowless room with three student desks, each with a large flat arm on one side for note taking. They are not suitable for a person holding a child, but I squeeze into the chair, because I don't want Amy crawling on the floor sprinkled with paper, dust bunnies, gum wrappers, and broken pencils. Once seated, she pulls a paper and pen from a drawer and fires questions at me checking off my answers with large slashing motions.

"Did you have a difficult pregnancy?"

"No."

"Was Amy's delivery normal?" She shakes her pen and scratches it on the paper.

"Yes." My voice is robotic.

"Was she ever sick?" She pulls open a drawer and grabs another pen.

"No."

"Had a high fever?"

"No." Another slash across the page.

"Are you Rh negative?" She brushes her blond hair out of her eyes. Her roots are dark.

This question can't be answered with one word. I swallow so my voice will not sound strained. "I'm not sure. I had a blood test when I was pregnant, but the test was inconclusive. To be on the safe side, my doctor considered me Rh negative."

"Was she transfused at birth?" She scribbles words and makes a small round circle instead of a period at the end of her comment.

"No."

Her voice changes from clinical to one of genuine interest. "What makes you think she doesn't hear?"

I clear my throat and lick my lips; my dry tongue makes a clicking sound. "Amy never vocalizes. Loud noises don't startle her. The only sounds she makes are crying and laughing."

"Hmm."

The grilling over, Amy and I are led to a different small room. "Wait here. I'll be back in a minute." She closes the door.

Foam with protruding bumps covers the entire room, including the door and ceiling. My feet sink into deep carpet. A huge mirror covers part of one wall. A small table with two chairs faces the mirror. Not certain if I am to sit or stand, I wait for instruction. I cough. The sound is dull and flat, absorbed into the foam. I'm trapped in total silence with my claustrophobia.

The door opens; I move to avoid being struck. The young woman enters and takes Amy from my arms. "Pull the door shut on your way out," she says.

My "okay" is muted by Amy's wail. Amy strains to free herself from unfamiliar arms. I back toward the door. Her howl increases. "I think she'd be calmer if I stayed in the room."

The woman sits at the small table facing the mirror. Amy strains and bucks against her grasp. Her crying has turned her face red. The woman speaks to the wall, "Can she stay here?"

Who is she talking to?

"Yes." A deep male voice booms into the room. "I'll have someone bring a chair."

Seeing my confusion, the woman points to a speaker concealed in the foam bumps above the mirror. "It's a one-way mirror. Dr. Zimmer is on the other side."

I chuckle to myself. *Pay no attention to the man behind the curtain, or in this case, the audiology wizard behind the mirror.* I feel as out of place here as Dorothy did in Oz. The door opens, an arm thrusts a folding chair into the room. I grab it.

"Sit in the back of the room," the baritone voice orders.

I offer to calm Amy before sitting, and the student sighs her relief. I hug Amy, rub her back and sit her on the small chair by the student. I kneel. "Mommy's right here." Amy watches as I retreat to the back of the room. When I sit, the squeak of the chair is absorbed into the foam.

"Let's get started." Dr. Zimmer's impatience is obvious.

The student puts colored blocks on the table. Amy pushes them around, making no attempt to stack them. The student watches in silence. Unexpected, a hideous noise, like radio static fills the room. I flinch. Neither Amy nor the student reacts. "What was that?"

"White noise." The student says. "It's used to test hearing because it can be generated with equal intensity on any frequency in the audio spectrum."

Huh? White, black, green, or whatever color this noise is, it explodes into the soundproof room with increasing volume. My ears ring. When I feel my ears will burst from the racket, Amy lifts her head, a quick movement, almost a jerk, and then she returns to the blocks. Several more intense static sounds assail my ringing ears, and then silence. My teeth separate, relaxing my jaw. A sigh escapes my lips. I slump against the back of the metal chair.

"That's enough for today," Dr. Zimmer declares.

The woman stands. "Come with me."

I pick up Amy and follow her. She nudges me toward an open door and leaves. The nameplate indicates I'm in Dr. Zimmer's office. The room is small and crowded with furniture. Every flat surface is stacked with papers, magazines, and books. The file cabinet could double for the leaning tower of Pisa. I squeeze into an uncomfortable student desk wedged between bookcases opposite his desk. Dr. Zimmer is less than three feet from me, but his head is bowed so all I see is black hair and a hand scribbling notes. He does not acknowledge me, introduce himself, or offer his hand; instead, he immediately launches into a barrage of questions.

"Does she walk?" His pen is poised, ready for my answer.

"No, but she's trying. She pulls herself up. I'm sure she wi—"

"Doesn't walk," he mumbles. "Does anyone in your family have a hearing loss?"

"No." I shift Amy to my other knee; her weight has numbed my leg. "I've heard talk that some people in my husband's family have a hearing problem."

"Who?"

"I'm not sure. Distant cousins, I think. And maybe an aunt or uncle."

"When did they lose their hearing?" His voice is hurried, aggravated.

"I don't know. I've never met them. I've just heard stories."

More scribbling follows his "Hmmm."

"Were you ill during pregnancy?"

"No."

"Did you have the measles?"

"No."

"Are you sure?" His voice is cynical.

My answer is definitive. "Yes."

"That's it. Come back tomorrow." He makes another notation and slips the paper into a manila folder.

"What about the hearing test?" I sputter. "What did you learn today?"

He lifts his head. His face is stern with dark eyes; the shadow of a heavy beard, even though it is only mid-morning, spreads across his cheeks and neck. "After I test her tomorrow, I'll give you my diagnosis."

"Can't you tell me anything today?" I plead.

"She has a hearing problem." His tone is matter of fact, as if he had said, "It's raining outside." He stands. The consultation is over.

My rehearsed questions will have to wait. I carry Amy upstairs. Mother looks up when I enter the waiting room, her face a plea for answers. I shake my head. "He'll tell me tomorrow."

I don't remember driving to my parents' home, but since Mother doesn't drive, and she's in the kitchen preparing lunch, I must have driven us here. I have a vague recollection of Mother encouraging me not to jump to conclusions as we left the Temple Building, but her words did not comfort me.

That night after supper, I bathe the children, put them to bed, and Mother suggests a game of Scrabble, a game we both love. "Maybe tomorrow." She does not press my refusal. Daddy, who is quiet by nature, seems solemn tonight, even keeping the volume on the TV low.

At nine-thirty, I dial Jack. I let the phone ring and ring, because at the other end of the line is a different world, one that has no knowledge of padded rooms full of white noise.

"Is he home?" Mother calls from the living room.

"No. I'll try later." The phone sits on a dainty antique sewing table. I rub my hand over the smooth top and wrap my fingers around spindled pieces that hang off each corner like wooden icicles.

A shrill ring surprises me. "Do you want me to answer it?" I call.

"Yes," Mother replies. "It's probably for you. No one ever calls us this late."

"Hello."

"What did the doctor say?" Jack asks.

"Nothing."

"Come on, Rebecca, he must have said something. What did he do?" In the background, a "squawk" followed by a "klunk" tells me Jack has relaxed in the recliner.

"They put us in this tiny room and blasted a rasping noise until I thought I'd go nuts, and then . . ." I detail the thirty-minute test concluding with, "and that's all he said."

"Amy responded to some of the noises, right?" Jack's voice is enthusiastic.

"One or two, I guess." My voice is despondent. I hear the click of his cigarette lighter.

"It's probably not as bad as you think." His voice is hopeful.

"Maybe, but she—" I'm silenced by my inability to express my fear. *If you'd been there, you'd know how bad this really is.* I mumble a promise to call him tomorrow and hang up.

That night, in my dreams, I'm pushing Amy in her stroller. John walks beside us. Strangers approach, they point and murmur comments. I can't understand them, but their eyes are full of pity. I hate them. "Leave me alone! Quit staring!" I shout. John tugs my hand. His eyes are filled with confusion and tears. "Why don't they like my sister?"

I jerk awake. Was that a nightmare or a prophetic dream?

4

Stunned and Numb

Rebecca

The next day after Amy's second hearing test is completed, the graduate student ushers Amy and me into Dr. Zimmer's office and leaves. I'm thankful she did not close the door to this stifling, cluttered place. Once again I jam myself into the student desk and attempt to hold Amy on my lap.

Minutes later Dr. Zimmer strides in and sits behind his desk in a high-backed swivel chair that squeaks when he moves. Like yesterday, he writes notes without speaking or acknowledging me. I wait, none too patiently. Like an unexpected bolt of lightning, he launches into his analysis of Amy's hearing loss.

"Two days of testing indicate your child does not respond to any sounds in the normal hearing range. At 110 decibels, she consistently reacted to white noise on lower frequencies which means . . ."

I'm trying to absorb everything he is saying, but I lose my focus when he uses unfamiliar words. I wish he would slow down and let me ask questions. Give me an opportunity to clarify his comments. His voice seems to fade in and out like a poorly tuned radio receiver. Words I don't understand in this context, threshold, sensorineural, and decibels pierce my foggy mind. He never speaks Amy's name and relates the information with as much emotion as a TV weatherman reporting the daily temperatures. I do not like the forecast.

Doesn't he realize Amy and I aren't lab rats? This is my daughter he's describing! Does he have any feelings? What does all this mumbo-jumbo mean? The meaning of his words become clearer with his next statement.

"Your child is severely to profoundly deaf."

"What exactly does that mean?"

He taps his pen on Amy's file and checks his watch. "She has virtually no hearing. A bilateral loss greater than 90 decibels."

I want to scream "Her name is Amy! She's not a nameless specimen to be studied under a microscope!" Instead, I ask, "Uh ninety decibels, how much is that? What's normal?"

With obvious impatience he states, "People with normal hearing respond to a whisper, which is spoken at about 10 to 15 decibels. A lawn mower's volume is 110 decibels or greater. She doesn't hear anything until the white noise is above 110 decibels, and then she probably perceives that noise as a garbled whisper."

I have many questions and no idea what to ask. Whenever he speaks, another question pops into my overloaded mind. "What caused Amy's hearing loss?"

"From what you've told me, her loss appears to be **congentital** and . . ."

Congenital . . . that means she was born deaf. If I have more children, will they be deaf too?

"her loss is definitely **permanent** . . ."

It will never get better.

"it's **uncorrectable** and . . .

"Does this mean nothing can help her?

"and it may be **progressive**."

She could become more deaf? How can it get any worse? I thrust my tongue between my dry lips to part them. "Will she ever talk?"

"I doubt it, at least not very clearly given the severity of her loss. You could try a hearing aid, but I don't think it will help her much."

Amy squirms; I pat her back to soothe her. *He doesn't sound very enthusiastic about a hearing aid. If that won't help, what can we do?* "Where will Amy go to school?"

For the first time, Dr. Zimmer looks directly at me. His dark eyes focus on me like a laser. "Don't harbor any hopes she'll attend school in Grand Island. That won't be possible; her loss is too severe. The only place for her is the Nebraska School for the Deaf in Omaha."

Omaha? That's 150 miles away from our home. I can't send Amy to a school that far away when she's only five years old! There must be another option. I hesitantly ask, "I thought Amy might have a hearing loss before I brought her here, but I'm also concerned she might be autistic. Do you think she is?"

"No. She's not autistic . . ."

Thank heavens. A bit of good news.

"but she might be **retarded**. Right now she's . . ."

No! I can't deal with that. What makes you think she's retarded?

"too young for me to determine if she's retarded without additional observation. You'll need to keep track of when she accomplishes simple feats, like walking."

"Okay." *Just because she doesn't walk, doesn't mean she's retarded. She's only thirteen months old.*

"If her hearing loss is progressive, she may not respond to any sounds the next time I test her. If that's the case, even the most powerful hearing aid in the world won't help her."

What's wrong with you? Every sentence you utter is filled with bad news! Can't you give me a spark of hope? What am I going to do? How can I raise a child I can't talk to?" He slaps the file shut. My time to ask questions is over. "Is there anything I can do to help Amy learn to talk?" I blurt.

"Not much. You could try a hearing aid."

Where? What kind? How much do they cost? "Who do I contact about an aid?"

"Look in the phonebook. After she's worn the aid for a month, bring her back here. I'll retest her to see if it's helping her." He stands and walks toward the door. "Make an appointment with my secretary before you leave."

That's it? Try a hearing aid and come back in a month. I mumble, "Uh, okay. Thank you for . . ." But Dr. Zimmer is already walking out the door. His final comment: "I'm late. I have a class to teach."

I watch him walk down the hall and disappear into a classroom. *Thank you for what?* Still holding Amy, I sling my purse over my shoulder and wander toward the stairs. My organized mind is in

Amy and John with Grandpa and Grandma Schmierer—Rebecca's parents, Al and Ruth Schmierer. Amy was named for her grandmother, Amy Ruth.

disarray, overloaded with new information. I feel lost with no map to guide me through this unknown territory that is my daughter's deafness.

On the drive back to Beatrice, I tell Mother about Dr. Zimmer's report. She tries to sound upbeat when she asks questions, but her trembling voice betrays her. I am glad I must keep my eyes on the road so I cannot see the distress on her face.

"I guess the next step is to buy a hearing aid, but I don't know where to go."

Thankfully Mother is ready with Plan B. While working part-time at the Beatrice Public Library, she meets a variety of people. One of the regular patrons is Mr. King, the local Zenith hearing aid dealer. Mother offers to arrange for him to see Amy. I nod my consent, relieved that I will not have to explain Amy's deafness to a stranger.

When we arrive home, I collapse in a living room chair. Mother prepares lunch. I'm not interested in food, choosing to remain like a slug in the chair. John and Amy eat and Mother puts them to bed for their naps. My mind endless replays Dr. Zimmer's diagnosis. The sound of the five o'clock TV news cast jolts me from my thoughts. My father is home from work. I hurry to the kitchen to help Mother with supper.

"Mother, did you call that guy about a hearing aid for Amy?"

"Yes. Mr. King works out of his home, so I invited him to come here after supper. Is that all right?"

"Whatever. It makes no difference to me."

"Have you called Jack and told him about Amy?" Mother asks.

"No. I suppose I could try now. He might be home for supper."

Jack answers the phone on the sixth ring, sounding breathless. He tells me he was outside when the phone rang and hurried to get inside, thinking it might be me calling. "Well?" he says. "What did the doctor say?" I tell him Amy has a severe hearing loss and a man is coming tonight to fit her with an aid. "That's good," he responds.

Good? I don't think anything about this day has been good. "I'll be home tomorrow. I'll give you a full report then." He seems satisfied with my simple explanation and has no other questions, but perhaps like me, he has too many questions.

At supper, I tell my father about Amy's exam. He listens and makes no comment, which does not surprise me. My father is intelligent, but slow to give his opinion without considerable thought. If he has questions or comments, they will come much later. After supper we await Mr. King's visit.

Daddy is seated on the sofa, near a table lamp working the newspaper crossword puzzle, his nightly ritual. John is occupied with a circus puzzle on the living room rug. Nearby, Amy watches, sucking her fingers. Mother sits on an ottoman by them. I am slumped in the chair where I spent the afternoon. I watch with little interest as John forces a puzzle piece into several open spaces.

"It's no good. It doesn't fit." John tosses the piece aside with disgust.

"It fits right here." Mother points to the correct place. "John, be careful with the puzzle pieces. These puzzles are old and fragile. I played with them when I was a child."

With the innocence only a child can muster, he says, "Really, Granmere? Then they must be really old."

Before I can tell John that wasn't polite, the doorbell rings. Seconds later Mother escorts Mr. King into the room. He is a small man, dressed in neatly pressed slacks and a plaid shirt. He carries a large briefcase. Mother conducts the introductions and motions toward the couch. Mr. King sits and places the boxlike briefcase on the floor. We indulge in meaningless small talk, skirting the purpose of his visit. An awkward silence soon fills the room.

Mr. Kings clears his throat. "Rebecca, did your mother tell you I have a son who wears a hearing aid?"

My father seems relieved that he can now return to his puzzle. I envy him. I cannot escape from this discussion. "Yes," I mumble, not at all interested.

"My son is in the sixth grade at Paddock Lane."

I lean forward with interest. Paddock Lane is a nearby grade school. "He goes to public school?"

"Yes. At first he had problems with the other kids making fun of him, but he's doing fine now. Each year we talk to his teacher before the school year starts to make sure she seats him in the front row. He wears two hearing aids now, but when he was younger he only wore one."

Ah ha! Perhaps Dr. Zimmer is wrong. If Mr. King's son can go to public school, why can't Amy? Maybe Amy's situation is not all gloom and doom like I thought. Feeling encouraged I say, "Dr. Zimmer said we could try an aid to see if it helps Amy. She has slightly better hearing in her left ear, so he suggested we try an aid in that ear first. If it helps her, we'll buy a second aid later."

"Great. Let's get started." Mr. King pulls a small zippered kit from his briefcase and puts it on the coffee table. He withdraws a container of pink powder and mixes it with a strange-smelling liquid. The powder is transformed into a malleable material which he packs into a large syringe. Next he ties a small piece of cotton on a long string and places it and tweezers on the table. "Okay. I'm ready. I'll need you to hold Amy on your lap and keep her still so I can make an impression of her ear."

I pick up Amy. We sit on the couch next to Mr. King. "What are you going to do?"

"First I'll insert the cotton with the string into her ear. The cotton keeps the mold material from going too far into the ear canal, and the string allows me to remove the mold once it has hardened." Using the tweezers, Mr. King inserts the cotton into Amy's ear canal. She shakes her head and reaches for her ear. "Don't let her pull the string out." He quickly picks up the syringe.

I gently pull Amy's hand away from her ear and hold it. "This will only take a couple of minutes, Amy. Then you can go play with John."

Mr. King inserts the syringe into Amy's ear and depresses the plunger. The pink material disappears into her ear canal. He gently presses the mold material into her outer ear, making sure he fills every indention. "If we're lucky, I will only have to do this once."

My father looks up from his puzzle to watch the procedure. Mother sits with her hands folded, her jaw tight with tension. John, ever the inquisitive and protective brother comes to my side. "Mommy, what's he doing to my sister?"

"Making a mold of her ear."

"Does it hurt?"

"No, John," Mr. King says. "It just feels weird to her."

"Oh, all right." Satisfied his sister is okay, he returns to his puzzle as does my father.

"It's not easy to get a good impression of a young child's ear be-cause their cartilage is so flexible," Mr. King explains. "That flexibility also makes it difficult to keep the earpiece in their ear, so I'll have Zenith embed a wire in the earpiece that will go around Amy's ear to hold it in place."

I can't envision the device he is describing, but I reply, "Okay."

"Did Dr. Zimmer give you a copy of Amy's audiogram?" He asks.

"What's that?"

"A chart that graphs hearing."

"He gave me a couple of papers. I think one might be an audio-gram." Amy reaches for the string with her free hand, determined to remove the offending mold material. I grab her other hand. She whines her distress. "John, bring me something for Amy to play with."

Mr. King asks to see the report, telling me it will help him de-termine which aid will be best for Amy. John brings Amy a stack of colored rings. She watches as he takes them off the center rod and replaces them.

"Thanks, John. Mother, those papers are in my purse in the bedroom. Will you get them for me?"

Once again, John returns to his puzzle and Mother leaves in search of my purse. Amy drops a colored ring. It rolls across the rug and stops against my father's foot. He hands it to Mr. King, who gives it to Amy. A sigh escapes my lips. A sigh filled with my unspoken frustration, confusion, and exhaustion.

As if having the ability to read my mind, Mr. King says, "Having a deaf child is difficult sometimes. My son has worn an aid since he was eighteen months old . . ."

He continues to relate the story of his son, but like my deaf daughter, I don't hear what he is saying. I'm lost in my own maelstrom of worry, fear, and disbelief. Stunned and numb by the events of the past two days.

Mother returns with Dr. Zimmer's report. Mr. King studies it before speaking. "Amy has a severe bilateral loss. That means the loss is in both ears. An in-the-ear type of hearing aid that older people wear won't help her. She needs a powerful body aid." He pulls the mold from Amy's ear and holds a perfect pink impression of her outer ear and ear canal aloft like a precious jewel. "Great! I got a good impression the first time." He places the mold in a small box.

I release my hold on Amy and she crawls across the rug to John. Mr. King puts the box containing Amy's ear mold into his briefcase and snaps it shut.

"I'll send Amy's impression to Zenith tomorrow. Her earpiece and hearing aid should be here in about a week. I'll order a hearing aid harness, too. I hope they have one small enough to fit her. When they arrive, I'll call you. Is that okay, Rebecca?"

Surprised to hear my name, I snap out of my reverie. "What? Oh yes, uh . . . I'm, uh, we're to come back in a week, right?"

"Yes, about a week. You won't have to wait long once the aid arrives, I live less than ten minutes from here."

"Wait! I live in Grand Island. It will take me three hours to get here. Call my mother. I'll try to come here the day after you call her."

He agrees. My parents walk him to the door. I move from the couch and plop onto the ottoman near John and Amy. She tugs at the ear that was filled with mold material. I reach for her hand, but realize it does not matter.

"Look, Amy. It's a lion." John points to the completed puzzle. "Grrrrr. I'm a lion."

Amy smiles. Daddy returns to his puzzle and Mother brushes small bit of the pink mold material off the coffee table into her hand. I stare blankly, seeing nothing.

Mother lifts Amy from the floor and calls to John. "Come on, John. It's way past your bedtime. Do you want me to read you a story?" They walk into the hall which leads to the bedrooms.

"Granmere, will you read the book about the three gruffy goats?

"Yes, if you hurry and put your pajamas on."

Sometime later my father yawns and asks me if I am going to bed now. I hear him, but don't reply. "Do you want me to leave the lamp on?" He waits. I'm mute. He turns off the lamp and walks toward his bedroom.

N-U-M-B. I'm alone in the living room of my parents' home, a room that holds many bright and happy memories from my childhood. Now the dim light from the hallway makes the room seem dusky and abandoned. The clock strikes ten, and then eleven. I massage the crick in my neck, arch my back to relieve my tension, and shuffle toward the hall. As I enter the hall, I snap off the light and enter the darkness in my bedroom.

5

Stomaching the Diagnosis

Rebecca

The next day, three hours after telling my parents good-bye, I arrive home and turn on *Sesame Street* for John and Amy. My throat is clogged with a lump of tension. I want to crash into bed and hide under the covers, but my life does not give me the luxury of escapism; I must cook supper. Nothing entices me, even though I am hungry. At last I decide on spaghetti. It's easy, and we all like it.

With robotic movements, I fill a pan with water, and place silverware with precision on our place mats, making sure each piece is straight and the same distance from the edge. I pull Amy's high chair to the table and place jars of strained baby food in a pan of simmering water. I watch bubbles form. Steam rises and dissipates. John's laughter at the antics of Grover drifts into the kitchen and fades away. Everything dissolves, except the lump in my throat.

By the time Jack arrives, my throat is so constricted that my ears hurt when I swallow. I force several bites of spaghetti past the lump in my throat by drinking milk. Before I replace my glass on the table, my stomach rebels. I rush to the bathroom and spew the contents of my stomach into the toilet. The vomit burns my throat, but does not dissolve the lump. I convulse with dry heaves. I gargle with mouthwash and return to the kitchen.

Jack looks up, but does not comment on my sudden departure. "What's that?" He points to an envelope on the table.

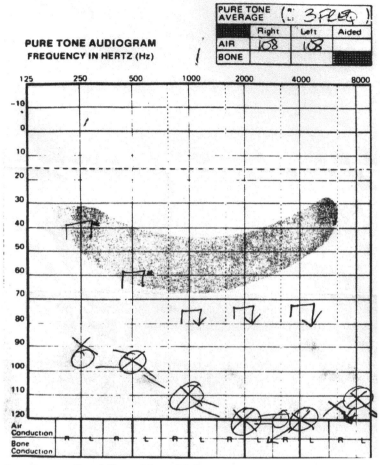

PURE TONE AVERAGE	(R: 3FREQ)		
	Right	Left	Aided
AIR	108	108	
BONE			

PURE TONE AUDIOGRAM
FREQUENCY IN HERTZ (Hz)

Amy's audiogram. O and X are right and left ear measurements.

"Amy's audiology report. I'll show it to you after supper." I ignore my food and feed Amy strained carrots. The smell makes my stomach spasm.

Jack pulls a sheet of paper from the envelope and studies the downward-sloping lines on the graph. Amy's response to sound enters the graph at 95 decibels and quickly slants off the bottom of the chart at 120 decibels. He frowns. "What's normal?"

"Normal people can detect a whisper. That's about fifteen decibels. I'm probably talking at forty to fifty decibels now. People with normal hearing respond to sounds in that shaded area on the chart and to quieter noises above it." Amy shakes her head at the strained turkey I offer.

"Will that hearing aid help?"

"Dr. Zimmer said we could try one, but he didn't sound very encouraging." I offer Amy strained peaches. She shakes her head.

"What other choices do we have?"

"If the aid doesn't help, I don't know what we can do." I wipe Amy's face with her bib and release her from the high chair.

Jack stares at the graph. If this chart portrayed a failing business, he could utilize his business degree to cut losses, increase sales, and make the business profitable, but like me, he's in uncharted territory; nothing can make the downward-sloping line of Amy's hearing climb.

Later that evening, after the children are in bed, Esther and J.W., Jack's parents, surprise us with a visit. Esther snaps on the light in the children's bedroom. John awakes and pulls his blanket over his head. Esther removes Amy from her crib and stares at her sleepy face, as if looking for a subtle difference in her appearance that would indicate she is deaf.

"How's my little sweetie? Are you sleepy?" Amy whimpers, upset with being woken. "You hear me just fine, don't you?" Amy pushes her hands against Esther's freckled face, rimmed with red hair. "Okay, sleepy head, back to bed." She puts Amy in her crib, pulls the blanket to her chin and says, "She looks fine. Are you sure this doctor is competent?"

"Let me show you Amy's report. It's on the kitchen table." My offer for coffee is declined. We all sit around the table, and I explain hearing requires clarity and adequate volume. "Amy doesn't hear any sounds until they are amplified to 95 decibels or greater. In addition, she can't hear the higher frequencies, which include the letters f, s, th, and z, so she has problems with both volume and clarity." I hand the report to J.W.

"Will an aid help?" he asks.

I shake my head. "Not much. Dr. Zimmer said Amy is severely to profoundly deaf. She has virtually no hearing. The best aids provide about a fifty-decibel gain, which means with an aid, Amy might hear shouting and other loud noises."

"So we'll all talk louder, and she'll be just fine." Esther pushes the report away when J.W. hands it to her.

"No amount of amplification will allow Amy to hear speech normally. A hearing aid only amplifies the sounds she hears. It can't restore hearing. She may hear speech, but it will be garbled." *Will this day never end?* I'm exhausted from driving and explaining the exam.

"Hmm," J.W. responds.

The room is smothered in silence. Finally a mundane issue rescues us.

"The forecast for Friday is snow," J.W. says.

"I hope the semi-truck of groceries arrives before the weather gets nasty." Jack sighs, knowing he'll have several backbreaking hours of work tomorrow.

Esther, a confirmed workaholic like her husband and son, usually joins their conversation, but tonight she stands and motions for me to follow her into the living room.

"You need to get another opinion." Esther is no taller than I am, but tonight her 5-foot 3-inch frame seems large and foreboding.

"Why? Dr. Proffitt and Dr. Zimmer both say Amy doesn't hear."

"It wouldn't hurt to have another doctor examine her to see if anything is really wrong."

"I could, but what's the point? Dr. Zimmer conducted two days of tests. I was there. I know Amy doesn't hear."

"He could be wrong. Did this Dr. Summer . . ."

"Zimmer. His name is Zimmer." I clamp my teeth together to keep from shouting, *have you heard anything I said tonight? Amy is deaf! Nothing is going to change that!*

"Did Dr. Sum . . . uh Zimmer say what caused this?"

My body tenses, unsure where this conversation will lead. "He doesn't think it's a birth defect, because generally babies injured during their birth have multiple problems. Amy's only problem is deafness. He said it's probably genetic."

"Genetic?" Esther scowls. "No one in *our* family has a hearing problem." She pauses a moment and then blurts, "You have some cousins who are retarded, don't you? Amy's must have inherited this problem from your family."

Her accusations catch me off guard. In a split second I shift from wary to red-flag-waving angry. I'm devastated by Amy's deafness. Instead of showing a little sympathy, Esther has questioned my ability to find appropriate medical care and insinuated that my family is the cause of her deafness. I can't believe this. "My cousins have nothing to do with Amy's deafness. For your information, they're distant third cousins." My stomach gurgles with stress.

"You had the flu when you were pregnant." Esther points her finger at me. "That's probably what caused this."

Why are you blaming me? I've already asked myself a million times if I did something to cause this! All the doctors assured me I didn't. I feel horrible, guilty, and punished by God! What do you want from me? A confession? My knotted fists massage my stomach.

"Did you tell the doctor about having the flu?" Esther's prominent jaw juts toward me.

My innards spasm; a trip to the bathroom will soon be necessary. "Yes, and Dr. Anderson said my bout with the flu occurred too late in my pregnancy to have caused Amy's deafness."

"You must have done something. Everyone in my family is normal."

My intestines churn and cramp.

"What you should do is . . ."

"Excuse me." I escape the inquisition and seek solace in the bathroom. Esther's accusation "you must have done something," can't be flushed away.

When I return several minutes later, Esther and J.W. are putting on their coats. "We better go and let these kids get some sleep," J.W. says.

Sleep? Are you kidding? I've just been brought up on charges, accused without warning or justification, and judged guilty! Sleep will be as fleeting as a gust of wind tonight.

Jack showers and goes to bed. After the 10 o'clock news, I slip under the covers beside him. *Why does Esther think this is my fault? Why does God allow things like this happen?* Please God, tell me what to do. I drift into an exhausted stupor.

My body rebels for days, refusing to accept the reality of Amy's deafness. My throat burns, my head throbs, my ears ache. Liquids seep past the emotional lump in my throat, but food is repulsed. Aspirins lodge in my throat, gagging me. Yesterday Mother called and told me Amy's hearing aid had arrived. *How can I drive to Beatrice to get her hearing aid tomorrow? I can't be more than ten feet from a bathroom.* I decide to stop eating. Coping with hunger is less stressful than the vomiting and diarrhea. By the end of the week I add coughing to my list of complaints. Two days later I drag myself to Dr. Anderson.

Our family doctor is an older man with gray hair and a soft voice. The night he delivered Amy, Grand Island was in the midst of a howling blizzard. I smile as I remember him rushing into the delivery room wearing his blue silk bowling shirt. He has not seen Amy or me since he referred us to Dr. Proffitt. I relate the results of Amy's hearing test at the university.

"I'm sorry. You'll need to watch for ear infections and high temperatures; they could damage her residual hearing. If you suspect an ear infection, take her to Dr. Proffitt immediately." I acknowledge his advice with a nod. "So, what brings you here today, young lady?"

"I feel like an outpatient from Livingston-Sonderman Funeral Home."

He smiles. "It can't be too bad if you can still joke about it. Hop up on the table and I'll take look." After peering into my ears and throat, he listens to my breathing for an extended period of time. "You have pleurisy. That's what is causing the pain in your side. I'm prescribing antibiotics, but it will take a week or more for that pain to go away."

What about the pain in my heart? Will that ever go away? Do you have a pill for it?

He scribbles prescriptions and hands them to me. "You take care, little mother."

That afternoon, I reschedule my appointment with Mr. King, the hearing aid dealer to a later date. The battle of acceptance ravages my body. At night, I drift in and out of nightmares. During the day, I torment myself. Why can't I cope? Who can I turn to? What can I do? I've been thrust into the role "parent of a deaf child," but I have no mentor to tell me how to proceed.

Several days later, the intestinal rebellion is over. My stomach and I have reached an uneasy truce, but digesting the heartbreaking diagnosis of Amy's deafness has not come without a price. I've lost more than 10 percent of my body weight in one week. I look svelte but feel lifeless.

6

The Mechanical Tyrant

Rebecca

The following week, John, Amy, and I travel to Beatrice where Amy receives her hearing aid on my twenty-fifth birthday. What a gift. Within a week, Amy has become accustomed to the small foreign object in her ear. She wears her hearing aid all day without complaint. Foolish me, I thought all was well, but a week later the aid is squealing unmercifully most of the day, setting my frayed nerves on edge, so I call Mr. King.

"What's that hideous noise her aid makes most of the time?" I clamp my free hand over my ear to muffle the high-pitched squeal from the aid so I can hear his response.

"Feedback whistle," Mr. King replies. "If the earpiece doesn't fit tightly, sounds enter the aid through the microphone on her chest and through the opening in the earpiece, which causes that squeal. She needs a better fitting earpiece. Bring her to Beatrice as soon as you can so I can make a new ear-mold impression."

The thought of a six-hour round-trip to Beatrice for a fifteen-minute appointment with Mr. King overwhelms me. I dislike long-distance driving, but I can't stand listening to the piercing squeal.

When I complain to Jack that evening about another trip to Beatrice he says, "You know Bob Burns, the beer distributor?"

"No, but I've heard you talk about him. What does he have to do with this?"

"Bob's a pilot." Jack reaches for the telephone. "Several weeks ago when I told him about Amy, he asked if he could do anything to help. Maybe he'll fly you to Beatrice."

"That would be great." I pray Bob would like to fly a mission of mercy.

Jack dials and after several minutes, he covers the mouthpiece and whispers, "Bob says he'll be glad to do it." He hands the telephone to me. "Here, you make the arrangements."

I love to fly, so the drudgery of the grueling drive to the hearing aid dealer in Beatrice is replaced by the anticipation of soaring over the countryside. The next morning, John, Amy, and I take off into a cloudless sky in a four-seat airplane. John delights in seeing little farms and highways from the airplane window. Amy is strapped in a seat beside him. I'm the unofficial copilot. After achieving our assigned altitude, Bob allows me to hold the yoke.

At age eleven I took my first airplane ride in a small plane like this. From that day, I wanted to be a pilot. The freedom of flight, soaring into the sky, and observing the world below still beckons me. The constant vibration of the engine has lulled Amy to sleep. John is engrossed in the miniature landscape, so for a minute I clutch the yoke and live my dream of being a pilot.

We're back home before supper. I feel like I've been pulled backward through a knothole. I'm exhausted and disgusted that my life is being orchestrated by a hearing aid. I don't like the music it plays: a shrill squeal.

That night, as I tuck John and Amy into bed, the theme song for *Hogan's Heroes* blares from the TV in the living room. "You know, Mother," John says, "That's marching music."

I'm amazed John has such a keen ear for music. His ability to hear and understand musical rhythms makes Amy's loss more poignant. *Will she ever hear music?* I remove Amy's earpiece; the aid squeals as if wounded until I turn it off. The cord connecting the earpiece to the aid is no thicker than the lead in a pencil and just as fragile. I hold the earpiece and aid together, so the earpiece does not swing on the fragile cord, which could break the wires inside it.

I return to the living room and watch mind-numbing sitcoms so I won't dwell on the hectic events of the day that have jarred my precise routine. At ten, when the news begins, I snap off the television. Jack won't be home until after ten-thirty. I'm accustomed to spending evenings alone, but tonight I long for comfort and companionship. I have three sisters, and while we are close emotionally, none are geographically near me. The closest sister is one hundred miles away and she's busy raising three young children. My other sisters live even further away. Of course I could call them or my parents, but tonight I need "in person" comforting. Having only lived in Grand Island three years, I have few close friends and none of them understand my feelings since they all have children without a disability. Jack is all I have.

A hug from him, and hearing him say, "There, there, it will be all right," would be wonderful. But Jack and I are unable to share our pain or comfort each other. He handles his pain by working more hours at the grocery store, and I cope by spiraling deeper into perfectionism.

I align the pillows on the couch, wipe dust off the end table with my sleeve, and center the lamp on the table. Satisfied that the living room is in order, I switch off the light and wander into the children's bedroom. I stand for a moment by Amy's crib watching her sleep, and then I lift her and clutch her to my chest. My hug awakens her. She smiles, yawns, and closes her eyes.

I sink into the rocking chair, resting Amy's head on my shoulder. Tears I have held inside since I heard *she does not hear* fill my eyes. In the dark, where no one can see, they escape, flowing in silent streams down my cheeks. A floorboard squeaks as I rock. *How can Dr. Zimmer expect me to send Amy to school in Omaha? That's too far away.* I've read about people who never send their kids to school, I could do the same. I sniff, a futile effort to control my tears. *If she went to that school, who would kiss her good-night?* I cradle Amy in my arms. Her finger sucking echoes John's thumb sucking across the room. *Amy's birthday's in January. I'd never be with her on her birthday if she's in Omaha.* I stop the rocker. Amy's my baby. *No one is taking my baby from me! I can't send her there; I won't.* The floorboard squawks, acknowledging my decision as I resume rocking.

I clutch Amy to my shoulder and rock. I cry for her, for me, for lost dreams, and for everything I will miss if she is away at school:

birthdays, proms, first dates, goodnight kisses, tender hugs, and a special mother-daughter relationship. The tears soften but do not dislodge the lump in my throat. Unaware of my tears, Amy sleeps. In my self-absorbed grief, I don't hear Jack enter the house.

"Rebecca, where are you?" Jack calls.

"In here. Rocking Amy." I return Amy to her crib and wipe my face.

"What's the matter?" He calls from the hall.

"Nothing." I blink several times forcing my tears to recede. "How can we send Amy away to school in four years?" I walk toward his silhouette. "I can't live without her."

"Don't worry about it now." We stand in the doorway. Four inches separates our bodies; neither of us moves to close the gap. "Everything will be all right."

Those were the exact words I wanted to hear, but they are not the least bit comforting.

Ten days later, the new earpiece arrives and the hideous squeal is gone.

Time flies, even if you're not having a good time. A month has passed. John, Amy, and I are once again in the Temple Building on the university campus. Today, Amy will be tested wearing her aid. I'm hopeful. In the past week, Amy has turned her head if there's been a loud unexpected noise near her.

We wait. Forty-five minutes pass. John and Amy are crabby and bored; I'm two seconds away from being short-tempered. "Stop swinging your legs, John." I grab the leg nearest me. Amy takes advantage of my relaxed grasp to squirm off my lap and toddle across the room.

"Why?" John's unrestrained leg moves faster.

"Because I said so, that's why." Amy sways by a sharp table edge. I spring from my chair.

"Amy Willman," the receptionist says.

"Come on, John." I swoop like a hawk on a defenseless bunny, grabbing Amy before she falls. With a backwards glance to make sure John is following me, we go downstairs.

Half an hour later, I'm seated in Dr. Zimmer's dismal office. John stands beside me, rigid like a toy shoulder, having been warned to keep his hands at his side and not touch anything. After several minutes Dr. Zimmer strides in, jerks open a file drawer, and tugs a folder from the overstuffed drawer. I wait for him to acknowledge me. Nothing happens.

Frustrated, I blurt, "Well? What did the test show? Is the aid helping Amy?"

"There's some improvement. Not much." He pulls a pen from his shirt pocket and writes in the folder. "Bring her back in six months." Without looking up he says, "You could try a Y cord."

"What's a Y cord?" I ask.

"Call your hearing aid dealer. He'll know." He stands, jams the file into the open drawer, and with one swipe of his paw-like hand slams the drawer and leaves.

My jaw tightens as does my stomach. Rebellion rises in my throat, but I squelch it. I've never been one to confront authority, especially male authority. "Come on, John, let's go."

On the drive home, I replay my short conversation with Dr. Zimmer. He said there was some improvement. That's encouraging. I wish there was another audiologist we could see. Dr. Zimmer is an impossible monster. I envision him snatched off the planet by aliens and tortured with their shock-inducing probes. The knot in my stomach relaxes.

෩

Over the telephone, Mr. King explains that a Y cord will allow Amy to hear sound in both ears without buying another aid. "The cord is shaped like a Y, hence its name. I don't have any in stock; they're not used often."

"How much are they?" I don't know why I ask. Regardless of the cost, we will buy it.

Mr. King quotes a price. "Y cords are a more fragile than the single cord she's wearing now. I'll order three, so you have a couple of spares."

Yikes! More fragile than the one she has now? Despite my careful treatment of the aid and cord, the first cord was rendered useless after ten days. "Thanks. I'll send a check right away."

"Rebecca, don't hang up. The Y cord requires two earpieces. I need to make an impression of Amy's right ear. When can you bring her to Beatrice?"

I groan inwardly. As much as I like Mr. King and his understanding demeanor, I need a local hearing aid dealer. "Go ahead and order the Y cords for me, but maybe I'll have the ear mold impression made here, if that's okay. I really like you, but I can't dri . . ."

"I understand," Mr. King says. "Laverne Almquist is the Zenith dealer in Grand Island. I'll call and tell her Amy will be coming in for an impression."

"Thanks. I appreciate that."

Laverne is a wisp of a woman, with a huge bouffant hairstyle. Her neck, ears, wrists, and several fingers are adorned with large jewelry. The weight of that jewelry would slow my pace, but not Laverne. She is spry and agile for a woman approaching retirement age. She's accustomed to fitting aids on older adults and has never made an ear mold for a client as young as Amy, but she has infinite patience. Laverne took three impressions before she was satisfied. She gave John the leftover pink mold material, which kept him occupied during this ninety-minute ordeal. Laverne promises to keep the Y cords and the batteries we need stocked. She's a breath of fresh air in my stifling life.

Amy's first Y cord is broken after three days of use. I contemplate putting her hearing aid harness under her dress. This would protect the fragile cord, but then Amy would constantly hear the sound of fabric rubbing against the microphone. Not a good choice. The Y cord was meant for adult use, so it's longer than needed to reach from Amy's ears to the aid on her chest. Her hands often become entangled in the cord and when she pulls them free, at least one earpiece is jerked from her ear and dangles on the fragile cord. The resulting squeal sends me running to reinsert the earpiece before the fragile wires inside the cord break.

This morning I am cleaning our spotless duplex before a visit from my parents and my older sister, Helen, who lives in Chicago. They arrive before lunch bearing gifts. Helen gives John and Amy red, white, and blue outfits from Marshall Field's.

Amy and John in the matching outfits their Aunt Helen, Rebecca's older sister, gave them.

"Thanks, Helen. They'll look like a million dollars on the Fourth of July." I wonder if Amy will hear the firecrackers this year. Many events in my life are measured as pre-deaf or post-deaf, filled with questions about how Amy reacted or might react now.

Mother hands me a box of Russell Stover's candy. All dark chocolates, my favorite.

"I made something for John," Daddy says. John and I follow Daddy outside and discover a huge wooden barn in his pickup. Daddy and I lug it into the house, and John follows carrying a toy tractor and plow. Soon Daddy and John are engrossed in farming the living room carpet.

Mother extends a book, and Amy walks to her. She lifts Amy onto her lap and together they turn the pages of *Pat the Bunny*. Amy touches the fuzzy bunny, but she's more interested in John's tractor. She wiggles off Mother's lap. Mother's lips smile, but her eyes are dull.

I offer coffee. Daddy declines, but Mother and Helen accept. As I pour the coffee, I pour out my heart. "I can't send Amy to school in Omaha in four years. I'm not going to do it."

"You have no right to deny her an education." Helen stands. Her five-foot-nine inch frame towers over me. "How can you be so selfish? Don't you care about Amy?"

I sink in my chair. My jaw tightens as Helen continues her harangue. My mind burns with ugly thoughts. *It's easy for you to tell me what to do; Amy's not your child. Grandpa was right, 'nothing like old maids and barren women to tell you how to raise your children.' You have no idea what I'm going through. You don't have any children. You don't know what this is like.* Three minutes into her accusing tirade, my familiar intestinal spasms start.

After my visitors leave, Helen's piercing words gnaw at me for days. *She had no right to be so mean. True, but you know she's right. Maybe, but she could have said it in a nicer way. If she had, would you have listened? Maybe, I don't know. I love Amy too much to part with her.* As I bemoan my fate, I realize the truth of Helen's words cannot be ignored. *Helen is right; I am selfish. I don't have any right to deny Amy the opportunity to learn, and to love knowledge as much as I do.* My selfish love must be replaced with selfless love. Do I love Amy enough to do what is best for her? I don't know. Do I really have a choice? No.

At that moment I decide Amy will receive the best education possible. *I must get off my dead butt and do something constructive and quit wallowing in self-pity.*

As I ponder what I can do for Amy now, my stomach is still tight with rebellion. But, for the first time in three months, I shift my focus from my feelings and contemplate what I can do for Amy.

7

Starting the Climb

Rebecca

The next morning I scan the telephone directory for agencies serving the hearing impaired. Grand Island, a town of 25,000, is the third largest city in Nebraska. If there are any services outstate, they'll be here. Midway through the list of schools, I stop: The Grand Island Speech and Hearing Program. Minutes later I have an appointment with the director, Mr. Snyder.

Jack's response to my news is, "Look for my initials on the wall at Connell School."

I frown, confused.

"Connell was a junior high school years ago. My friend Larry and I carved our initials by the gym when we went there."

"You defaced school property? I find that hard to believe."

"It wasn't my idea. Larry suggested it." He defends his behavior, but his smile betrays him.

His impish smile attracted me to him in college, but Jack's demanding job and Amy's deafness have wiped the smile from his face. "I'll look for them, but I don't think I'll show them to John. I don't want him writing on our walls. Like father, like son."

Our smiles give us a brief respite from the tension.

The following Tuesday, John, Amy, and I arrive at Connell. Lack of landscaping, the age of the building, and the grim exterior concern me, but the inside is remodeled. The walls are freshly painted, indoor-outdoor carpet covers the floor, and colorful posters decorate the walls.

Mr. Snyder's office is on the second floor. Instead of a stairwell, a ramp leads to the second floor. I'm certain the architect never imagined the ramp installed so rowdy teenagers could move quickly between two floors would be ideal for special-needs children in wheelchairs forty years later. The slope stretches my calf muscles, making them twitch as I carry Amy, who now weighs twenty-three pounds. John enjoys climbing the "big hill."

Mr. Snyder ushers us into his office and motions toward chairs opposite his desk. He asks the usual questions. I have answers for all of them, except the one that torments me.

"What caused your daughter's deafness?"

"I don't know; neither do the doctors. They think it's genetic, because she hasn't had an illness that could cause deafness." I add my silent prayer, *Please God; tell me why Amy's deaf?*

Mr. Snyder explains that he supervises therapists who work with the special-needs children attending Connell and those in regular public school classes. "We offer speech and language therapy."

"Speech *and* language?" I ask. "What's the difference?"

"Language therapy encourages children to speak. Speech therapy helps a person pronounce words properly. Children like Amy who were born deaf need language therapy to encourage them to vocalize. In the future she may need speech therapy."

"How do you do this?"

"The children in our program wear hearing aids and are taught lipreading skills. This is an oral program. The deaf here learn to speak. We don't use sign language."

Amy quits squirming as if interested in what Mr. Snyder is saying.

"After a child is assessed, appropriate therapy is arranged. Some kids receive therapy two days a week, others every day. We have individual and group therapy. Kids progress differently, but we have many success stories. Parental involvement is encouraged. Children progress faster if their parents repeat the exercises at home."

"I'll do whatever it takes to help Amy." My voice is a combination of excitement and apprehension. I have no idea what I am promising to do, but my enthusiasm is genuine.

"There's a group session here now. Would you like to see it?"

"Yes." I rise. "Come on, John." He scoots off the chair and follows me.

Mr. Snyder leads us down the hall awash with fluorescent light to a small, narrow room dimly lit with recessed bulbs. I stumble over a chair before my eyes adjust to the low light. The long wall in front of us is a one-way mirror. On the other side of the glass, a therapist sits at a U-shaped table facing several preschool children wearing hearing aids. She holds a ball aloft. "What is this?"

"Ball." A girl speaks. Her voice has a slight nasal quality. She reaches for the ball.

The therapist holds the ball higher. "Melissa, sit down. What is this? Use a sentence."

"It's a ball." Melissa grabs the ball and plops onto her chair. Her voice is flat, but her speech is clear and understandable.

A boy beside Melissa says, "Let me see it, puh-leez." His speech is slow and deliberate.

"It's mine!" Melissa pushes away the boy's outstretched hands. "You can't have it."

"Melissa, stop that," the therapist says.

Amazed, I watch and listen as Melissa defends her right to the ball. She shoves the boy away. I ignore her rough actions. "She has great speech." This is the place for Amy. If she can speak like that in four years. I drift into my future. I see Amy in that chair, speaking in sentences.

"Melissa speaks very well," Mr. Snyder says, "but her speech came at a price. Her family was determined she'd speak, so they invested a lot of time and money in therapy, but they failed to realize a hard of hearing child such as Melissa needs more than good speech. Melissa lacks social skills. She'll have a difficult time in kindergarten next year when she learns the world does not revolve around her."

My happy vision disappears. *Rebecca, don't become so focused on Amy's speech you forget she's a child.* Amy must be taught the same social skills I'm teaching John. But, I hear Melissa speak again and pray that one day Amy will speak as well.

Mr. Snyder opens the door of the observation room, and we return to his office. The exterior of Connell may be dilapidated, but the hearing program has excellent equipment and qualified staff who produce results. I'm ready to enroll Amy.

"Amy will definitely benefit from the programs we offer here," Mr. Snyder says. "When she's four, bring her back so she can start."

What! Anger bubbles inside me, my stomach churns. Amy needs therapy now. If she can't start for three years, she'll be years behind "normal" kids by then.

I squelch that thought and calmly say, "I think Amy should start now. If she doesn't, she'll be lucky to have the speech of a two-year-old when she's five." I sit in a chair facing Mr. Snyder.

"We don't accept children until they are four." Mr. Snyder tilts in his swivel chair.

"Couldn't you make an exception?"

"No. We're not equipped to handle children younger than four."

"What difference does it make if the deaf child is sixteen months or four years old? They both need to learn language skills, right?" Mr. Snyder nods. "Hearing children Amy's age already speak. She shouldn't wait three years." I feel like a teenager begging a stern parent for a favor.

He swivels his chair from side to side, and then stops to face me. "This program provides language therapy, not daycare. Children as young as Amy wouldn't benefit from our program."

"How do you know that? You've never had a student this young?"

"As an educator I can tell you, children less than four years . . ."

We continue our stalemated dialogue several minutes. I try to understand his viewpoint, but he makes no attempt to see mine. I plead through clenched teeth. My stomach tightens and gurgles; ominous noises I'm sure he can hear. *There's no justice. Damn it! Why can't anything be easy?* The roadblock is now a "bridge out." We are at an impasse.

Mr. Snyder offers a parting peace offering. "You could try the John Tracy Clinic."[1]

"What's that?" I shove my arm in the sleeve of my coat.

"You know the actor Spencer Tracy?"

I nod, wondering what an aging actor has to do with Amy's education.

"His son is deaf. His wife operates a correspondence course for families of deaf children. You might find it helpful." He extends a pamphlet in my direction.

I stuff it in my purse and pick up Amy. "Thanks. Come on, John, let's go." I stomp to the car before realizing I forgot to look for Jack's initials in the scarred woodwork, but I'm in no mood to return to the building. Life isn't fair. I thought I'd found a place to help Amy, but it's a dead end. At home, I contemplate my next step. Surely this guy has a boss. Someone he answers to. I'll speak to whoever is in charge of special education for the entire school district. I'll fight my way to the State Department of Education if I have to. Amy needs to start therapy now.

I open the telephone book, and after several calls I have scheduled a meeting with Mrs. Fishbach, the Director of Special Education for the Grand Island School System. Nothing to do but relax and wait until Tuesday, but relaxing is not my strong suit.

The next week John, Amy, and I are seated on no-nonsense wooden chairs in Mrs. Fishbach's office. She's an old lady compared to my twenty-five years. Her hair is gray, streaked with strands of chestnut brown; facial wrinkles mark deep smile lines.

As I explain why I want Amy to start therapy now, she listens with interest. Her eyes are thoughtful, focused only on me, not on the stacks of papers that clutter her desk or the blinking light on her

---

1. The John Tracy Clinic is a private, nonprofit education center founded by Louise Treadwell Tracy in 1942. Its mission is to offer hope, guidance, and encouragement to families of infants and preschool children with hearing losses by providing free, parent-centered services worldwide. The clinic has more than sixty years of expertise in the spoken language option. Contact them at http://www.johntracyclinic.org/.

telephone. When I finish, she folds her hands on her desk blotter and leans toward me, silent. I wait for her response, planning what I will say when she refuses my request.

"You're absolutely right," Mrs. Fishbach says. "Amy should start language therapy now. I'll speak to the school board and Mr. Snyder. I'll call you as soon as it's arranged."

Not sure if I have achieved my goal or am being politely dismissed, on the way to the car I think, that was quick. Too easy, actually. She said she'd try, but she's retiring in six weeks. I suppose I'll never hear from her again. Then what?

A month later, Mrs. Fishbach called. Amy is a pioneer, led by her determined scout: me. She's the youngest child ever to be enrolled in the Grand Island School System. I'm frazzled, but claim my victory, small though it may be. I challenged the school's policy and prevailed, but I have no time to bask in glory. Tomorrow is my sixteen-month-old daughter's first day of language therapy at Connell.

8

Twenty Minutes of Torture

Rebecca

At ten-thirty Monday, Wednesday, and Friday mornings, Amy has language therapy with Charmaine, the speech and language therapist at Connell School whom I observed through the one-way mirror weeks ago. Today is Friday, Amy's twelfth session. I thought I'd feel better once Amy started therapy, but I don't. My life is more complicated and stressful than before. For the past two weeks, when I park in front of Connell and remove Amy from her carseat, she begins to cry and my stomach cramps. I make a conscious effort to relax my clenched teeth. "Here, John." I hand him a cloth bag filled with small toys and books. "Carry this for Mommy."

He shakes it. "What's in here?"

"I don't remember." I placed the items in the bag fifteen minutes ago, but my short-term memory is overloaded. I grab Amy and hurry toward the door. Once inside, I take slower steps as I walk up the ramp so John's short legs can keep pace with me. Walking up is slow, but John and Amy love going down the slope, which allows them to run faster than they could on flat ground. Shrieks always accompany their tumbling charge, and I worry their screams will disrupt the children in the classrooms or they will fail to make the U-turn and smash into the wall.

As we enter the now-familiar therapist's office, Amy hides behind my skirt. I hear rhythmic sucking sounds and know her fingers are being transformed into shriveled, wet digits. I make no effort to stop her finger-sucking; this is the least of my worries. Amy avoids Charmaine's outstretched hand. My eyes brim with tears as Amy pulls several tissues from a box and follows Charmaine down the hall for language therapy.

I know Amy will return in twenty minutes, and the therapy is necessary, but Amy doesn't. Explaining this separation to a sixteen-month-old hearing child would be difficult; to a deaf child it's impossible. After Charmaine and Amy are in the therapy room, John and I enter the observation room. Two speakers fill the room with Amy's cries. Piping in sound from the therapy room isn't necessary; I see her distress through the one-way mirror and hear her gut-wrenching cries through the glass.

I stare at my reflection in the glass and tell myself, *I am doing the right thing. I am doing the right thing.* But, if this is the right thing, why does it hurt so much? *I am doing the right thing.*

"Why is Amy crying?" John asks.

"She . . . she's unhappy."

John presses his nose against the mirror. "Why? They have lots of toys. Why doesn't Amy play with the toys? Huh, why?"

John prefaces many of his questions with "why." Usually I have an answer for his "why" questions, but when his questions concern Amy, I have too many "why" questions of my own to give him reasonable answers. "I don't think she notices the toys, John."

"Why not?"

"Because she's too busy crying."

"Why?"

"Because she doesn't like being away from me."

"Why?"

"Children like to be with their mommy or daddy, don't you?"

"Yeah, but why?"

My only hope to stop the incessant questions is to change the subject or to ignore them. I choose the latter and feel guilty, but John does not notice. He changes the subject.

"Amy goes to school so she can learn to talk, right?" John repeats what he's heard me tell him numerous times.

"Yes." I wonder if that will ever happen. I open the book *Goldilocks and the Three Bears*. "Come away from the window, John, and sit by me."

He climbs upon a chair and I read, "Once upon a time . . ." I enjoy giving each character a distinct voice, but today I read with little expression.

"Wait, Mommy. That's not how the Papa Bears talks."

"What?" My attention is focused on Amy's mournful cries.

"He sounds like this." John lowers his voice. "Who's been sitting in my chair?"

"You're right." My eyes brim with tears as the intensity of Amy's cries makes her chest heave. I sniff and tip my head back, but my tears escape.

"What's the matter, Mommy?"

"Nothing. I have something in my eye. Do you want to hear the rest of the story?"

"Yes."

I continue reading, hoping Amy will stop crying; she doesn't. The twenty minutes pass. As John replaces the book in the bag, I rush to meet Amy. I speak words she does not comprehend, "Mommy's here. You have to go to school, Amy. It will be all right." My hug calms her.

"Amy, you want a book?" John holds a book behind his back and runs toward the ramp.

Amy smiles and toddles after him. She's happy now, but my relief is temporary. On Monday this scene will be replayed for the thirteenth time. I rush toward the ramp and my screaming children.

"John, don't yell in school," I call. "And slow down, before you kill yourself."

Several weeks ago I took Mr. Snyder's suggestion and contacted the John Tracy Clinic. They instruct students in lipreading skills and oral communication at their clinic and distant students, like Amy, through correspondence lessons. Their initial packet included a lengthy questionnaire. The first section was easy: name, age, birth date, et cetera. The second section: medical history, hearing evaluations, type of aids worn, and history of deafness in the family took longer. Three blank lines at the bottom of the page were for my questions. Unable to decide what to ask, I left it blank and mailed it.

Also in the packet was the first of twelve lessons that I'm to use to encourage Amy to vocalize. I'm intrigued by the lesson, but more interested in the one-to-one personal responses I will receive from Nancy Kelley, my John Tracy advisor. She'll provide feedback on our completed lessons and respond personally to my concerns. I hope she's prepared; I have plenty of questions.

Amy and I began Lesson One two weeks ago. Every afternoon we sit at a small table and I encourage Amy to look at my face. Whenever she looks at me, I speak. I stop when she turns away. Throughout our twenty-minute session, I turn her face toward me and hold her hand to my throat so she feels the vibration of my voice when I speak. The goal is for Amy to associate my lip movements with sound. After speaking, I put her hand on her throat hoping she will make a sound. So far there have been no results. Today I completed the feedback sheet on Lesson One. Under the special concerns section I scrawled: "I've done this lesson with Amy every day for two weeks with no results. When will I be rewarded with a response from Amy?" I mailed the form and began Lesson Two while waiting for Nancy's response.

During the day I cope by attempting to make my environment perfect. I can't control how quickly Amy learns to speak, but I need control over some aspect of my life so I don't feel like a failure. The challenge of perfectionism makes my mind race and stomach hurt, but I can't stop. At night my guilt keeps me awake. *I didn't spend enough time with John today. I snapped at Jack for no reason. I should have done the ironing tonight. I need to wash the clothes tomorrow. God is punishing you, Rebecca. Wait, that makes no sense. Why would God punish me by making Amy deaf?* Jack rolls onto his back. I'm thankful he doesn't snore. *I can't do anything right. Amy will never talk. God, give me patience.* My prayer is like the old joke, "Give me patience, Lord, and give it to me now!" *I mustn't spend so much time with Amy that John suffers.* Before going to sleep, I promise to give John the same amount of one-on-one time I give Amy. I have no idea how I can do this, but I never want John to say, "Mommy, you love Amy more than me."

Monday, before we leave for therapy, the mail arrives. I sort through junk mail searching for a letter from Mother or the John Tracy Clinic; I'm not disappointed. Hoping for a miracle, I rip open Nancy Kelley's letter. *What kind of answer is this?* Patient! She wants me to be patient. She explains that hearing children listen to their language for five or six months before they babble. After another three to six months of being exposed to language, a hearing child speaks simple words. Nancy's closing sentence crushes me. "Even though Amy is seventeen months old, she's only heard sounds for three months. You need to devote more time to Lesson One." I shove the letter in my purse and exhale before shifting the car into reverse. More weeks on Lesson One. It's hopeless.

Fifteen minutes later John and I are sequestered in the claustrophobic observation room listening to Amy cry. Midway through reading *The Cat in the Hat*, a strange sound fills the room . . . silence. Amy has stopped her mournful wailing. The book slips from my hand; I stand and press my nose against the one-way mirror. Charmaine holds a colored cube by her mouth and says, "block." She pulls Amy's hand to her throat and repeats the word. Amy takes the block and drops it into a container. Charmaine repeats the exercise with other blocks, reinforcing the John Tracy lesson we've been doing at home.

"Mommy, are you going to finish reading the book?" John's voice is impatient.

"Yes."

"When?"

"Right now." I retrieve the book from the floor. "What were we reading about?"

"Thing One and Thing Two. They were being naughty."

"Oh, yes, I remember now."

Today, when I go home, if I discover Dr. Suess' demonic Thing One and Thing Two have wrecked our house, I won't care. Amy stopped crying; her learning can now begin.

9

Gibberish

Rebecca

Four months after Amy was plugged in and tuned on to the hearing word, she vocalized, "Buh-buh, buh," Her first sounds, were music to my ears. My hands shook with excitement as I telephoned of my parents.

"Mother, Amy's started babbling!"

"Wonderful!" In the background I hear Daddy ask, "What happened?" Mother repeats the good news. Returning her attention to me, she asks, "When did she start? Tell me all about it?"

"Yesterday was the first time. I thought it was a fluke, but she's done it several times today. It's not much, but it's a start. I've done the first John Tracy lesson every day for more than a month. Yesterday, when I put her hand to my throat and spoke, like I've done a zillion times, she said 'buh.' I was so excited I almost fell off my chair!"

"Perseverance," Mother says, "that's the key. I'm sure it seems hopeless at times —"

"It does. Most of the time."

"What about Jack and his parents? What did they say?"

"Jack never does the lessons with Amy, so he doesn't understand how frustrating it's been, but he's excited about Amy's progress. As for J.W. and Esther, that's another story. J.W.'s a lot like Daddy; he doesn't say much, so I don't know what he thinks. Esther still hasn't accepted Amy is deaf, so she doesn't understand the significance of her accomplishment. Esther always tells me Amy is fine. I don't see how she can ignore the facts." My voice is tense.

"Some people can't accept things they don't like or understand. Don't worry about what she thinks. You're doing what's right for Amy."

"I hope so, but sometimes I wish she'd . . . oh well, it's pointless." I snort my frustration. "I almost forgot the other good news. Jack and I bought a house. We'll be moving later this month."

"Where is it?"

"Not far from where we live now. It's new. Has three bedrooms, two baths, and a basement door I can lock. That was my number one priority. Since Amy's learned to walk, I can't let her out of my sight, and since I can't yell to warn her about anything, I have to have a lock on the basement door."

"Tell me more about the house."

"I can't talk longer, I need to start supper." A persistent tug on my tee shirt interrupts my farewell. "Wait a minute. John wants to talk to you."

Mother's voice cracks as she says good-bye, but this time I know her tears are the result of joy. I give the telephone to John.

"Hello, Granmere," John says. "I'm going to have a new bedroom. One all by myself."

Saturday is moving day. John is standing by the front door holding his cardboard suitcase that contains his most valuable possessions: his stuffed dog, Pooh bear, and his blankie.

"Before the movers arrive, Jack, you need to take Amy's crib apart." I call from the kitchen where I am removing the last food items from the cupboards.

"Okay. By the way, Amy needs her diaper changed," Jack replies.

"Am I the only person in this house who knows how to change a diaper?" I shout.

"I'd do it, but you told me to take her bed apart," Jack hollers.

"Yeah right," I mutter as I pick up Amy in the hall and take her to the bedroom. After changing her, I reach for her hearing aid.

For the past few weeks, as soon as I put on her aid, she babbles, but this morning she is silent. I turn her face toward me. "Amy, can you hear me?"

Amy shakes her head, but not in response to my words. She pulls an earpiece from her ear. I reinsert it. She pulls it out again. I inspect the earpiece, clean off wax and examine her outer ear. In the ear canal is a small red area, rubbed raw by the earpiece. *It's always something. I'll have to have a new impression made Monday.* I rub Vaseline on the mold to reinsert it, and then I realize the earpiece is not squealing as it should when the aid is turned on and the earpiece is not in her ear. *The battery must be dead. What next?*

The spare batteries are in my dresser, which is wedged between our mattress and box springs in the living room against a wall. I weigh the effort of moving the furniture against Amy missing six hours of sound. Jack and I haven't had an evening out since Amy started wearing hearing aids. I can't enjoy a movie knowing I've left the expensive aids in the care of a teenage girl who's more interested in talking on the phone to her boyfriend than watching Amy. I believe Amy hearing for three hours is more important than Jack and me having a night out, but today I decide six hours of sound for Amy is not worth moving the heavy furniture when my back already aches. I take Amy from her changing table, stand her on the floor, and put the aid in my pocket. As I gather scattered toys and toss them into a box, Amy's eyes fill with tears.

"Amy, I'm not taking your toys away." I drag the box to the living room. "We're moving." I place the box on the couch, ignoring her worried expression.

The movers arrive and I return to help Jack who is struggling to remove the last bolt from the crib. Before I enter the room, he pulls the bolt free and the crib collapses near Amy. She cries.

"Amy, are you all right?" A quick scan of her body reveals she is unscathed, but her crying continues. "What's wrong?"

Amy stands among crib pieces clutching her pink, cat-shaped pillow. She watches with frightened eyes as everything is stripped from the room. My words of explanation literally fall on deaf ears. The enormity of our inability to communicate overwhelms me.

❧

Four hours later, our sparse furnishings are distributed throughout the rooms of our new home. Assembling Amy's crib is the first order of business. She watches with interest as we erect the familiar brown crib. Minutes later, she toddles from her room, clutching her stuffed cat pillow and sucking her fingers. The moving crisis is over.

I locate the spare batteries and install a new one in her aid. As I insert the earpiece and turn on the aid, Amy babbles, "Buh-buh bub. Muh-muh. Eye-eee." She runs off to find John.

I survey a stack of boxes in the living room. *I might as well start with these. My most precious possessions: books.* I rip tape off a box and remove the lessons from the John Tracy Clinic. I stack the manila envelopes on a bookshelf within easy reach and think, *if Amy can make sounds, she should be able to speak words.* The rest of the box is filled with my college textbooks.

The Psychology of Behavior. Why did I keep this book? I hated that class. Without an ounce of guilt, I toss the psychology book aside and withdraw several sociology books. Shelving the books is time-consuming, because I must adjust each one so its spine is aligned on the edge of the shelf. I don't know why I take the time to make everything perfect. No one cares but me, and it makes me crazy most days because nothing remains that way for long, but still I do it. While mulling over what motivates me to be a perfectionist, a hopeless pursuit since I have two young children and a husband who are not neat, I gain a flash of insight. Motivation! That's the key. If I can figure out what motivates Amy, I can use that to teach her to speak.

Amy is a stubborn, strong-willed child, not easygoing like her brother. A stern look from me will make John comply, but Amy is unfazed by my scowling face. She's too young to be bribed with money, toys, or clothes. Denying TV time is no incentive since the talking heads are meaningless. By the time the bookcase is filled, I realize what I can use to motivate Amy.

10

Pavlov's Daughter

Rebecca

Amy is like me in many respects: intelligent, strong-willed, and motivated by something good to eat. As a child, Mother used Fig Newtons as a reward for my good behavior, and it never failed to work. I still love Fig Newtons today.

Today, my lofty goal is to have Amy vocalize to obtain food. My stomach tightens as I set plates of food in front of Jack, John, and me. Amy's plate is empty. I hold a piece of chicken near her. "Amy, say 'buh.'" For two minutes I repeat my plea. My food grows cold. "Say 'buh.'" Amy cries, not liking or understanding why I'm withholding her food. "Say 'buh,' and then I will give you your supper."

Jack and John eat, but without enthusiasm. Amy screams with anger and frustration. I take a bite of mashed potatoes, a comfort food for me, but have trouble swallowing.

"Say 'buh,' Amy." I repeat for the umpteenth time.

"Geez, Rebecca, do you have to be so mean?" Jack asks. "Give her something to eat."

"No. If I do, she'll never learn she has to tell us what she wants."

"Why can't Amy have anything to eat?" John asks.

"Because she didn't say the magic word," I reply.

"Amy, you have to say 'please,'" John says.

Amy's body quivers. Her mournful sobs increase my guilt.

"For heaven's sakes, Rebecca, give Amy her dinner. Make her speak for dessert." Jack pleads.

"No!" I drink a glass of milk, swallowing with difficulty. I stick to my plan, begging Amy to speak. An ugly silence grows between Jack and me. Amy provides relentless wailing for our dinner music. Her cries twist my stomach into an angry knot. *God, tell me, am I doing the right thing? Give me a sign.*

I clear away our dirty dishes and retrieve a carton of rainbow sherbet from the freezer, Amy's favorite. My voice is strained; my nerves frazzled. "Amy, say 'buh.'" I extend a dish of sherbet in her direction. "Say 'buh.' Amy you have to say 'buh,' if you want the ice . . ."

For a nanosecond the crying stops. As tears stream down her face, Amy says, "baa."

My joy is unrestrained. *Thank you God!* I give Amy her sherbet. I hug her. I am jumping up and down with joy. I scoop generous dishes of sherbet for Jack, John, and me. The cold dessert slips past the lump in my throat and soothes my stomach. *Thank God.* If Amy hadn't said something, I don't know what I would have done when the meal was finished. I didn't want to give in, but I'm not a monster. I wouldn't let her starve. I honestly don't know what I would have done if she hadn't said "buh." John doesn't understand why I did this, and Jack thinks I'm horrid. I don't know what to do. I'm frustrated. I babble to God.

My ray of hope that Amy will learn to speak burns a bit brighter tonight. I reward myself with a Fig Newton before I go to bed.

During the next few weeks, the ray flickers. Many of our meals are bedlam, but I believe if Amy vocalized once for food, she can and will do it again. I must infuse my determination that Amy speaks into her strong will.

Today Amy has her three-month review after her therapy. I don't expect Mr. Snyder to report any progress, since Amy cried during the first four weeks of her therapy sessions, but the last few weeks she's made a variety of sounds. We arrive at Connell early. I examine the doors by the gym. After several minutes, I locate "J M W" scratched in the worn woodwork.

"Look, John." I point to the initials a few inches above his eye level. "Your Daddy carved his initials here years ago, when he went to school here."

"Daddy went to school here? Why? Did he have to learn how to talk?" John asks.

I smile. "Daddy didn't come here for speech therapy; he went to junior high here."

"Can I write my name on the wall?" John asks.

"Absolutely not." I nudge him toward the ramp. Once on the second floor, I put Amy down and she and John race to Mr. Snyder's door. I finish a poor third.

"You can sit there, Mrs. Willman." Mr. Snyder points to a padded armchair opposite his desk. "After Charmaine takes Amy to therapy, we'll talk." He scans a file on his desk.

Charmaine arrives, and Amy leaves with her without a fuss. John is engrossed in new library books, and I'm as ready as I ever will be for my first parent-teacher conference.

"This conference is mainly a formality," Mr. Snyder says. "I'm required by law to inform you of Amy's progress. She's only been here a short time, and we both know she wasn't very happy for weeks, so I don't have much to report. Charmaine's notes indicate Amy is beginning to make a variety of sounds. That's a good sign."

I nod in agreement.

"After she can make a wide range of sounds, Charmaine will try to teach her simple words. Right now, encouraging her to vocalize is important. Are you using the John Tracy lessons?"

"Yes. I've been doing Lesson One for two months. I think she understands lip movements are associated with speaking, so I guess it's time to move onto Lesson Two."

"Good. It's important to re-enforce the skills she learns here at home."

"I work with Amy twice a day. About twenty minutes every morning and afternoon."

"Good, but don't become so focused on her speech you forget she's a child. You remember Melissa, don't you? You saw her the first day you came here."

"Yes." How could I forget? You made it clear that teaching a deaf child excellent speech and verbal skills aren't enough. "Amy's not a problem here, is she?"

"No, and I want to keep it that way. Do you have any questions?"

"No?"

"Good. Keep doing what you're doing. We'll meet again in three months."

"Okay." I stand and motion for John to follow me to the observation room.

"Read this book to me, Mommy." John places a Curious George book on my lap.

"Not now, John. I want to think. I'll read it to you when we get home?"

"Okay." John takes the book and studies the pictures as I drift into my thoughts.

How can I teach Amy everything? Speech. Social skills. Emotional development. Language. I can't do it all. Amy's not an only child. I need to consider John. He deserves my time and attention, and so does Jack. I'm behind on the laundry. The yard needs attention. The only time I get five minutes to myself is when I take a bath. *God, I'm not up this task. Why did you give Amy such a hard row to hoe? If you expect me to do right by her, the least you could have done was given me a sharp hoe.* I give God no time to answer and shift from praying into demeaning myself. *I'm incompetent. I'll never do justice by Amy. If I had more patience or had studied speech therapy in college instead of sociology, maybe I could do something for her. My nerves are shot. I'm a complete failure. I might as well be dead.* After a moment of wallowing in self-pity, I wonder what would happen to Amy if I died. Who would look after her? Who would help her? She has no one but me.

In spite of my feelings of impending failure, I know I must try harder. I cannot quit. I must be Amy's hoe, clearing her road until she can do it herself.

11

Hard Lessons

Rebecca

The next three months are filled with the same exhausting routine. At home, I've mastered the art of multi-tasking, long before it became a buzzword. While in the observation room, John and I read books, do puzzles, and play games. This is our special time together.

Since Amy makes a variety of sounds, I now work with her thirty minutes every morning and afternoon. We're doing a John Tracy lesson on lipreading the words "ball" and "airplane." These words were chosen because the lip movements look very different when the words are spoken. The lesson explains that many words have similar lip movements, like "Mama" and "bye-bye," and thus aren't good words to learn first. The extra information in the John Tracy lessons has expanded my knowledge of deafness. I'm grateful.

I place a ball, a toy airplane, and pictures of balls and airplanes on the table. Amy and I sit opposite each other, with the light at her back so my face is illuminated. I put her hand to my throat and say, "ball." Then I reverse the actions. Sometimes I'm rewarded with a sound from Amy. I repeat the same actions with the airplane.

As I say "airplane" for the umpteenth time, I hear an airplane overhead. I grab Amy and run outside screaming, "Airplane. Look, Amy. Airplane." I point to the sky. All I gained from that burst of energy was exercise. I'm not sure if Amy understood what I yelled or saw the airplane. I realize language is more than words. The object or idea a word represents must be understood on many levels, as the actual object, in a picture, and as a toy. How can I convey all this to Amy?

We return to the table; John joins us. Since we've done this lesson for several weeks, I prepare to test Amy's ability to lipread "airplane" and "ball." If she can lipread these two words accurately, I can add new words.

"Amy, give me the ball." I place her hand on the ball to re-enforce her choice. "Amy, give me the airplane." I repeat the requests several times, moving her hand to the appropriate object each time. Then I put my hands in my lap and pray for a miracle.

"Ball. Amy, give me the ball. Ball, Amy. Give me the ball."

Before Amy can respond, John grabs the ball. "Here Amy, give this to Mother."

"John! Don't do that. Amy has to figure this out herself." I snatch the ball from him and slap it on the table in front of Amy.

"Don't you want the ball?" John's eyes are full of hurt and confusion.

I ignore him and repeat my plea. "Amy, give me the ball. Ball." Amy looks from me to John for an indication of what to do. "Ball, Amy. Give me the ball."

While Amy stares into space, John puts the ball in her hand.

"John, get out of here! I told you not to bother me when I'm working with Amy."

"I'm only trying to help," he sputters.

"You're not helping. You're making it worse. Go away. Go to your room. Go watch TV, go play outside. I don't care what you do, but just go!"

"Mommy . . ."

"GO!"

John leaves in tears. Amy doesn't understand my stinging words, but she sees the effect they have on John. Her howls join his. The lipreading lesson is over. I need another lesson on patience.

12

Gain and Loss

Rebecca

Amy has worn her "ears," as we call her hearing aids, for six months. The squealing demon has the power to make or break my hectic schedule. I can tolerate an occasional squeal, which occurs when Amy turns her head, but a long piercing squeal sends me running. That means the heavy earpiece is no longer in her ear and is swinging on the fragile Y cord. Rarely a week goes by that I do not visit Laverne, our hearing aid dealer, for a new Y cord, batteries, or to have minor adjustments made to Amy's earpiece. In the past six months I have amassed a collection of broken cords, dead batteries, and old earpieces.

"Jack, listen to this." I read a section of "Hints from Heloise" from our local paper. "Some woman has saved hundreds of those cardboard tubes from rolls of plastic wrap, tin foil and paper towels. She wants to know what to do with them. I'd tell her to 'Throw 'em away.' I can't believe the junk some people save."

"One man's junk is another man's treasure." Jack turns on the TV. "What about you? You have a box of broken hearing aid stuff on your dresser. What are you going to do with it?"

"I don't know, but I hate to throw away all that expensive stuff."

"Yeah, but none of it works, does it?" Jack flips the TV to another station.

"No, but I might be able to use it for something."

"Like what?" He props his feet on the coffee table, content to watch an old movie.

"I could use the cords for wire to hang pictures." I refold the newspaper, smoothing the creases.

"If Amy can break the cord, I don't think it will work for hanging pictures."

"You're right. It's stupid. I should toss —"A high-pierced squeal interrupts me. I'm off and running. Moments later I sink on the couch beside Jack. "I know what I can do with all those worthless cords."

"What?"

"Bundle up my frazzled nerves."

The following week Amy, John, and I return to the university for Amy's six-month hearing test. Dr. Zimmer is his usual brusque self. He pulls a paper out of Amy's file and compares it to the one he holds. "The audiogram I just plotted indicates the hearing aid is helping. She responded to some sounds at a lower volume than she did three months ago."

"I knew she was hearing better because I've noticed . . ."

"Your daughter still has a severe hearing loss," he interrupts. "That has not changed. Since she's benefitting from one aid, buy her one for the other ear. Come back in six months and I'll test her again." He tosses Amy's chart into a basket of items to be filed and leaves his dingy office. "Who's next?" I hear him call as he goes down the hall.

On the drive home, I refuse to let Dr. Zimmer's surly mood diminish my joy that the hearing aid is helping Amy. *If one aid helps her hear, then two aids will help her hear more.* I'm spinning off into a delightful fantasy about Amy speaking when the realization of the cost of maintaining two aids hits me. I'll need twice as many cords and batteries.

Her hearing aids are expensive. I'd planned to deduct their cost on our income tax return as a medical expense, but IRS regulations state hearing aids are an elective purchase, the same as cosmetic surgery, hence not an allowable deduction. "Since when is wanting your child to hear a cosmetic choice?" I argued with an IRS agent, to no avail.[2]

We can afford to buy the aid, by dipping into our savings, but I decide to explore the possibility of having a charitable organization help us with this expenses.

My brother-in-law, Rick, in Beatrice is in Sertoma. I know Sertoma promotes hearing awareness, so I contact our local chapter. A member tells me, "I'm sorry for your loss, but currently Sertoma does not provide assistance to individuals."

Strike one.

Next I try Easter Seals. After minutes on hold and being referred to several people, I am told, "Easter Seals rarely gives grants to individuals. I'll send an application, but the process is involved and lengthy, and in your case it would probably be futile."

Strike two.

The area March of Dimes representative responded, "No," before I finished my request.

"But your literature states your main focus is on birth defects. Amy was born deaf," I countered.

"I'm sorry, but our donations are allocated to research. The March of Dimes' goal is to prevent birth defects."

"Great, but what about the children already been born with birth defects who won't benefit from your research?" My voice took on a peevish tone.

She mumbled an apology and hung up. Strike three.

Thank God Jack and I can afford to buy the aid, but I wonder what happens to deaf children who have the misfortunate to be born into families who can't afford this expense?

"Mother!" I scream into the phone. "Amy said a word today! A real word!"

"What did she say?" Mother's voice is full of excitement.

---

2. The IRS now considers hearing aids and their batteries a deductible medical expense.

"'Eye.' We've been looking at pictures of faces and pointing out facial features for weeks, and today when I did this Amy pointed to her own eye and said, 'eye.'"

"I'm at a loss for words," Mother says. "And you know that rarely happens!"

We laugh. Both of us are known for our quick wit and our love of talking.

"Charmaine said Amy's language development is at least a year behind a hearing child since she didn't hear sound for thirteen months. Hearing children start babbling at about six months, so Amy's right on target. She's worn her aids for more than six months now. Charmaine said a child has to hear the same word a bazillion times before they try to say it. It's a good thing I like to talk."

"Yes, but don't talk so much Amy can't get a word in edgewise." We chuckle. "Have Jack's parents heard Amy speak?"

"No. Esther's still in denial, and she and J.W. both work all the time. I rarely see them except on special occasions, like holidays and birthdays."

"I bought a surprise for Amy months ago. I planned to send it to her for a special occasion. I'll send it now. Having my namesake say a word is very special."

"What is it?"

"Wait and see. It won't be a surprise if I tell you."

A week later a beautiful porcelain ballerina musicbox arrives. I place the ballerina on the palm of Amy's hand so she can feel the vibration of the metal roller playing *Lara's Theme*. Tears well in my eyes because Amy will never experience the wonder of music. As *Lara's Theme* plays, I realize I need to bury my "hearing dreams" for Amy. Listening to Fats Domino or Beethoven will never be a part of her life. As I ponder the significance of her loss, I fail to notice her bright blue eyes are mesmerized by the ballerina twirling on her hand.

Sunday, August sixteenth. Today is Esther's birthday. I baked a cake, and John and Amy decorated it. This evening when they arrive to celebrate, J.W. looks more tired than usual. His skin is ashen,

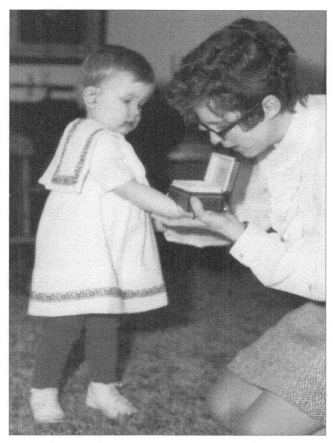

Amy with her mother feeling the music from the musicbox, about January 1971.

and his breathing strained after ascending the four steps to our door. Once seated, he extends his arms to Amy; she runs to him. With effort, he lifts her to his lap. He doesn't speak, just smiles. Amy grins.

"Momo," John tugs his grandmother's hand. "I made you a birthday cake. Amy helped."

"It's gorgeous, John. Almost too pretty to eat," Esther replies.

"Come and see my room." John pulls Esther toward his bedroom. Amy follows.

Esther picks up Amy, dislodging an earpiece. It squeals. "You should take these *things* out of her ears," Esther says as I replace the earpiece.

"Let me show you the wallpaper I bought for Amy's room." I change the subject, not wanting to have another discussion with Esther about "these things."

"These things can't be comfortable. They probably hurt her ears," Esther says.

I'm being sucked into another pointless discussion. "What do you think of this?" I unroll the wallpaper.

"If she has to wear them for therapy fine, but when she's at home . . ."

"She needs to wear them all the time if she's ever going to talk," I state.

"She'll be talking before you know it. I don't know why you're so worried. All children talk. She's just a late bloomer."

"No, she's not. She's deaf." My words shoot from my mouth like bullets.

"You should have another doctor examine her, and then you could stop all this needless therapy and worry."

"Come on Momo, look at my room." John's persistent tugging allows me to escape.

"Esther, you better look at John's room before he pulls your arm out of the socket. I'll get the ice cream ready. Don't be long, John. It's almost time to sing Happy Birthday to Momo."

Ninety minutes later Jack's parents leave. I put John and Amy to bed and sink onto the couch beside Jack. "Your dad looked really tired tonight. I'm worried about him."

"He'll be okay after a night's sleep." Jack opens the sports page of the paper.

"I hope so." Two blue eyes peek around the corner. "Amy's out of bed."

Jack stands, and Amy runs to her room.

"Your mother wants me to have another doctor examine Amy?"

"I don't think there's much point in it, but you know my mother. She won't . . ."

"Amy's out of bed again." I'm exhausted, in no mood for our usual two-hour bedtime ordeal. Amy's laying in the hall, resting her chin on the palms of her hands. "Amy! Go to bed!" I know she can't hear my words or read my lips; my command is one of habit and frustration. Amy notes my scowling face and takes a few steps toward her room. She's out of my sight, but not being able to hear, she doesn't realize I know she's still in the hall.

"Jack, put Amy in bed, please."

"Why? She'll be back out here before I can sit down. Did you write the Tracy Clinic about her bedtime behavior?"

"Yeah. I received a letter today, but haven't had a chance to read it." I locate the letter on the coffee table and use fingers with gnawed off nails to rip it open. "Nancy suggests leaving a light on in her room, because 'when a deaf child goes to bed in the dark, the child theoretically becomes deaf and blind. Removing her sight, her most vital link to the world is frightening and confusing for Amy.' Hmmm. I hadn't thought of that. It's worth a try." I refold the letter and stuff it in the envelope. "Do you want me to take Amy to another doctor?"

"Might as well, Mom won't quit harping on it until you do. She mentioned a doctor in Hastings to me who is supposed to be good. Dr. Shin. Call him?"

"Are you kidding me? An ear doctor, named Dr. Shin."

"Nope, that's his name."

I sigh with exasperation and weariness at the thought of one more thing to do. "I'll call him tomorrow. Amy's in the hall again."

"It's late. I'm going to bed." He chases Amy to her room on the way to our bedroom.

As we prepare for bed, Amy creeps from her room and leans against our bedroom door-frame. I wonder how many more times I will return her to bed tonight before I give up and let her sleep in the hall again. Then I remember Nancy's suggestion. I don't have a night light, but our porch light is outside Amy's bedroom window. I turn it on, open her drapes, and tuck her into bed. "Good night, Amy. Sleep tight."

I return to bed, snap on my bedside lamp and pick up a book. I'm anxious discover why everyone is talking about a seagull named Jonathan. I expect to be interrupted by Amy, but thirty pages later I realize she hasn't disturbed me. The porch light worked a miracle.

In the middle of the night, the persistent ringing of the telephone awakens Jack and me.

"Hello?" Jack mumbles.

I watch as Jack's eyes, heavy with sleep grow wide with fright. "What is it?" I ask.

"My dad. He's dead. Mom found him on the bathroom floor about five minutes ago."

"Oh, no."

At age sixty-one, J.W., the gentle giant, is dead. Sorrow fills my heart for Jack, Esther, and my children who will only have vague memories of their Grandpa. I'll miss J.W. He was an honest, hard-working, soft-spoken man who loved his family and accepted people as they were.

13

The Scarlet Letter

Rebecca

Several weeks after J.W.'s funeral, Amy had her appointment with Dr. Shin. After a comprehensive ear examination, he tells me what I already know.

"Physically Amy's inner and outer ears are fine, but she doesn't hear. She has a lot of wax in her ears, which can reduce a person's ability to hear substantially. I'll wash out her ears, but this won't restore her hearing."

"I know. She's deaf." I reply. "I'm here because my mother-in-law thought we needed to get a second, or in this case, a third opinion."

Dr. Shin prepares a bowl of warm water and plunges a bulb syringe, which reminds me of a turkey baster, into the solution. He gently squeezes the water into Amy's ear and clumps of horrible looking gunk washes out.

"Yuck," says John.

"Yuck is right. Where did all that stuff come from?" I ask.

"Everyone has wax in their ears." Dr. Shin continues rinsing Amy's ear. "Her ear molds pack the wax against the eardrum where it dries, making it difficult to remove."

"How can I get it out?"

"You can't. Don't use cotton swabs. They pack the wax tighter against the eardrum and embed cotton fibers in the wax. She'll need her ears washed periodically by a doctor."

I agree to have Dr. Proffitt wash Amy's ears every few months, and we return home. That evening I telephone Esther with the result of our visit to Dr. Shin.

"I suppose he knows what he's talking about," Esther says.

I know she's unconvinced, but I'm not dragging Amy to another doctor to pacify her.

Since J.W.'s death, Jack works longer hours at the grocery store. I see less of him as he now closes the store most evenings. In addition, I must now squeeze mowing the lawn, the only chore he did at home, into my schedule. While mowing last week, I remembered the day I brought Amy home from the hospital. When Jack arrived to take me home, I sobbed, "There's no way on God's green earth I can raise two children. You can take me home or Amy home, but I'm not going if she does. I can't handle two children under the age of two. I never should have had a second child." Jack replied it was a little late for this discussion now. *You underestimated yourself, Rebecca. You're doing more than you ever imagined possible.* But secretly, I'm afraid my ability to cope will soon reach the breaking point.

Sleepless nights and stomach problems remain my constant companions. To avoid flopping like a frustrated fish in bed, which disturbs Jack, I retreat to the living room and read. Tonight it's a new mystery from the library by Mary Higgins Clark. I read deep into the night before falling asleep.

Five hours later I jerk awake. 8:15 a.m. *Ye gods, we have to be at Connell in less than two hours.* "Jack!" No answer. I'm amazed that I slept through his noisy morning routine.

I follow the muffled sounds of *Captain Kangaroo* to the family room and find John and Amy perched side by side on the couch eating handfuls of Cheerios from a box.

"How about some milk with your cereal?" I ask.

"Sure," John replies.

"I'll get it, and then you two need to hurry and get dressed. Amy has school today."

Even though only John can hear my verbal commands, I always

include Amy in any orders I give, so John will not feel Amy does not need to obey what I say.

John and Amy's personalities are as different as night and day. John is easygoing, a cheerful Mother's helper who is quick to obey. Amy is strong-willed and defiant. John's extensive vocabulary is in stark contrast to Amy's lack of speech. Amy's first word was a six-month uphill struggle. Now, after nine months of tireless work by Charmaine and me, Amy speaks two words, but I'm certain if she had the vocabulary John did at her age, she'd be sassy.

As soon as I insert Amy's "ears," she babbles various sounds for an hour or more nonstop. Most days this is music to my ears, but not on Sunday. For the last two months, Amy's become increasingly difficult to control in church. We usually sit on the back pew, so we won't disturb others, but today that pew is occupied, so we sit near the front. The people seated near us are engaged in silent meditation. John sits on the pew without speaking; Amy squirms on my lap. Her babbling increases as she struggles to be free. People turn to see who is causing the commotion.

"Be quiet, Amy." John puts his index finger to his lips and hisses, "Shhhhhh!"

Amy spits a sloppy raspberry at John. I cup my hand over her mouth, which muffles the noise and covers my hand with warm spit.

"Can't you make her be quiet?" Jack asks. "Everyone is staring at her."

People always stare at Amy. I remove my spit-covered hand from Amy's mouth and she rewards me with "lad-er ladder lad-er" a noise she makes by flicking her tongue in and out. Her mouth is a noisy, gaping hole, dripping saliva.

"Amy, don't spit!" John pushes her away and knocks out an ear-piece, which squeals.

I switch off the first aid I reach. The squeal continues. *Damn! It's the other aid. Sorry God, don't hurl a thunderbolt at me for swearing in church.* I fumble for the other aid. Click. The squealing stops. Amy is instantly silent; she collapses on the pew like a deflated balloon.

"Jack," I whisper. "We have what every parent wants. An 'off switch' for a child."

We giggle. I hope God likes my joke and forgets about the cursing.

My need for perfection and my hectic schedule result in every morsel of food dropping like acid into my tension-filled stomach. I visit Dr. Anderson, hoping he can wave a magic wand and make me feel better. When he enters the exam room I give him my list of complaints. "I think I am going nuts. My stomach hurts all the time. Doesn't matter what I eat, it hurts. The squeal from Amy's hearing aid gets on my nerves. Total strangers ask me all sorts of rude questions about Amy, which hurt my feelings. If I don't say anything they probably think I'm rude, and when I snap back at them to mind their own business, I'm sure they think the parents of deaf kids are mean and nasty. "Did you ever read *The Scarlet Letter* by Hawthorne?"

"Yes, years ago, but what does that have to do with you?"

"I feel branded, like Hester Prynne. Is there a giant 'D' on my forehead marking me as the parent of a deaf child?"

He smiles and brushes my bangs off my forehead. "Nope, no 'D.' Sounds to me like you have a nervous stomach, not an ulcer. I'll give you a prescription to calm your stomach, but I want you to have an upper GI exam to be sure nothing is seriously wrong."

The report the following week is good: no ulcer. Dr. Anderson's prescription is not a miracle drug, but taking a pill before I eat calms my innards, sometimes.

14

Blessings and Fellow Travelers

Rebecca

Today Charmaine will discuss Amy's progress and outline future goals. After twelve months of intense therapy with Charmaine at school and with me at home, Amy can now say four words.

"I'm sure you feel Amy isn't making any progress," Charmaine says, "but that's not true. She vocalizes all the sounds needed to speak every word in the English language. She comprehends more words than she speaks, and she understands the connection between sounds and communicating. Learning new words will be easier and faster for her now."

"I hope you're right." As I say this, a book I read recently pricks my conscience. *I must be doing something wrong.* The book, written by the mother of a deaf son, related how every night before bed, she told him, "I love you." After several months, her son said, "I love you" and soon spoke in sentences. Now at age five, he spoke as well as most hearing children. *Why isn't Amy progressing like this? I talk to her all the time.*

"Part of the reason Amy's doing so well is you work with her at home. I wish more parents were as diligent as you." Charmaine leans back in her chair; her smile is genuine.

"Thanks." *But I'm not getting results that other mother did.* "In books, it always seems easy."

"Don't become discouraged." Charmaine rests her elbows on the desk and leans toward me. "The words will come. Nothing happens overnight." Her voice is full of confidence.

One day I'll write a book about raising a deaf child. An honest one. Books with fairy-tale endings give parents unrealistic expectations. "What else can I do to help Amy?"

"I have two suggestions." Charmaine opens a drawer and withdraws a stack of index cards.

"Mommy, can I have my snack now?" John asks.

Charmaine pauses while I rip open miniature boxes of Froot Loops. "Here, John. Give this one to Amy. I'll be done in a few minutes and we can leave. Go on, Charmaine, I'm listening."

"Most deaf people learn visually. Labeling items at home will help Amy understand that everything has a printed word associated with it." Seeing my perplexed face, Charmaine adds, "Deafness is an educational, not a physical, disability. Deaf people must see language, since they can't hear it." She hands me a card with "chair" written in block letters.

"This won't be hard." I slip the card into my purse. "What's your other suggestion?"

Charmaine hesitates. "I know coming here three days a week is time-consuming, and I'm sure John finds it boring, but I'd like Amy to come for therapy on Thursdays also."

"Why?" My voice betrays my disgust at another demand made on my shrinking day.

"Another deaf child is enrolled here. I'd like to have group therapy on Thursdays."

I can't believe it. There's another mother out there struggling to raise a deaf child. "Who is she? How old is she? When will you start the group?" My excitement is obvious.

"Next Thursday. Her name's Teena Eaton. She's three months younger than Amy and has only worn her aids four months, so she doesn't vocalize as much as Amy, but I think they'll both benefit from group therapy."

"What time?" *I won't miss the opportunity to talk to someone else with a deaf child.*

"Ten o'clock." Charmaine hands me a flyer. "Will you be at this meeting tonight?"

"What meeting?"

"The Central Nebraska Association of Parents of Deaf and Hearing-Impaired Children is meeting tonight in the gym at eight o'clock."

"I'll be there if I can get a sitter."

That afternoon, as I attach 3 × 5 cards labeled with words to lamps, doors, and other items, I recall a Bible verse. "Be joyful always, pray continually, and give thanks in all circumstances." Maybe St. Paul could be joyful in all circumstances, but I'm not very good at that. Pray continually. I have that one down, but I've yet to receive any answers. Give thanks in all circumstances. What blessings have I received as a result of Amy's deafness? None that I know of. Oh well, one out of three; it's a start. I take my stack of cards to the bathroom and ponder where to tape "bathtub."

"Mother! Amy won't give me the blue color," John calls from the kitchen.

"Use a different color, John." I put "bathtub" above the soap dish and tape it in place.

"But I want the blue one," John whines.

"Amy will put it down in a minute, and then you can have it."

"Amy's arting on the wall," John calls.

"Tell her to stop." I adjust the sign and step back to look at it. *Now it's straight.*

"Amy, Mother said to stop," John says with authority. "Give me the blue color now."

Shuffling of chairs alerts me to a fight. "Buh-mmmmmm. Eeeee," Amy screams.

"All right. All right. I'm coming. No wonder I can't get anything done." When I enter the kitchen, John and Amy are still squabbling over the crayon, but my attention isn't focused on their struggle. I'm transfixed by blue crayon slashes on the wall. The artist is still at work.

"Amy! Get off that table. Give me that crayon." I snatch the offending blue crayon from her hand. "What's the matter with you?" Amy's eyes twinkle as she grabs another crayon. "Give me that crayon." I pry a yellow crayon from her hand. "No more crayons for you." I collect the scattered crayons. "Do you have the red one, John?" I kneel on the floor.

"No. Look, mommy." John extends a picture toward me. "It's for you."

Under the table searching for crayons, I can't see it, but answer, "That's nice."

"It's a refrig-a-ray-tor."

Crawling from under the table, I see John's art is a lopsided purple rectangle with a small red handle. The drawing is crude, but what amazes me is that at age four, he's written FRIGADOR on it. "It's wonderful." While pondering John's accomplishment, I notice Amy has the missing red crayon. Before I can grab it, she adds an ugly red slash on the wall. Picasso she is not.

That night Jack watches as John sounds out words on the 3 × 5 cards and places them by the appropriate item on the table: fork, knife, spoon, plate. "When did he start reading?" Jack asks.

"Today." I show him John's "frigador" picture secured by a magnet to our refrigerator. "Our days of spelling words so John won't know what we're talking about are over."

Jack spells a mild expletive.

"Daddy spelled a dirty word," John says.

Thankfully, a neighbor girl can babysit on short notice and Jack has the evening off from work. When we arrive at Connell, the small parking lot is filled. In the gym, two dozen adults of various ages are engaged in noisy conversations. Not knowing anyone, we sit by ourselves. A woman breaks away from a group and joins us. "Hi, welcome. I'm Vodis Dahlke."

"Nice to meet you. I'm Rebecca Willman, and this is my husband Jack."

A man with gray hair approaches. "This is my husband, Calvin." He shakes Jack's hand.

"I didn't know about this group until today," I say. "I thought I was the only person in Nebraska with a deaf child."

"We've all felt that way. We lived in the Nebraska panhandle when Julie was born. Very few people out there and none deaf. I never met another deaf child until we took Julie to NSD," Vodis says.

"What's NSD?" Jack asks.

The Nebraska School for the Deaf," Cal says. "It's in north Omaha. Really nice."

"How old is Julie?" I ask.

"Thirteen. She's in the seventh grade at NSD."

Thirteen! People do survive after learning they have a deaf child; Vodis is living proof.

Tonight the members discuss buying a neonatal testing device for the hospital. A local pediatrician that was invited to the meeting says, "This device is new and I don't trust the results." Parents argue that identifying a deaf child in infancy is worth the risk of some inaccurate results. The doctor is not swayed. "Go ahead, buy it, but I'll never use it." I vow not to take my children to this doctor.

"Does Amy wear aids?" Vodis asked.

"Yes. She wants them on first thing in the morning. What about Julie?"

"Julie stopped a year ago. I expect Amy will do the same when she's twelve or thirteen."

"Why?" Jack asks.

"Many reasons," Vodis says. "Peer pressure. They don't want to look different in public. And, many deaf people prefer their silent world instead of trying to interpret sound."

"I can't imagine Amy ever giving up her aids."

"Maybe she'll be different." Vodis smiles, a hopeful smile.

Sleep does not come easy tonight, but my wakefulness is due to the excitement of meeting kindred spirits. Even though all the parents at the meeting had older deaf children, our bond was instant and strong due to our shared experiences. I'm no longer alone. In our quiet dark bedroom, an inaudible voice speaks to my spirit. *I knew you could do it. That's why I gave you Amy.*

Thursday we race up the ramp. "They're not here, yet," Charmaine says.

The patter of small running feet, followed by a female voice shouting, "Wait! Slow down," announces the arrival of Teena and her mother, Bernice Eaton.

Teena is a mirror image of Amy; the same height with blonde hair and bright blue eyes. They wear similar hearing aid harnesses. The girls stare at each other. A hearing aid squeals.

As if cued to speak in unison, Bernice and I say, "Come here. Let me fix that." We reach for their earpieces, but the blonde imps dodge us. We look at each other and shake our heads.

"That squealing drives me nuts," Bernice says.

"Me too." We nod like old friends who have years of shared experiences.

After introductions, Charmaine beckons the girls to follow her. "I'd like the girls to spend thirty minutes together."

Teena darts out the door and Charmaine dashes after her. Amy runs to keep pace with them. "Feel free to watch through the window," Charmaine calls over her shoulder.

"I don't envy her." Bernice shakes her head.

"She'll have her hands full with those two live wires. Come on, let's watch."

Bernice, John, and I pull chairs near the one-way mirror. Charmaine is on the floor with the girls. They watch as she withdraws an apple from a bag. "Apple." Charmaine extends the apple like the witch offering the poisoned apple to Snow White. "Teena, say apple."

Teena grabs the apple and runs around the room shrieking. Charmaine leaps up in hot pursuit and corners Teena, but not before Amy joined the race. A few minutes later, Charmaine has corralled the girls, and they are once again seated on the floor.

"Looks like organized chaos," I say.

"Good thing she has plenty of patience," Bernice responds.

"More than I have some days, that's for sure." I relax in my chair. John is reading a Dr. Seuss book, which allows me time to converse with Bernice without feeling guilty.

"When Charmaine told me about you last week, I could hardly

wait to meet you." Bernice turns toward me. "I thought, at last I'll meet this woman I've heard so much about."

"What do you mean? I'm not famous."

"I've followed you around the state for months. When I took Teena to Dr. Proffitt, he said he'd diagnosed a little girl with deafness a few months ago. At the university, Dr. Zimmer asked if I knew you and about the speech program in Grand Island. I called around, and here I am."

"Did you have trouble enrolling Teena into this program?"

"No, it was easy. All Mr. Snyder wanted was a copy of Teena's audiogram."

"You have no idea what I went through." While detailing my struggle to enroll Amy in therapy, I realize my actions are a blessing to the parents of deaf children who follow me. God used me to accomplish something good for others. This revelation surprises and humbles me.

"When I learned Teena was deaf, I cried for weeks." Bernice says.

"I couldn't eat. I lost a lot of weight."

"Too bad that didn't happen to me." Bernice pats her bulging stomach. "I ate everything in sight. After crying for six weeks, I said, 'crying isn't getting you or Teena anyplace. Get off your big butt and do something.'"

"Sounds like my story. Do you know why Teena's deaf?"

"No. My husband and I are in the process of adopting Teena. We got her when she was six weeks old. We don't know much about her parents. What about Amy?"

"I don't know why she's deaf. You're lucky Teena's adopted; at least you don't have family members telling you your child's deafness is entirely your fault." My voice is tinged with anger and bitterness.

"Yeah, but the adoption agency wants to take her away from us."

"Why? How can they do that?" My anger is replaced with surprise.

"The adoption isn't final yet. The agency thinks raising a deaf child might be too difficult for us, so they want to put Teena in foster care."

"That's terrible. What are you going to do?" I watch Bernice's reflection in the one-way mirror, an unwilling voyeur as she wipes tears from her cheeks.

"We're fighting it." Bernice dabs her eyes with a tissue. "We've had Teena two years; she's family. If Teena was our biological child, we wouldn't try to exchange her because she can't hear. Our caseworker agrees and supports us. We'll know the court's decision in a month."

I look through the mirror; Charmaine is beckoning us to join her. "I think the first session went well. We'll be working on colors for a couple of weeks. If you have any small red, blue, or yellow items at home, have the girls bring them next week."

"I have some crayons I'd be happy to donate." Having shared the story of Amy's artistic endeavors with Bernice and Charmaine, my offer is met with laughter.

Three weeks later Bernice's face is flushed and beaming when we meet her at Connell. "The adoption was final yesterday. Teena's all ours now."

"Wonderful! I'm so happy for you." We enter the observation room and John slumps into a chair. This morning he begged to stay home. He swings his feet so they hit the wall making a dull thump. When I frown, he glares and kicks faster and harder. I feel guilty for making him come here four mornings a week, but I have no choice. "Let's go to lunch and celebrate the adoption after therapy. How about McDonald's? My treat."

At the mention of McDonald's, John halts a kick midair. "Can I go too?"

"Of course, you're my number one son." I pat his knee. "I love you."

"I love you too, Mommy. Will Ronald McDonald be there?" The swinging legs are still.

"Maybe." John retrieves a small car from his toy bag and pushes it along the frame of the one-way mirror. "Bernice, be prepared for rude remarks and impolite stares at McDonald's."

"What do you mean?" Bernice frowns.

Bernice and her family live in Central City, a small, rural Nebraska town. News spreads like the flu in a small town. Everyone in Teena's home town knows she's adopted and wears hearing aids, so Bernice hasn't been subjected to the prying questions of strangers as I have.

"You won't believe the dumb questions people ask me in public, like, 'Does she have to wear those hearing aids?' I want to tell them, 'Of course not, you idiot. We spent a small fortune on these squealing demons so we could get a little sympathy.'" My prophecy becomes reality for Bernice later.

When Bernice is in the "big city," she often shops in Grand Island before returning home to Central City. Several weeks after hearing rude comments at McDonald's, Bernice told me, "I was in the children's department of Penney's and a total stranger said, 'What have you put in that child's ears? She's jabbering like an idiot. What's wrong with her?' That really hurt my feelings. Boy was I mad."

"Did you tell her to mind her own business?" I ask.

"No. I was too stunned, but after she left, I thought of several snippy remarks."

"Remember them. Maybe you can use them another time. I always think of my best lines when I'm lying in bed trying to sleep."

Bernice and I make jokes about how ignorant people are about deafness to hide our pain, but we both know that having a deaf child isn't the least bit funny.

15

Terrible Twos

Rebecca

"Mother," John screams, "Amy is ruining my race track! She took all my cars. I asked her for them, but she won't give them back. I even said please and told her she could have one."

I'm in the next room ironing, so I welcome a break, even if it is to referee a squabble between two preschoolers. John and Amy are so different. He's a little gentleman, a diplomat, but Amy . . . she's no lady, she's a terrorist.

"Amy! Stop kicking the race track!" I scream. Yelling is pointless; she does not hear me even though she has on her aids, but I'm as frustrated as John. I grab Amy and spin her around to face me. "Amy, play with your own toys. It's not nice to ruin your brother's race track, he's . . ."

Midway through my lecture, Amy gives me an impish smile and covers her eyes with her hands, rendering herself deaf and blind. I shake my head at her cleverness.

I return to my ironing, but before I can finish the next shirt, John alerts me to an overflowing toilet. "What next?" I mumble as I rush toward the bathroom. I know who is responsible for this, Amy. I'm trying to toilet train her, without much success. Her solution to wet underwear is to flush it down the toilet. This time, the plunger unclogs the toilet, sparing a costly visit from the plumber.

That night I write my frustrations to Nancy at the John Tracy Clinic. Two weeks later I have her response: "Amy doesn't appear ready to be toilet trained. I suggest you try again in a few months. Don't worry, she'll be toilet trained long before she starts school. Ninety percent of all children, hearing or deaf, are toilet trained before they are three."

Today after group therapy, Bernice and Teena come to our house so we can discuss the bombshell Charmaine lobbed at us last week. "Now what are we going to do?" Bernice takes the iced tea I offer.

"I don't know." My frown reveals my own concerns.

"Teena was just getting used to Charmaine. When a new therapist arrives, Teena will be back at square one again trying to adjust."

"Didn't Mr. Snyder tell you? They're not hiring a replacement for Charmaine."

"Why?" Bernice sips her tea.

"The program at Connell loses its federal funding in June." I squeeze lemon in my tea. "Charmaine quit now, because she was going to be out of a job by the end of the month anyway."

"What about the summer program?" Bernice leans forward, anxious for my response.

"There isn't going to be one. Mr. Snyder said the Grand Island schools can't provide any language therapy this summer or in the fall if they don't get funding."

"If Grand Island doesn't offer a program, what are our kids supposed to do?"

"I've made some calls. There are no programs being offered anyplace in central Nebraska. The closest program is at the university in Lincoln. They offer speech therapy for preschool hard of hearing and deaf children three days a week. The kids get forty-five minutes of private therapy and thirty minutes in group. It's not free, but I plan to enroll Amy. The Tracy Clinic material is good, but that's not enough. This program is our only option. I don't like the idea of driving 600 miles a week, but what choice do we have? I want Amy to continue therapy. If she doesn't, how will she learn to talk? When I asked Jack,

he said 'Fine. Go ahead, but don't expect me to help with the driving.'
Are you interested? Maybe we could carpool."

The anger on Bernice's face is replaced with concern. "I'll talk it
over with my husband, but I don't think we can afford it. How much
is it?"

I quote the price.

"I don't know. I'd have to quit my part-time job to go, and we need
that money."

"Think about it, please," I beg. "It would be great to have your
company."

"I will, but right now, my answer is no."

"If you change your mind, let me know." My gnawed off nails
return to my mouth.

Bernice's dejected mood is contagious. We shuffle in silence down
the driveway to her car. After waving goodbye, I pull puffy seed heads
from dandelions. I should dig out the weeds, but I'm not in the mood.
I toss the seed heads in the trash and walk into the garage.

16

Miles and Moments

Rebecca

On the first Monday in June, at three forty-five, I drive into our garage having completed my first two-hundred mile round trip to Lincoln for Amy's language therapy. I arch my back and rub my neck to relieve tight muscles. One down, twenty-six more to go this summer. We left mid-morning. John and Amy rode in their car seats with a box of toys wedged between them. After an hour, John said. "Are we there?"

"No, but it won't be long and we'll stop and eat lunch." I looked in the rearview mirror; neither John nor Amy was in their car seats. I slowed from seventy-five miles an hour to a dead stop, which galvanized John into action. He climbed into his car seat and stuck his thumb in his mouth.

"I'm sorry, Mommy. I dropped my dog."

Amy was on the floor behind my seat. I reached over the seat to grab her dress; my short arms clawed the air. I had no choice but to get out of the car on the shoulder of the interstate, pull her off the floor and stuff her in her car seat. Minutes later we enjoyed sack lunches at a rest stop, which gave us time to stretch and the opportunity to use a bathroom. Amy refused to use the strange toilet, so the extra underwear I brought was used before we reached Lincoln. Twenty-five minutes later I enrolled Amy in the university's program without talking to Dr. Zimmer. I saw him skulking about the halls, but his assistant, Mrs. Kramer, a middle-aged woman with gray hair, handled the paperwork.

"How many children are in the group?" I asked.

"Fifteen. Group therapy is at the other end of this hall." Mrs. Kramer was all business, rattling off the information while typing a form. "The viewing room is on the left, behind the green door. Individual therapy is upstairs, you can't watch that. You," she lifted her head and peered over her glasses, "and your son can wait in there until, uh . . ." she consulted the form in the typewriter, "until Amy is brought downstairs. Bathrooms are in the basement." She jerked the form from the typewriter, rolled her chair across the uneven wooden floor to a file cabinet, and jammed the form inside. She turned, surprised that we were still there. "Did you have a question?"

"No," I mumbled as we walked toward the crowded waiting room.

Minutes later, Mrs. Kramer and fifteen young coeds arrived. Several children rushed to greet them, calling the coeds by name in a flat monotone, a voice typical to many deaf people.

Mrs. Kramer flipped a page on her clipboard. "Each student therapist will be matched with a child. Pay attention, so this can be done quickly. "Marsha Reimers, Karen Johnson."

A tall girl rose with a nudge from her mother and followed the coed. More names were called in quick succession. "Judy Simmons, Thomas Lawson."

A woman grasped a small boy by his hand. He tried to pry her fingers from his wrist. Unsuccessful, he leaned on his heels while she pulled him across the room. "Oooooow." He howled as if in mortal pain.

"Come here, Tommy. We have lots of toys to play with upstairs," his therapist said.

"OOOOOOOWWW."

In a reversal of actions, his mother tried to pry her son's hands from her arm. "He's never been in therapy." Her face was crimson. "Go on, Tommy." She pushed him into the outstretched arms of the coed who pulled him across the room toward the elevator.

"OOOooooowww." Tommy flung his free arm back and forth and kicked the elevator door until it opened. After a brief struggle, they entered; the solid elevator doors closed but didn't mute Tommy's howl. His mother sank in a chair, exhausted.

"My son acted like that when he first came here," a mother said.

Tommy's mother sank lower in her chair. I could read her thoughts. *I can't go through this three times a week until he adjusts.*

"Sandra Minor, Amy Willman."

Having attended therapy in Grand Island for a year, Amy was accustomed to being taken from me. Like a lamb going to the slaughter, she made not a sound.

Thirty minutes later, the coeds with their young charges walked past the waiting room where we sat toward the group therapy room. Like rats following the pied piper, John and I, and most of the other mothers followed the group. The small observation area was filled with twelve chairs in two rows. John and I spent the next twenty minutes jockeying for a good view in the stuffy room.

"How much longer?" John leaned against the door, bored and sleepy.

I shifted from one foot to the other. "Let's wait in the other room." The campus carillon chimed two. "Amy will be done in twenty minutes, and then we'll go home."

"Good." John climbed on a chair and swung his legs.

I made a mental note to bring something special for him on Wednesday. Poor John. He never complains, but it's not fair. Our entire life revolves around what Amy needs.

At home now, I arch my back. Free from the confines of their car seats and having slept most of the way home, John and Amy are rambunctious. They pull paper, crayons, and a pair of scissors from a kitchen drawer. Four hands clutch the blunt-tipped scissors, twisting and turning to loosen the two unwanted hands. To deter an impending squabble, I shout, "John, go outside and play. You need some fresh air after being cooped up all day."

"All right. But I had them first." He clumps toward the sliding door.

Amy clutches the scissors. I watch as a puddle grows between her feet. "Oh Amy." I sigh, frustrated and exhausted. After changing her underwear, we go outside to remove clothes from the line. "One, two, three." She drops the pins in the clothespin bag to my repeated counting.

❧

Our thrice-weekly trips to Lincoln blend into an endless road trip. I cross off the days slowly moving toward August 6, the last day of the summer session. Often the viewing room is packed with university students, leaving no room for the parents. To escape the tedium of the waiting room, John and I enjoy the paintings at the Sheldon Art Gallery or walk across the campus to see the dinosaur skeletons in Morrill Hall. The Etch-a-Sketch I bought him for a special treat keeps him entertained giving me the opportunity to converse with the other parents. Today I turn to the woman beside me, who's fanning herself with a two-year-old magazine. "Hi, I'm Rebecca."

"Sure is muggy in here today. I asked the janitor to adjust the air conditioning, but he says it's broken." She brushes damp strands of wavy brown hair off her forehead.

"Here comes someone with a fan. That might help." I point down the hall.

A janitor shuffles into the room with a box fan. Several people move so he can locate an electrical socket. After finding one, he stretches the cord to its full length, but it doesn't reach the socket. "I'll have to go find an extension cord." He shuffles from the room.

"Par for the course," someone says.

"Yeah, no one cares about the parents," another adds.

The woman beside me says, "You better grab a magazine before they are all gone." Her answer confuses me. I want to talk, not read. Seeing my perplexed face she adds, "For a fan. I doubt he'll be back before we leave. I'm Melinda."

I snatch a tattered journal from a table. "I'm Rebecca. And this is my son, John."

"How long has your child been in the program, here?" Melinda asks.

"Amy's been here four weeks. She'll be three in January. How old is your child?"

"Lucy's five. This is her third year. In the fall she'll go to kindergarten at our neighborhood school. They don't have speech therapy for kids her age, but that's okay. I'll work with her at home. In six more weeks I'll be done with this place forever, except for Lucy's annual hearing exam with Dr. Zimmer."

"Why? Do you have a long drive?" Since my main complaint about the university's program is its distance from our home, I assume that's her complaint.

"No, we live on the south side of Lincoln. Takes me less than fifteen minutes to get here."

"Hasn't this program helped Lucy?"

"At first, but she hasn't learned much the last eighteen months."

"Why? What changed?" I stop fanning; it's pointless. The air is heavy with humidity.

"Nothing changes. That's the problem." She tosses her magazine-fan aside.

"What do you mean?" I lean forward in my chair.

"The university has a twelve-week program of language therapy lessons that the student therapists use with your child regardless of their age or hearing loss. The lessons are repeated every semester."

"I thought they had different programs for different age groups." Sweat trickles down my back. I resume fanning myself.

"They should, but they don't. Lucy's done the same lessons for three years. I suppose some repetition is necessary, but . . ." her voice fades.

"I can't believe the university does that." My brow furrows with unspoken thoughts.

Melinda shrugs her shoulders. "Wait and see."

"I only plan to bring Amy here this summer. She was attending therapy in Grand Island, but they ran out of money last month. If they obtain funding, they'll resume this fall."

"You drive a hundred miles to come here." Melinda's remark is an exclamation, not a question.

"Yes. Takes a big bite out of my day." My mind races to the chores I must complete later.

"For your sake, and Amy's too, I hope Grand Island gets funding. This program will be a waste of your time and not much help to Amy after another semester."

"Look, Mommy. I drew a house." John extends his Etch-a-Sketch.

"Good job. Draw something else for me." He shakes the Etch-a-Sketch, erasing the picture and I return my attention to Melinda. "Why is Lucy going to a public school instead of the Nebraska School for the Deaf?"

"Lucy has a moderate hearing loss. Her speech is quite good. I think she'll do fine in public school. Dr. Zimmer's against it, but we don't want to send Lucy to school in Omaha when she's so young. If she can't keep up with the other kids, we'll send her to the Nebraska School for the Deaf [NSD] in a few years."

"You're lucky. Grand Island only offers special education for mentally challenged students. Dr. Zimmer says since Amy is profoundly deaf, NSD is her *only* option." I imagine the day I must leave Amy at NSD and drive home to Grand Island, one hundred fifty miles away. I shake my head like the Etch-a-Sketch, but the unhappy vision is not erased. I make a mental note to research other options.

Other mothers in the room, who are ringside to our conversation, share their educational plans. Some haven't decided, but most are opting for local schools and will only send their child to NSD as a last resort. That topic exhausted, someone asks, "Why is your child deaf?"

From strangers on the street, I'd consider this nosy and would bite my tongue to refrain from telling them to mind their own business. But in a room of parents with deaf children, I'm not threatened and have the luxury of expressing my feelings honestly without fear of censure. Having no definitive answer to the question that haunts me, I launch into a brief history about Amy's life. "When Amy was about ten months old, I was filling out her baby book and realized I had nothing to write on the page, 'Baby's First Words.' I looked in John's baby book and saw he spoke several words at the same age. Amy never reacted to loud noises, so I took her to our family doctor, who told us he wasn't qualified to say if Amy could hear, and referred us to a specialist, and here I am. Dr. Zimmer thinks she was born deaf, but no doctor knows for sure." Once again, God hears my oft-repeated plea: *Why is Amy deaf?* God must be busy; I receive no response.

"What about your child? What caused his deafness?" I ask a teenage mother.

"Drugs. Some drugs I took during pregnancy." She bows her head and flips the pages of a worn magazine. Her posture tells me she will not expand her answer. I'm afraid to ask if they were prescription or street drugs.

"Drugs caused my daughter's deafness too." The woman speaking does not raise her eyes from the sweater she is knitting. "When my daughter was two, she had a sore throat. The doctor prescribed an antibiotic that got rid of the sore throat, but one of the side effects of the drug was hearing loss. For two years Amanda was normal. She was beginning to talk. Now she's four and doesn't say much more than she did when she was two years old."

"My child had meningitis when he was three." Another mother says. "Between the disease and the high fever, his hearing was destroyed."

A bleached blonde rubs her bulging belly. "I hope this baby's not premature, like Doris was. I can't deal with two handicapped children."

"How far along are you?" I ask.

"Seven months." She props her feet on a table to elevate her swollen legs. "Doris was born two months premature. The doctors don't know if she was born deaf or if the high fever she had when she was in the incubator caused it. Her deafness wasn't anybody's fault, but there's no excusing the doctor who . . ." Her jaw tightens, her body fills with tension. She spits words full of anger. "Doris wasn't breathing well at first, so a doctor in the delivery room gave her a blast of pure oxygen. He got it in her eyes and blinded her. Deaf and blind. It's not fair."

I'm unable to respond I clench my jaw with anger and despair. My stomach knots.

"A few months before I was pregnant with Lucy, I had a miscarriage." Melinda's voice is flat, devoid of emotion. "Thursday was my carpool day. That morning, my obstetrician confirmed I was seven weeks pregnant. I called my husband and shared the good news. That afternoon when I dropped off Sara, she's one of the kids in my carpool, she asked me to come into her house. She said, 'My mom wants to talk to you about the Girl Scout meeting.' Sara's younger sister greeted me at the door; she had the measles. I broke out with them several days later. For the rest of my pregnancy I wondered how much damage the measles had done to my child. Would my baby be born blind, deaf, retarded, or worse? I'm thankful Lucy's only deaf."

"How terrible." I sense her statement, "I'm thankful Lucy's only deaf," was said for her benefit. Melinda's faraway stare says, "I wish I didn't know why Lucy's deaf. It's all my fault."

My God. Most of these women know why their child is deaf. If Melinda hadn't gone into Sara's house that day, she never would have gotten the measles, and Lucy wouldn't be deaf. If I were in her shoes, I'd never stop blaming myself.

Today, a thunderstorm with brilliant lighting and rolling thunder accompanies my drive home. John and Amy slump in their car seats, heads lolling to one side, heavy with sleep. I'm haunted by Melinda's story and those of the other parents I've heard in the past few weeks. The windshield wipers swish across my vision. After a crack of lighting, followed by an ear-shattering clap of thunder, I realize that relating how you discovered your child was deaf is like rain on the windshield. The wipers can't remove all traces of the torrential rain, and neither can the pain of having a deaf child be eliminated by retelling your story.

The wipers swish, *if only, if only. If only* I hadn't taken drugs. *If only* my child didn't have meningitis. *If only* my child wasn't born premature. *If only* I knew why Amy was deaf. *If only* I hadn't gotten the measles. *If only, if only.* A few minutes later the thunderstorm is over and I drive toward the sunny, western sky. The wipers swish *if only* one more time before I shut them off. I stare through the clean windshield and realize God has blessed me with ignorance. He knows me well. Suffering the torture of *if only* would be more than I could bear. I thank God for not revealing to me why Amy is deaf.

Summer school is finally over. The university will start their fall semester in five weeks. Tonight as I prepare for bed, Jack watches as I comb my hair, wet from my recent shower.

"I need a vacation. During the past twelve weeks I've driven seven thousand miles. Do you realize that's almost a third of the way around the equator, and all I've seen is cattle and corn. I can't do this for two more years." I jerk the comb through a snarl.

"Maybe you won't have to." Jack flips through several TV channels and settles on the Tonight Show. "Hopefully the program here will get funding this fall."

"I hope so." I move closer to the mirror to part my hair. *What's this?* I squint. No. It can't be. I'm only twenty-six years old. But it is. My first gray hair.

17

Respite and Renewal
Rebecca

The longest day of summer was two months ago, but my days defy the laws of nature; they have increased in length. Since the university is on hiatus, my days seem endless. I have the luxury of being a stay-at-home mom who actually stays at home, and I love it. Most days I finish my chores by noon and enjoy the afternoon reading or working in the yard. John and Amy are drawing pictures on our concrete patio. After Amy's artistic expression with crayons, I bought chalk. It's not permanent and washes off any surface.

"Do you want to help me?" I step outside with two small buckets. They are too young to help with weeding, but they like to pick raspberries.

"Yeah." John grabs a bucket. When Amy sees where he's going, she disappears with him into the three-foot-high prickly raspberry canes. Amy loves raspberries, which surprises me, since less than a year ago she refused to eat anything with lumps, and raspberries are full of seeds.

The day is gorgeous, so I decide to have a picnic supper. Before Jack arrives home, I set up a card table and place bottles of catsup, mustard, and pickles on the paper tablecloth to keep it from blowing to Kansas. When Jack arrives he places burgers on the grill and fills his glass with iced tea. John and Amy are seated, anxious to have their hamburger. A gust of wind raises a corner of the tablecloth, threatening to set it soaring.

"Quick, put this on your plate before it blows away." I hand Jack a jar of mustard. Too late. His paper plate with potato chips whips across the yard scattering its contents. I shoo flies off Amy's plate and fan a swarm of gnats away from her face. "Cheee, chee, chee." Amy kicks the underside of the table, frustrated. The catsup bottle vibrates from her mini-earthquake, but remains upright.

Jack hands her a slice of cheese. "Is this what you want?"

Amy shakes her head and hollers louder. "Chee, chee, Chee." Her plate blows away.

"Wow," John shouts. "They're Frisbees." He runs after Amy's airborne plate.

"I think she wants Cheetos," I say.

Jack grabs a handful of Cheetos and puts them near Amy. "Rebecca, let's eat inside. The bugs are terrible and nothing is staying on the table. He flips the burgers and then uses the spatula to kill a fly. I raise my eyebrows, but make no comment.

"It's impossible to enjoy a pleasant evening outside with the wind and bugs." Out of my grumbling, an idea is born. "We should screen the patio."

"What?" Jack swats another fly with the spatula. "Hand me a paper plate."

"You're not going to use that spatula on the burgers are you?"

"Sure, why not."

"You just used it to kill flies."

"The heat from the charcoal will kill the germs." Jack scoops the burgers onto the plate and closes the grill.

I shake my head and wonder if the five-second rule about food being dropped on the floor can be applied to food served with a spatula used to kill flies.

"Go ahead and have it screened. Hire somebody; I don't have time to do it," Jack says as he opens the sliding door. "I have more than I can handle at the store. Come on, John. We're eating inside."

❧

At noon the next day a salesman and carpenter arrive from a local lumber company. "Sure is hot outside, isn't it?" I comment. The carpenter nods and smiles. The salesman wastes no time with pleasantries.

"Okay, let's get started. What do you have in mind?" The salesman asks.

"I'd like a porch big enough for a picnic table, a hammock, room for the kids to—"

"Show me where you want this porch, so I can see what's possible," the salesman says.

As we walk toward the sliding door, the carpenter wrinkles his forehead and runs his fingers over the 3 × 5 card "sliding door." I smile, wondering what he's thinking.

Twenty minutes later the men have measured the area and given me a price. As we enter the house, I ask, "How long will it take to build the porch?"

"About a week, if the weather is good," the salesman says. "The guys can work in the rain, but we can't use the electric saws outside when it's raining."

"You could put the saws in our garage to keep them out of the rain." I don't want any delays.

"Is it through this door?" The salesman points to our hall closet.

For the first time the carpenter speaks. "No." He smirks. "The label says it's a closet."

"Ahem . . . uh . . . right." The salesman clears his throat to mask his embarrassment.

The carpenter and I share a smile.

Two weeks later, not one as I was promised, the porch is finished and I'm swinging in a hammock while John and Amy enjoy snacks at our picnic table. Amy tips over her tumbler of Kool-aid; red liquid drips onto the concrete floor. I'm unconcerned. Tonight I'll hose off the porch; I only wish the kitchen was as easy to clean. I reach for something to read from the stack of books and magazines under the hammock. I grab a paperback Mother sent me about a missionary's experiences in the Far East in the late 1800s. I push my foot against the cinderblock wall below the screens to set the hammock in motion and turn to chapter one. Midway through the second chapter, the author makes a profound statement about spreading the gospel to non-English-speaking people.

> At first our efforts were spent on teaching the natives how to read and write English, so they could read the gospel's message of salvation and understand our teachings. This proved difficult since many of the tribes we encountered had no ability to read or write the language they spoke, and their harsh living conditions did not provide them the luxury of furthering their education. After enduring months of frustration, due to my inability to communicate with these people, I realized that learning someone else's language, rather than expecting them to learn yours shows how much you love and value that person.

The author's last sentence stuns me. I rest the book on my chest and listen to Amy's incoherent babbling. Soon she'll be three years old. She speaks less than two dozen words, and few of these are intelligible except to Jack, John, or me. Amy's trying to communicate, but more times than not her effort only brings frustrations: hers and ours.

Last night at supper, Amy tried to tell us something. She said the same sounds over and over with increasing volume, and then she cried. Jack shook his head, and I spent the next fifteen minutes guessing if she was tired, hungry, or thirsty. I removed the peel off her apple slices and she stopped crying, but next time I may not be so lucky.

As the hammock sways, I look at Amy and wonder: will I ever know what she thinks and how she feels? If her ability to learn and understand language continues at her present pace, her personality will remained locked inside her. After biting off two fingernails, I continue reading.

Learning someone else's language . . . Learning someone else's language is an expression of love. That sentence plagues me as I read. Three pages later, I snap the book shut.

"John. Amy." I push myself out of the hammock; the book drops to the floor. "Go to the bathroom and get in the car. We're going to the library."

An hour later we're back on the porch. John and Amy have stretched an old bedspread over the picnic table and are playing in their makeshift tent. Relaxing in the hammock doesn't enter my mind. I'm upright in a chair, poring over a book on sign language for deaf people.

The first page is devoted to the manual alphabet and numbers. I scan it and flip through the subsequent pages. The words are listed alphabetically, like a dictionary, but with one major difference: there are no definitions. I note that one gesture conveys an entire word and many incorporate letters from the manual alphabet. I return to page one and in less than an hour master the manual alphabet and can count to ten. I practice the sign "ice cream" several times.

Minutes later I'm holding two cones. "I have ice cream cones. Who wants one?"

John's head pops out from under the bedspread. "I do." He tugs on Amy's arm, alerting her to the treat I hold.

I hand John a cone filled with rainbow sherbet and kneel to Amy's level. I form my hand into a fist, like the letter "s" and move it in a circular motion by my mouth: the sign for ice cream. "Amy, do you want ice cream?" I make the sign again.

She grabs the cone and watches as I repeat the sign. I point to her cone while saying "ice cream" and making the sign for it. She sits by John licking the orange and pink treat from her cone.

By using this simple hand sign, I've crossed the invisible gorge that separates parents and professionals who espouse using *only* oral communication from those who encourage manual communication for deaf people. Once again I'm on a journey into the unknown with no guide.

During the next two weeks, I learn and use a number of signs including eat, water, bed, toilet, book, car, stop, yes, no, and tricycle. I use these signs daily, but Amy hasn't mimicked any of them. Today I must return the sign language book to the library. I sign "car" followed by "book." Amy runs to her room and returns with a book. Tears fill my eyes. That awful lump of hopelessness and pain that too often clogs my throat shrinks to a manageable size.

I continue using the John Tracy lessons, but now I incorporate sign language. Amy is able to understand a new word sooner than she ever did when I just used the tedious process of lipreading. Labor Day passes. I call the director of Special Services for the Grand Island schools. The phone rings numerous times before an unfamiliar female voice answers.

"Do you know anything about the program for the hearing-impaired children?" I ask.

"No. I just answered the telephone to keep it from ringing, but I've heard a teacher was hired. She won't be here for a month or so. Call back in a couple of weeks?"

"Okay. Thanks." She hangs up; I'm left listening to a dead phone line. A line as dead as I feel. I have no choice but to start driving to the university again next week.

18

On the Road Again

Rebecca

It's Monday, September 20, and John, Amy, and I are on our way to Lincoln. During my six-week reprieve from taking Amy to therapy, by adding sign language to my verbal queries Amy now understands, "Do you need to use the bathroom?" At last she is toilet-trained.

At the university, I greet the mothers I met last summer and nod "hello" to the new ones. Joyce, who was seven months pregnant, is now holding a squirming infant dressed in blue.

"Amy. Look. A baby." I sign "baby." John and Amy hover over the baby.

"He's so little," John says.

"You were that little once, John." I sign "baby" again for Amy.

Joyce places the hand of Doris, her deaf-blind daughter on the baby's head. "Donald was born screaming. No incubator or oxygen needed for him. Thank God."

Before Joyce can hand me Donald to hold, Mrs. Kramer strides into the room with twelve coeds following her like ducklings. Without so much as a hello, Mrs. Kramer's launches into the assignments. "Doris Muenster, Kathryn Davis."

"Here." Joyce puts Donald in my waiting arms. She leads Doris to the therapist. "Can Doris feel your face?"

The therapist's face reveals she's uncomfortable with such close contact. Her lips form a false smile. "Of course." She kneels to Doris' level.

"This is Kathryn." Joyce places Doris' hand on Kathryn's cheek. Doris rubs her hand across the unfamiliar face. "She's blind, as well as deaf. You knew that, didn't you?"

Kathryn shakes her head "no." The uncomfortable look in her eyes is replaced by fright. "I'm sure we'll get along just fine." Her voice is not convincing.

"Let's move along or there'll be no time for therapy today." Mrs. Kramer calls several names. She glares at Tommy's mother with piercing eyes. "Janet Parker, Thomas Lawson."

Tommy's mother nudges him toward Janet. This time he takes the therapist's hand and enters the elevator without a howling battle. She heaves a sigh. I give her a thumbs up.

Amy's name is called last. I didn't understand the name of her therapist and Mrs. Kramer left the room before I could ask her to repeat it, but it doesn't matter; we're not allowed to have any contact with the student therapists. Our comments must be directed to Mrs. Kramer, who then informs Dr. Zimmer.

Today group therapy is bedlam. At first, Amy remained seated when other children ran around the room shrieking, repelling any efforts their therapist tried to make them behave. Before long, Amy joined the mayhem. At a loss on how to regain control, the therapists converse among themselves in one corner of the room.

Amy is sweaty and rambunctious when we leave the Temple Building, supercharged by forty-five minutes of undisciplined activity. She tries to break away from me and run toward the car on the opposite side of the street.

"Nooooo!" Amy swings her free arm to swat away my hand.

"Amy! Stop it!" After several minutes of pulling a screaming child down the street, I put her into the car and sign, "Bad. You were bad at school. You're supposed to sit down, not play."

Amy is more familiar with the meaning of my stern face than she is with hand signs. She climbs into her car seat, pulls the restraining bar over her head, and pops her fingers in her mouth. I sign, "bad" again. She puts her left hand over her eyes, shutting out my discipline.

***

Wednesday is no better. By Friday I'm frazzled and fuming. I wish Karen was here so she could tell me, "I told you so." She was right; the university has one twelve-week program of instruction to use with the deaf children. Amy didn't master all of the language skills this summer, but she will before this semester is over. If I bring Amy here until she starts school, she'll be doing the same lessons for the next two years. It's pointless and nonproductive. I come to the unhappy conclusion that if a deaf child receives any benefit from the therapy here, it is purely by chance. The university's objective is to train *their* students, not help the children.

"Have you talked to Mrs. Kramer or Dr. Zimmer about this?" I ask several mothers.

"No."

"Why not?" I snort with disgust.

"This is our only option."

"You can't buck authority."

"It wouldn't do any good."

I ponder their passivity. Saying nothing is not the solution.

The more I observe Amy's therapy at the university, the more dissatisfied I become. The therapists are inexperienced and unable to properly discipline the children. During one session, a young deaf boy who refused to behave was placed in a chair facing the wall for more than thirty minutes. The money his family spent on therapy that day was wasted. The therapists rarely change their discipline tactics. I wonder how often instructors observe and critique the student therapists.

Three weeks into the fall semester, I speak to Mrs. Kramer. "I'm concerned that the therapists aren't skilled in disciplining the kids. What does a child learn by sitting in the corner for thirty minutes?"

"It takes time for the therapists to learn what discipline works with these children." The edges of her mouth form a brief smile.

"You could correct the therapists instead of letting them punish a child for an entire session?"

"We don't believe in interrupting a therapy session. We routinely observe the students and they receive a written critique each week."

My fingers curl into tight fists. My bitten-off nails save my palms from being scratched. My jaw tightens; my head throbs, warning of an impending headache. *How can you call this a teaching program when you let a therapist continue the same mistake for a week?* I swallow, to suppress my overwhelming urge to spew angry words at Mrs. Kramer.

"I realize therapists need to learn discipline tactics, but does it have to be at the expense of these deaf children? Couldn't they learn to work with hearing children first?"

"I see no need for that. We've conducted our program this way for years with no complaint." Mrs. Kramer straightens papers on her desk. She considers the matter settled.

I have just begun.

The next Monday a notice is taped to the door of the observation room: Parents are not permitted to observe therapy. This room is reserved for student therapists and university staff.

The other parents are as upset as I am. When Mrs. Kramer marches by the waiting room, I halt her progress. "Why can't we watch group therapy?" My hands are planted on my hips.

"The room's too small. Faculty and students are required to observe one session a week. There's not space in the room for them and *you* people." She pushes past me.

I retreat to my chair. How can I tolerate two more years of this? And now I can't even see what they are doing with Amy. I scan the face of the other mothers. Are they blaming me? *I'm sorry; it's not my fault. I was only trying to help.*

At supper, I tell Jack about my conversations with Mrs. Kramer. ". . . and now I can't even see what they're doing with Amy." My voice sounds like a child's plea.

"You'll have to put up with it until there's a therapist here." Jack takes his plate to the kitchen. He never clears the table. I'm moved by his uncharacteristic behavior; his way of showing he's concerned. "I have to go back to work. It's my night to close the store."

I wave my hand in front of Amy's eyes to get her attention. "Say good-bye to Daddy."

Amy waves and John says, "Bye, Dad."

I swallow one of my little yellow pills. In twenty minutes I'll feel better. Instead of the usual miracle cure, my stomach spasms. Like a two-year-old sick child, I want my mommy. After putting the children to bed, I call my mother.

"Hi, Mother, it's Rebecca." I know my voice conveys my sense of failure.

"I know who it is. What's wrong, Rebecca?" she asks.

"Nothing. I just wanted to talk to someone."

"I'm glad you called. How are John and Amy?"

"Fine. John's reading quite well now. I hope he won't be bored in kindergarten next year."

"He'll be fine." A voice in the background distracts her. "Your father says 'hi.'"

"Tell him 'hello.' Does he still have tomatoes? We had frost last night. Mine are dead."

"No frost here. I have tomatoes coming out my ears. How is Amy doing in therapy?"

"Mother, I don't know what I'm going to do." Tears fill my eyes; I am thankful she cannot see them. I rattle off what the university is doing and that Grand Island still has no program.

"Have you talked to the people in charge at the university?"

"I've tried, but it's pointless." I huff. "They're pigheaded and stubborn."

"Well, it takes one to know one," Mother jokes.

I laugh in spite of my pain. "Yeah, but I think I'm right."

"I'm sure they do too. Why don't you try again next week?"

"Maybe I will. Did I tell you I'm using sign language with Amy?"

"No. How's that working out?" Mother's interest is genuine.

"Good, but if Dr. Zimmer hears about it, he'll have a fit and fall into it."

"So be it." Mother's voice is emphatic. "You have to do what you think is best for Amy."

"I don't know what's best."

"Rebecca, you don't have to decide anything now. Think about it this weekend."

And think I did.

Over the weekend I ask Jack and my friends. Jack's answer is much like my mother's. "Do whatever you think is best for Amy." My friends offer consolation but no solutions.

When I ask my best friend Pat, she says, "Tell Dr. Zimmer to take a flying leap. Who does he think he is, God?"

"Yes."

"Well, I've got news for him; everybody in Nebraska knows Bob Devaney is God."

I laugh. Devaney is Nebraska's football coach. He coached a team that lost consistently for years to a national championship last year. "I'll tell Zimmer we took a vote and decided there's not enough room on the throne for him and Devaney, so he'll have to take a hike." The laughter relieves my tension, but does not provide a solution.

Saturday night, wide awake at two in the morning, I mull over my options. I could try to have the university change their program. Fat chance. They've been running their program this way for years. I suppose I could just work with Amy at home. That's possible, but I'm not qualified. Maybe someone will call from Connell tomorrow and say the therapy program will start next week. That's wishful thinking. Maybe I'll do nothing. That's an option but that won't help Amy.

I'm not the same person I was a year ago, cowering in my chair before Dr. Zimmer, speechless, while he and other professionals told me what was best for Amy. Doing nothing is no longer an option for me.

19

Ready, Aim...

Rebecca

Sunday as we dress for church, I pray the pastor's sermon will contain words of wisdom giving me the courage to confront Dr. Zimmer. A sermon about Daniel in the lion's den or those three guys in the fiery furnace would be nice. The pastor's sermon is lackluster; I come home discouraged.

On Monday, as I drive to Lincoln, I decide to give the university another chance. This is the third week of the semester; perhaps they pulled their act together over the weekend. Even if they didn't, their program is better than nothing, which is what I have in Grand Island. *You're kidding yourself, Rebecca.* I imagine confronting Dr. Zimmer, a bear of a man with the personality of a grizzly. I've never seen him smile. He prowls the halls as if stalking prey. *He'll devour me alive.* Four hours later I'm home. If it were possible to kick myself in the butt, I would. Today was a replay of last Friday, but fear of being ripped apart by Dr. Zimmer, fear of the unknown, fear, just plain old fear kept me from speaking to him. *Wednesday I'll definitely talk to Dr. Zimmer.*

I'm at a decided disadvantage Wednesday. Dr. Zimmer has heard about the rabble-rousing mother who confronted Mrs. Kramer and he's ready for me. I knock on his office door. I see his face in profile. It is pinched, sour-looking, as if he's just bitten a grapefruit rind. "Come in," he growls.

"I'm Rebecca Willman." I sit in the chair opposite his desk. "I'm Amy's mot —"

"I wondered when you'd get around to talking to me." He leans back in his chair, self-confident, at ease with my presence. His dark eyes stare at me, unmoving.

"I'm ... I'm dissatisfied with several things happening in the therapy program."

"Such as?" He remains tilted back in his chair, giving the impression he's humoring me.

"First of all, I want to see what Amy's doing in group therapy."

Dr. Zimmer snaps forward, shoves his chair back, and stands, towering over his desk. "Until you and your child enrolled in this program, everyone thought our program was just fine." He walks around his desk. "And now, all the mothers have the attitude of 'just what the hell are you doing with my child!'"

I'm surprised he reacted with anger to my simple request to observe Amy. I stand. "Amy's *my* daughter. I have every right to know what the hell you're doing with her."

I'm as surprised by my response, as is Dr. Zimmer. His dark eyes narrow. He straightens his shoulders so his six-foot two-inch frame towers over my five-foot two inches.

"It's my job as Amy's mother to see she receives the best education possible. These deaf kids shouldn't be in a program that considers their education a secondary goal. You're more interested in educating your therapists than helping these deaf kids."

He glares and steps toward me, speaking with a raised voice. "This program is part of the university's curriculum. Upon graduation, our students are experienced therapists, ready to help deaf children develop speech and language. Your child is one of the many tools we use to accomplish this goal."

Can't you see the idiocy of your remark? You're using the very children you profess you want to help as guinea pigs. "What about the deaf kids here now? They don't have the benefit of trained therapists. These kids only have once chance for pre-school education."

"I oversee this program. I designed it. The program works as it should."

Sensing I'm beating a dead horse, I shift gears. "Have you considered using sign language with the children?"

He whirls toward me, his face red, his nostrils flaring. "This is an *oral* program! We'd never do that. If you allow a deaf child to use sign language, they'll never learn to speak. They'll become isolated from everyone except for a small group of other deaf-mutes who sign."

"Signing allows me to communicate with Amy. Lipreading isn't enough."

"Sign will never be used here as long as I direct this program." He jabs his index finger toward me. "You shouldn't be using sign language with your child."

I shake my head. This man is impossible. He brushes past me. He may know how to teach a deaf child language, but he doesn't have a clue on what it's like to live with a child you can't communicate with.

Today as I drive into the garage, the telephone is ringing. "Hello," I gasp. "Hello? Hello?"

"Hi, I'm Marge Beatty, the new speech therapist at Connell. I'm starting therapy next week. Do you plan to bring Amy this year?"

Now there's a stupid question. "Yes, but I'd like to meet you first." I want to make sure this program won't be a mirror image of the university's. "Could we talk tomorrow?" I hope my voice does not sound pleading, like the desperate beggar I am. "I'll need to bring my son along."

Marge agrees to meet as at eleven and adds, "It's fine to bring your son. He can play with toys in the therapy room while you and I discuss what's best for Amy."

Wow! What's best for Amy! I reconfirm the time and hang up. "Hallelujah, hallel . . ." I burst into the chorus of Handel's *Messiah* and dance around the kitchen waving a dish towel.

"Mommy?" The screen door slaps shut behind John. "What are you doing?"

"Dancing for joy." I grab his hand and we twirl, while I sing. Amy does her own little jig. I grab her hand. "Come on, Amy. This is your celebration."

"A breath of fresh air." "A ray of sunshine." "A light in the darkness." "A godsend." These trite expressions are inadequate to describe my first impression of Marge Beatty. Her voice suits her effervescent personality. Blonde curls frame her porcelain complexion. Her smile is frequent, generous, and genuine.

After taking John to the therapy room to play, Marge returns with a stacking ring toy. She spread the rings on a small table near Amy and pockets one of the rings. "I thought Amy might like something to play with." Marge observes Amy as she stacks rings of various sizes on the spindle. The blue ring is missing, leaving an awkward gap. Amy takes off the rings and replaces them in a different order. Dissatisfied with the result, she looks under the table. Marge extends the blue ring to Amy. She grabs the ring and completes the stack.

"She's quite bright." Marge looks at me. "I hope you'll enroll Amy here, but before you decide, I want to explain my teaching philosophy."

I relax. Marge's demeanor is not threatening like Dr. Zimmer's. "What's your educational background?" I ask.

"I have a master's degree in deaf education from Ball State University in Indiana."

I'm impressed. I want to ask if she's open to other methods besides oral communication, but I don't want the good feelings I have about her to vanish if she gives me the wrong answer. She's my only hope. "What method of instruction will you use to teach Amy language?"

"I'll use every tool available." Marge's smile is replaced with a determined look. "That includes Amy's residual hearing, lipreading, the printed word, and sign language."

Once again an exuberant performance of the "Hallelujah Chorus" explodes in my head.

Friday morning it's raining when we leave for Lincoln. While Amy's in therapy, I tell the other parents I won't be returning. They'll have to fight their battle without me.

When Amy finishes therapy, she's accompanied by Dr. Zimmer and Mrs. Kramer. My mother's scary rendition of James Witcomb

Riley's poem "Little Orphan Annie" springs to mind. "And there were two great big black things a standing by her side . . . and the goblins will get you if ya don't watch out."

"Amy won't be coming here anymore. She'll be attending a program in Grand Island."

"Who's running it?" Dr. Zimmer asks.

"Marge Beatty."

"I know her." Mrs. Kramer's response is an acid-filled aside to Dr. Zimmer. "She's an older lady. She used to work for the Lincoln school system."

"Oh yes, I remember her." He shrugs. "I guess she'll be okay."

"You must be thinking of someone else. Marge is young, just out of grad school."

"No, she isn't," Dr. Zimmer's voice is authoritative. "She's been around for years. What sort of program will your child be in?"

"Amy will have private therapy three times a week." John and Amy fidget beside me. "You two, go over there and sit on the steps."

"Will she have group therapy?" Dr. Zimmer asks.

Why does he care about Amy's schooling? "Not for a while. There aren't enough students yet, and Mrs. Beatty wants to become accustomed to each child before she starts a group."

My simple statement blows the cork off their bottled-anger.

"You're making a big mistake taking your child out of this program." Dr. Zimmer's voice echoes in the hall. "Without group therapy your kid will never learn to interact with other children."

My response is rapid; my mothering skills are under attack. "Amy has a brother and there are a lot of kids in our neighborhood for her to play with."

"She needs group therapy. Without it, by the time she's five no one will want to be around her. She may have speech, but she'll have no social skills or emotional maturity. No school will accept her. She'll be an outcast among her peers and family members won't like being around her either."

Tears well in my eyes; I blink them away. I'd rather have my arm gnawed off by wolves than let this tyrant see me cry. "I don't see why you think your program is superior to the one in Grand Island. You're mistaken about Mrs. Beatty. She's not an older lady, she's a young teacher with a master's in deaf education. Much better educated than the therapists here. Amy isn't the only person in our family. I have to consider the needs of my husband and son. It's not fair to them I spend so much time away from home." I take a quick breath. "I don't think the lack of group therapy will be Amy's ruination. You don't know me. Amy will have children to socialize with. She'll go to Sunday school, nursery school, dance classes, and play with the kids in the neighborhood. I may not know everything about deafness, but I know to teach her social skills. You look at Amy and all you see is her deafness; I see a child."

Amy rises from the steps. She looks at me; I sign "sit." Her fingers sign "no, go."

"No, sit," I sign.

Dr. Zimmer and Mrs. Kramer watch our manual exchange, horrified, as if we had made a series of obscene gestures.

"I warned you about using sign language," Dr. Zimmer snaps. "Your daughter will never speak if you do that. How will she communicate with normal people if all she knows is sign?"

"Her lack of speech already isolates her. Signing gives her the opportunity to express herself. Why shouldn't I utilize every means possible to communicate with my daughter?" I inhale. "John and Amy, come here. We're going home."

The angry voice of Dr. Zimmer follows us to the door. "It won't work. You're kidding yourself. In two years she won't be ready for school. She won't have any friends or the ability to communicate. Just you wait and see."

"None are as deaf as those who will not listen," I call over my shoulder.

Outside it's pouring rain. After John and Amy are strapped in, I shift the car into reverse, check the review mirror and accelerate. Whump! *What was that?* "John and Amy, stay in the car." In the "no parking zone" behind me are three motorcycles. I've knocked one over. I struggle to upright the undamaged heavy bike. Ugh! I'm glad this beast didn't create a domino effect and topple all three bikes.

"Do you need some help?" A male voice surprises me.

"Yes. That would be nice." I turn to face my good Samaritan: a Lincoln police officer.

"What happened here?" He takes the motorcycle from my shaking arms.

"I was hemmed in." Tears, the lingering result of Dr. Zimmer's harsh words stream down my cheeks. "I was just trying to leave." Rain merges with the tears on my cheeks.

The officer is perplexed. My hysterical sobs are an inappropriate response to a minor accident with no damage. "That's okay. Don't be so upset." He gestures toward my car. "Go on." His command is gentle. "Get out of here."

"Yes, sir. That's exactly what I want to do."

20

Dreams and Reality
Rebecca

By the time I arrive home, my head throbs. I only want to soak in a hot bath with a good book, but that will have to wait until the children are in bed. When Jack comes home, I pop garlic bread under the broiler. "Supper will be ready soon."

"Good." Jack washes his hands at the kitchen sink. "I could eat a horse. Took me four hours to unload the truck today. I'm beat."

"Me too. I told Dr. Zimmer we're not coming back anymore. He was really nasty. Said Amy wouldn't amount to anything if I took her out of *his* program." My temper's hotter than the flame in the broiler as I relate Dr. Zimmer's stinging words. ". . . and then, I hit a motorcycle."

"What? Was anybody hurt?" Jack asks.

"No." Several hours after the fact, I see the humor in the motorcycle incident. Jack laughs as I describe standing like a drowned rat in pouring rain, trying to upright the heavy motorcycle. "I'm sure the policeman thought I was nuts."

"Be glad you don't have to go there again." Jack calls the children to the table as I spoon macaroni and cheese on our plates. Once seated, we bow our heads for prayer.

"God is great and God is good, we thank him for this food—"
Beep! Beep! Beep! The smoke detector blares.

"Well, probably not this food," I say. The pungent odor of burnt garlic bread fills the room.

That night I take a hot bath and then relax with a book I've heard a lot about recently: *On Death and Dying*. Soon I'm engrossed in the Kübler-Ross grief cycle. As I read, I find myself comparing accepting the death of a loved one to the shock of learning Amy was deaf and the loss of the dreams I had for her. My dreams were nothing out of the ordinary, just common things like seeing her walk to school with her brother, going to her dance recital, and watching her leave for her senior prom. In the past two years, professionals have suggested ways to help Amy, but no one offered grief counseling to me or other parents of handicapped children, and we sure could use it.

Educated as a sociologist, and hoping one day to earn a master of social work degree, I visualize how the stages Kübler-Ross describes could assist parents to accept the life-altering changes that occur when a child is born with a disability, any disability, not just deafness.

Stage one, shock: the initial paralysis of hearing the bad news. Been there, done that. I was a robot for weeks. Shock is filled with questions that begin with why, how, and what.

Stage two, denial: ignoring the truth and trying to avoid the inevitable. I did that before Amy's diagnosis when I ignored subtle clues that she was deaf. I can't deny she's deaf now. Her squealing hearing aid won't let me. Esther still denies Amy's deaf; I'm glad my family doesn't. Denial is a dead-end road. Denial doesn't change the situation; it only delays progress.

Stage three, anger: the frustrated outpouring of bottled-up emotions. Kübler-Ross writes that anger is a common reaction to situations we can't change or control. God knows I'm angry. Life isn't the least bit fair for me, Amy, John, or Jack. Parents of handicapped children are angry about many things. Bungled deliveries, medications with side effects, family members who berate them, prying questions, accusations. I've spat plenty of angry words to nosy strangers, and that confrontation with Dr. Zimmer was no picnic either.

Unlike some parents who are angry because they have a handicapped child, I'm thankful Amy was entrusted to me. I feel sick when

I read about parents who mistreat handicapped kids, locking them in rooms, beating them, and doing other unspeakable acts. Anger is wasted energy, unless you put it to work. *Hmm, maybe I should write something for the newspaper. Try to educate hearing people about deafness.*

Stage four, bargaining: seeking in vain for a way out. I chuckle. At least I'm not guilty of this. I know there's no way out, but I've seen plenty of people run from doctor to doctor, hoping to find a miracle cure. What could I promise God so he would restore Amy's hearing? I contemplate what I have to offer. Not much, and I know I'm not good at keeping promises.

Stage five, depression: final realization of the inevitable. The stage when a person at last realizes that the loved one is dead. Or in my case, deaf. I realized the inevitable in a small, soundproof room in the basement of the Temple Building. Since then I haven't had time to be depressed; I've been too busy trying to determine what's best for Amy. Onward and upward, that's my motto, and yet, sometimes I have overwhelming feelings of failure and sadness. There are days I feel my life is hopeless. I'm unsure of my decisions. I have no one to talk to. If I screw up Amy's first few years, I will have doomed her future. Depression is a dark mummy, ready to bind you in yards of guilt, anger, and unexpressed pain.

Stage six, acceptance: finding a way to move forward. *Am I moving? I don't know.* Most days I feel like I'm spinning my wheels, going no place fast. Seeking realistic solutions is the first step toward acceptance. I've been in this stage since Dr. Proffitt said Amy didn't hear. I've explored lipreading and oral communication; put labels all over the house; and fought to get her into therapy when she was only a year old. I don't know if what I did was right. Books, doctors, and educators all have different ideas, but how many of them actually live with a deaf child? Maybe there is no right answer. What works for one child may not work for another, but I think I'm on the right track with total communication.

As I ponder the deeper meaning of acceptance, I realize acceptance is more than moving forward; it is moving forward in an altered state of reality, one that is achievable. I accept that Amy's journey to adulthood will be difficult, but with a good education she can function as a deaf person in a hearing world. Amy will never speak with the clarity of hearing people, but she can learn to communicate by other methods. When I think about Amy attending NSD I'm sad, but I know if I hadn't changed my vision of her life to incorporate the reality of her deafness, we would both be frustrated and disappointed.

I doze off, holding the book. In the fuzzy world of my dreams, I see children playing. One child stands alone; her back is toward me. Even though I cannot see her face, I know her feelings are hurt and she's crying. She's different: an outcast. It's Amy; she's crying because she has no friends, and believes no one cares about her. Sobs wrack her body. The child turns; it's not Amy, it's me. I'm crying, because Amy is upset that she can't communicate with anyone. I cry for both of us, because I hear the ugly remarks and see how they affect Amy. Her eyes are my blue eyes. Our eyes brim with tears. I jerk awake.

The next morning, before breakfast, John makes a funny face at Amy, and runs in a silly fashion like only a four-year-old can toward the kitchen. Amy smiles and runs after John, imitating his strange gait.

Acceptance. No wonder John and Amy have such a close relationship. He accepts her as she is. No expectations. No demands. Amy can't tell me what she feels, but her actions indicate she adores her brother.

Marge had planned to start group therapy in November, but decided to wait until January. I'm disappointed, fearing Dr. Zimmer's prophecy about Amy becoming a wild animal might be fulfilled, but Marge assures me Amy's social skills are comparable to hearing children her age. Teena's therapy follows Amy's, so Bernice and I are able to chat for a few minutes each week. Marge notices the girls' excitement on being reunited and plans a Halloween costume party. She invites John to join the party.

Deciding on a costume for John was easy. He enjoys watching reruns of *The Lone Ranger*, and told me months ago, "I'm going to be Indian just like Tonto when I grow up." I explained he could be a faithful scout, but not an Indian, so he's excited about the costume I'm making him. I quickly completed his Indian costume from an old sheet and dyed it tan in a pan of strong tea. Deciding on a costume for Amy was difficult. She has no interest in being a princess, and it would not suit her personality. She needs a costume that doesn't require a mask that would slip over her eyes, blocking out her primary way to keep in touch with the world.

"She could be a monkey." John jumps up and down and makes convincing "oo-oo-oo" sounds. "I want to be a monkey next year."

"I don't have any monkey material. Think of something else."

"What about a pumpkin?" John pulls orange fabric from my box of fabric scraps.

"That's a good idea." A short time later, Amy is dressed in an orange shift with black triangle eyes and a wide toothy grin.

The party is a wild success. Teena is dressed as Tinkerbelle, a character that suits her tiny frame and exuberant personality. Amy describes herself as a "pumpee," and John is thrilled that he can wear face paint and clothes like Tonto. After the party, I decide to stop at the grocery store to pick up a few items. The employees who know us slow our progress with greetings and comments about the clever costumes.

Jack offers to keep John occupied while I shop for groceries. "You want to help me put out the apples?" he asks John.

"Sure."

Jack ties an apron on John and pushes a cart filled with apple boxes to the produce aisle.

Thirty minutes later, the groceries are ready to load into the car. I've opened the car door and the trunk. As Jack pushes the grocery cart toward the car, John stands on the bottom rung for a free ride to the car. Amy runs ahead of them. Two feet from the car, she slips on loose gravel and tumbles forward, smacking her face against the metal doorsill. Her screams bring me running.

The scrapes and bruises on her knees are minor; it's the blood streaming from her mouth that worries me. I'm unable to determine the extent of her injuries due to her screams. The next few moments are a jumble of confusion, hollering, and questions, which all lead to the same conclusion: Amy must go to the emergency room.

After an exam, the emergency room doctor says, "Her facial wound is superficial, so are the scrapes on her knees. There will be no scarring. The real damage is to her front teeth, which appear to be broken off at the gum line; that's a dental problem."

By the time our dentist can see Amy the next morning, her face is swollen and bruised. As I hold Amy, the dentist pulls her fingers from her mouth; she screams whenever he tries to determine the extent of the damage. After a cursory exam he states, "I'll have to extract her front teeth, but I can't remove them today because of the swelling. Bring her back here in three days."

"How do you plan to remove her teeth here? She won't even let you touch her mouth."

The realization that Amy will not be a cooperative patient dawns on him. He sputters, "You're right. She'll have to be admitted to the hospital."

Three days later, Amy's two front teeth are removed under general anesthesia. After surgery, the dentist gives me her front teeth in a small plastic bag. I hold two perfect little teeth with their complete root attached. Amy did not break off her teeth at the gum line as the doctor suspected, instead she hit them so hard they were driven upward until they were flush with her gums. My mouth aches thinking about the pain Amy has endured for the past four days.

As Amy returns to consciousness, my thoughts focus on her missing teeth. How will Amy learn to talk now? Teeth are necessary for the formation of certain sounds. Will she need false teeth before she is three?

My fears are calmed by the dentist and Marge Beatty. "She'll have beautiful permanent teeth by the time she's seven," the dentist says. "The X-rays taken when Amy was under anesthesia indicate the formation of her permanent teeth was not injured by her fall."

"Amy will adapt her speech patterns." Marge reports after consulting several journals.

With Christmas nearing, John asks, "Are we going to decorate cookies today?"

"Yes." Happy memories of Mother and my sisters decorating Christmas cookies bring a smile to my face. My sisters are scattered across the United States. Their jobs and families make it impossible for us to share the holidays. Jack, John, and Amy are my family now. "I have sprinkles for you and those little silver balls you like to put on the cookies." Visions of cookies, heavy with decorations, not sugar-plums dance in my head.

"Cookies, Amy." John signs. "We're going to make cookies."

"Oo-kee-mo, oo-kee, oo-kee-mo." Amy repeats over and over.

"John, you and Amy go to the kitchen. I'm going to run outside and get the mail, and then I'll be right there."

Our mail box is curbside, about seventy feet from our door. I sort junk flyers from the electric bill and several Christmas cards as I walk up the driveway. Near the house I sense unrest. The sounds coming from inside the house are not happy children at play, but a duet of screams.

What now? I shake my head and open the door. Amy is sprawled on the floor, kicking and screaming. John stands over her sobbing. "John, what happened?" My voice is filled with concern and anger.

"It was Amy." He rubs the back of his hand under his nose. "She kept saying the same word over and over and I couldn't understand what she wanted and she wouldn't stop so I hit her." His crying intensifies. "I hit her with my fist on her back but she still wouldn't stop."

A quick examination reveals Amy has no physical injuries. Frustration and anger, not pain, have triggered her tantrum. My arms allow me to comfort only one child. "Oh, John." I kneel, my arms surround him. "I know exactly how you feel. I'm often exasperated with your sister, because she can't understand what I'm telling her. There are times I'm so frustrated I don't know what to do, but it isn't Amy's fault, and we mustn't take out our frustrations by hitting her."

"But she wouldn't quit." John sputters. "I didn't know what she wanted."

"Neither do I, sometimes. But remember, Amy's frustrated too. Can you imagine how she feels, wanting to tell us something but none of us can understand what she's saying?" I squeeze John close to me in a loving death grip, not wanting him to see my face, which I'm sure betrays my concern about his feelings.

"Mother, stop." John squirms to free himself. "You'll squeeze the juice out of me."

After a quick kiss, I release him. "I know it isn't easy for you to have a deaf sister, but you're a good big brother to her. She's lucky to have you. The next time you're this upset, tell me, don't hit her. Amy's doing the best she can. We have just to help her do better. Okay?"

"Okay." John smiles, comforted. "Are we going to do the cookies now?"

Happy to change the conversation, I ask, "What color should I make the frosting?"

"Purple!"

"I should have known; it's your favorite color." I try to imagine purple Christmas trees as I lift Amy from the floor. Her crying has long since ceased. "Do want to help with the cookies?"

"Oo-kee, oo-kee."

Bottles of sugary decorations line the table. At the direction of John and Amy, I slather frosting on a cookie and place it before them to decorate. As purple bells, green trees, and yellow stars are produced on our makeshift assembly line, a conveyor belt of thoughts pass through my mind. *You expect too much of John. He's not even five.* A green tree. *All kids squabble with their siblings.* A yellow star. *Yes, but Amy is different.* A red bell. *If John hit her because she wouldn't give him a toy, that's not acceptable, but it's understandable. But he hit her because he couldn't understand her, that's not right.* A purple bell. *It's not Amy's fault she can't communicate.* A white star. *John's young, but he can learn compassion.* As I frost a green tree I ask myself. *What will John do if neighbor kids make fun of Amy?* The devil's advocate torments me. *Next you'll expect him to defend his sister.* I scrape the last of the red frosting from the bowl onto a bell. *Having a deaf sister could make him a better person, more compassionate, tolerant, and understanding.*

"What do you think of this one?" John holds up a purple bell laden with silver dragees that make the letter A. "I made it for Amy."

"That's beautiful, John." *The cookie and your love.*

Early the next morning, as I shift between dreams and wakefulness, I hear whimpering. *What's that noise?* Silence. *Good. I can sleep another hour.* Jack rolls over, but does not awaken.

A vision of dancing flowers chased by a goat entices me to deeper sleep, but the whimpering halts my spiral to dreamland. *What is that?*

I shuffle from our bedroom and stand in the hall, daring the noise to happen again. My challenge does not go unheeded.

"Mommy. No. I couldn't help it," a voice whimpers in the darkness.

"John, what's wrong?" I rush into his room and sit on the edge of his bed. He rolls over, wide awake, shaking with fright. "Did you have a bad dream?"

"Yes. It was horrible." John pulls the sheet over his head.

"It was a dream; it didn't really happen." I tuck the sheet under his chin. "Here's your dog."

John clutches the worn animal and whispers, "It could happen, if I'm not fast enough."

"What do you mean? What did you dream about?"

"I dreamed Amy and I were playing in the front yard. She ran toward the street and a car was coming. I yelled at her to stop, but she didn't. I ran as fast as I could, but I wasn't fast enough. The car hit her and it was my fault." He buries his head in his pillows and cries.

He dreams my worst nightmare. "John, John. Don't cry. It was only a dream."

"But it could happen." He shoves his thumb in his mouth, but it offers no comfort. "And it would be all my fault."

"No, it wouldn't. It's not your job to watch Amy or take care of her; that's my job. I'm the mother." His brow is full of wrinkles; he's not convinced. "John, even if Amy got hit by a car, just like you dreamed, I would never blame you, ever."

I lie beside John and hold his trembling body. "It would never be your fault, John. I would never blame you." *It would be my fault, all my fault, and I would never stop blaming myself.* My voice and patting his back reassure him; he falls asleep.

I return to bed, but my nightmare of Amy dead, killed by a speeding car, crushed under a falling tree, or floating face down in the swimming pool because of my inability to warn her of eminent danger torments me. To chase away the visions, I rise and read a book on the major causes of deafness that I borrowed from the library. Perhaps one of these causes will explain the source of Amy's deafness. Measles (*Rubella*) during pregnancy. Nope. The child had an illness with a high fever. No. Amy is as healthy as a horse, except for a serious bout with the flu, but that was after we knew she was deaf. Side effect of certain medicines. Can't be that; Amy has never taken any medication except vitamins. A genetic disorder. Hmm. Amy doesn't have any of the symptoms for well-known syndromes that cause deafness like Waardenberg or Usher's, but the author indicates there are numerous recessive genes that sporadically cause deafness in some families. This might be a possibility. Jack has told me family rumors about relatives in both his mother and father's family who had hearing problems. If I ever have some extra time, I'll do some genealogy research and see what I discover.[3]

3. Years later I researched my side of the family, the Schmierers and Kelleys, and Jack's family, the Willmans and Meyers. My research took me back several generations in each family. No proof of deafness was discovered in the Schmierer, Kelley, and Willman lineages. In the Meyer family, starting five generations ago, deaf family members, both male and female, were discovered in all generations, with Amy being the latest deaf person in the lineage.

21

Pets and Playmates

Amy

My earliest memories include animals. When I was about three, Mother bought my brother and me a cream-colored rabbit for a pet. I expected the rabbit to play with a ball, but of course there is no way a rabbit can fetch a ball. Sometimes we were rough with the rabbit. I liked to carry the rabbit like a toy, and it often scratched me with its back claws. After several nasty scratches, Mother gave the rabbit to Teena's parents, who raised rabbits. Now I had no pet.

The next pet we had were goldfish. They were not my style of pet. I wanted a pet I could play with. After awhile the fish died, I suppose because I poured glue in the fish bowl. Anyway, once again no pet.

Then we had a tropical fish tank. A child who came to visit us turned up the heater on the tank. My mother did not know this and all the fish were boiled. More dead fish, but at least it was not my fault.

Later my parents decided to get a black puppy. John named the puppy Bobo, a word I could say. I played with Bobo, but got bored. We had Bobo for several weeks, but Mother was afraid I would hurt the puppy as I hugged it so hard or dropped it when I no longer wanted to hold it. She could not watch me and the puppy all the time, so Bobo was given to an older lady. Then Mother said, "No more pets!"

Amy with her beloved first Kitty, given to her by her father.

This conversation took place in the kitchen. Of course I did not hear it, because I was in another room, but Mother told it to me later. She said one day when I was about four, my dad came home for lunch and asked her to come to the garage. He was waiting for her there, standing like Napoleon with one hand inside his coat. When he pulled out his hand, he held a kitten. He asked my mother, "Would Amy like this?" The cat was crying.

Mother was not sure about another pet, but she knew I would love to have one. John of course, could hear the cat, and he was excited when dad brought it into the house. "A cat. Dad has a cat," he cried. Mother said she told John to be quiet, that the cat was a surprise for Amy, but that was not necessary. I could not hear them.

I was in the living room watching TV and did not see my dad come into the room. I felt a thump, thump on the floor. I turned. My father had stomped his foot to get my attention. He kneeled and showed me a kitten. The cat was wet, because it was raining outside. Father told me he heard a cat meow when he threw boxes into the trash bin behind the grocery store and discovered the kitten.

My mother was not excited about another pet, but I was so thrilled when I saw the most beautiful silver tabby kitten. I cuddled and cradled him like a sweet baby in my arms. The kitten was not supposed to stay with us long; my father only brought him home because the weather was wet and cold.

John asked what I would name it, and I said, "Kitty." I played with Kitty all that day. I loved him. He was my style of pet, one who could play and who loved to be held.

Kitty never bit or scratched me, and if I dropped him, he always landed on his feet, not hurt. After a few days my parents decided that I could keep Kitty. I was so happy. He became mine.

From that day, I have always had cats as pets. They are so fluffy and peaceful to look at when having a catnap or fun to watch and play with. I say, "Cats rule."

Most of the time I played with John in our house and yard. In our neighborhood were many children, but most of them were boys. I was lucky: next door to me was a girl, Sue, who was my age. She was hearing, but we played together like any girls our age would. She was the only hearing child on my street I had for a friend. We got along well as we had things in common. Usually we played games or with our dolls. Sue also had a cat, and we often petted our cats together. She came to my birthday parties, and I went to hers. When we were older, we rode our bikes to the Riverside swimming pool, which was not very far from our homes. We also went to summer camp together.

How did we communicate? I'm not sure how it started, but she used sign with me. A child usually picks up sign fast and is able to express themselves through gestures better than adults do. Of course, I taught her some sign language. Sue and I never really had a communication problem.

Amy and Sue Snyder in our backyard. Best of friends.

Strange, but there was another deaf girl in our neighborhood. Her name was Samantha. She was more hard of hearing than deaf like me. She was two years younger than me and went to public school. She did not sign as much as Sue, possibly because her parents encouraged her not to sign. I find it ironic I didn't play with her often compared to my hearing friend. Sue was more fun than Samantha. Sue and I were childhood friends until I was eleven, when there was a tornado in our area, and she moved to a different neighborhood.

At first I would still see her sometimes when I came home for the weekend, but since I only had two days at home, I preferred to be with my family and cat. Sadly, our friendship faded away. Sue was my first and only hearing childhood friend. She was a fun, and I enjoyed hanging around with her.

22

Hearing in a Deaf World
Rebecca

The year 1971 slides away without fanfare. Amy has private therapy two mornings and group two afternoons a week. Three new deaf children, two boys and a girl, will soon join Amy and Teena. I'm anxious to meet them and their parents. Amy is now three, and John will soon be five.

For two years I've taken John with me to Amy's therapy. Each week Amy brings home school papers and objects she's made, and John, who by birth order should have been the first child to impress us with his academic handiwork, has been relegated to second place. I worry he has no identity of his own. Even though he does not need the intellectual challenge of preschool, I decide to enroll him in Humpty Dumpty Preschool. He'll be at preschool when Amy's in group therapy. I'll have two hours alone! My mind whirls with possibilities. Since John won't be with me, I can converse with the other parents without feeling guilty. I could run errands, or if the other parents don't stay to observe therapy, I'd be alone in the quiet viewing room for two hours. As a harried mother of two preschoolers, any of these options sounds great.

John telephones his grandmothers to tell them his "big news." Both are excited for him. Monday night John selects the clothes he'll wear on his first day of school. Early Tuesday morning, a small hand taps my shoulder, awakening me. "I'm ready." John is dressed, his hair combed, and shoes tied.

I blink several times. 6:15 a.m. "You're up early. School isn't until this afternoon."

"I need to be ready." He stands tall and smiles. "This is the biggest day of my life."

The weather is unseasonably warm for January, fifty degrees when I park by Humpty Dumpty Preschool. John steps onto the curb. "You don't need to go with me, I can go by myself."

"Okay." My voice is cheerful, but I'm disappointed. I wanted to participate in his new experience, savor a bit of his excitement, be a part of the biggest day of his life, but I respect his desire to do it alone. I'm filled with pride and sadness. Proud he is so grown up and independent, but sad and guilty for the same reasons. John behaves more like an adult than a five-year-old child.

When Amy and I arrive at Connell, Bernice and Teena are waiting outside Marge's office.

"Marge is at a meeting." Bernice answers my question before it's asked. "She'll be back in fifteen minutes."

I sit beside her and we share the events of our holidays. A few moments later a small woman about my age carrying an infant and nudging a small blond, deaf child hurries toward us and sinks into the empty chair beside me.

"The calves broke out of their pen this morning, and I had to help my husband round them up before I could leave. Then I was stuck at a railroad crossing for fifteen minutes. I thought I'd be late." She inhales, and exhales. Her sigh is long and full of exhaustion. "The group hasn't started yet, has it?"

Bernice and I shake our heads, exchanging glances that reveal neither of us knows who this woman is.

"I'm sorry. I didn't introduce myself. I'm Norma Wruble. This is Cindy." She smooths the hair of the child on her lap. "And this is Jeannie." A younger, smaller version of Amy and Teena, but one wearing glasses in addition to hearing aids, stands beside Norma.

We introduce ourselves and Bernice and Norma discover they live about ten miles apart, Bernice in Central City and Norma on a farm near Clarks, Nebraska.

"Mama, no." Cindy pushes against Norma's chest, struggling to be free. Norma places Cindy on the floor. She takes a halting step, and then drops to her knees and crawls toward Amy, Teena, and Jeannie who are occupied with a tennis ball they found.

"How old is Cindy?" I ask.

"She'll be one in a couple of months." Norma looks at her daughters. "Jeannie's almost three, but already Cindy has a larger vocabulary."

Bernice and I nod, knowing the pain of comparing children. I recall past discussions Bernice and I had about Amy and Teena's lack of speech compared to their older brothers at the same age. The difference was evident and painful. How much more so for Norma, since Cindy is younger than Jeannie, her deaf sister.

I drift into my own world of doubt, while Norma and Bernice discuss carpooling.

Will Amy ever understand the world around her? Even with the use of sign language, she misses hundreds of hours of ambient conversations at home, in stores, and at church. Much of what is said is not important, not worth signing to her, and I'm not that good at signing anyway, but those overheard conversations provide children with a wealth of information.

While contemplating the ramifications of all the input Amy is missing, Marge rushes down the hall. Cindy hears Marge's voice and waddles away from Jeannie, Teena, and Amy toward Marge. The deaf girls react to Cindy's movement by turning to see what prompted her departure. They spot Marge and rush to her, clutching her legs making it difficult for her to walk.

Marge bends and hugs the girls, prying them off her legs in the process. "Bring them to the therapy room. As soon as Kay Darnall and her boys get here, I'll start the group."

Unintelligible sounds direct our attention toward the opposite end of the hall. Two young boys are being hurried along by their mother, a tall woman with long auburn hair.

"The older boy is Linsay Jr.," Marge says. "The younger is Daniel. He's too young for the group, but I'm going to include him anyway. They live in Polk, about forty miles east of here. She's a stay-at-home mom, and her husband is a barber."

Marge walks into the therapy room; the five children run after her reminding me of *The Pied Piper of Hamelin*. After the therapy door is closed, Bernice, Norma, Cindy, Kay, and I select chairs in the viewing room.

I turn toward Kay, who has chosen a seat at the far end of the observation room. "You have a long way to drive." My eyes make contact with Kay's. We exchange smiles.

As Bernice, Norma, and I watch the activities in the therapy room, we engage in an animated conversation about how we're coping with our kids. Through it all, Kay is silent. She nods or smiles, but makes no effort to join our conversation.

"Kay," I ask, "I'm half crazy raising one deaf child; how do you cope with two?"

No answer. I wait. Her long auburn hair shines like copper in the dimly lit room. With a sweep of her long fingers, she catches her hair behind her ears. She smiles again. Her index finger taps her ear.

My goodness, she's deaf! I'm a dunce. I slump in my chair, hoping my face reflects how sorry I am for my stupidity. I smile again. A smile is the universal sign of friendship, but now it seems inadequate, the easy way out, a distant, nonthreatening way to say I care, without getting involved. I sign "hello," and fingerspell my name.

She smiles again, but this time her smile is a "nice to meet you smile," not like her earlier vacant ones. I fingerspell the names of Bernice and Norma. My attempt to include Kay in our conversation is difficult. Her method of communication is sign language, and none of us are proficient signers. Norma and Bernice soon return to their conversation.

Kay and I sit at opposite ends of the room, silent. Our bodies are less than ten feet apart, but our lives seem worlds apart. I'm uncomfortable with this silence. Perhaps Kay does not mind. Maybe she's accustomed to being left to her thoughts while hearing people converse, but our language barrier bothers me. My silence is painful, full of helplessness, guilt, and frustration.

One Saturday, Vodis Dahlke, my mentor from the Central Ne-braska Hearing Association, calls to ask if I would like to attend a deaf social club tomorrow at a local church.

"Maybe, what time?"

She challenges my lackluster response. "Several other members from the parents' group will be there. You'd have an opportunity to practice your sign language and meet deaf adults."

I agree. Vodis is waiting for me outside the church when I arrive. We enter a room of people engrossed in conversations. Everyone is busy chatting, moving around the room introducing themselves to new people and greeting old friends, but shuffling feet, laughter, and chairs scraping across the floor are the only sounds; the conversation is all in sign language.

I watch, fascinated, as flying fingers and hands, along with expres-sive faces convey messages. My signing is limited to the vocabulary of a three-year-old, so I'm reduced to watching. A deaf woman ap-proaches and signs something. I wrinkle my forehead. I have no idea what she said. She waits, expecting a response. At last, I have the presence of mind to sign, "Again. Slower, please."

She repeats her signs. This time her gestures are accompanied by her monotone voice which helps me realize she's told me her name: Marilyn. She wants to know mine. I fingerspell, "R-E-B-E-C . . ."

"Rebecca." She nods, anticipating my name before I finish. "Wel-come. Do you have a deaf person in your family?" she signs.

After asking her to repeat her question, I sign, "Yes, my daughter Amy is deaf."

Marilyn signs, "How old is Amy? Where is she? Do you have a picture of her?"

In a hearing world, my responses would be quick and include un-asked for information, such as "She's at home with my husband, Jack, and her brother John. She just turned three. I don't have a picture of her." But here, in a world that uses a language of which I know very little of the vocabulary, I am silent, struggling to communicate.

Marilyn is patient, far more than I might have been were our circumstances reversed. She waits while I spell most of the words in my reply, often nodding before I finish a word because she knows what I am spelling. She demonstrates signs I should use instead of my clumsy spelling. If there is such a thing as pidgin signing, that is what I am using.

When Marilyn leaves to rejoin her deaf friends, Vodis and I join the two hearing people in the room who are from our parents' group. The chairs are arranged in a large circle, which allows the deaf people to see each other and converse with ease. We pull our chairs to the edge of the circle.

The speed of their signed conversation mesmerizes me. Fingers fly, arms swoop, faces are animated. With extreme concentration, I recognize isolated signs, but I have no idea what is being said. The deaf people often look in my direction, nod, and smile, and then return to signing. My fascination with their speaking hands soon changes from interest to paranoia.

Several hands have a rapid-fire exchange and laughter erupts. The Deaf people look at Vodis and me; they continue laughing. I have no idea what's so funny. I wonder, *did they tell a joke, or are they laughing at us? At me?* I shift my weight on the padded folding chair. Five minutes ago this chair was comfortable; now it is irritating. The laughter and smiles continue. My paranoid feelings push reason away.

They are probably laughing at me, because I don't know how to sign. Maybe they're making fun of me. They could be talking about me right now, and I wouldn't even know it. I can't defend myself, because I have no idea what they are saying. I have no way to communicate with them. With them? What's the matter with you, Rebecca? These are people, not THEM. They are not an alien force to conquer; they are merely people who do not hear.

Forty minutes later, I prepare to leave. The deaf people wave and smile. Marilyn signs, "Bring Amy next time."

I leave their silent oppressive world and go outside to a world of sounds. Sounds I have often wished would cease, because my nerves are frayed by the constant noise, but now I'm relieved to hear people talking, children screaming, car tires screeching, horns blaring, and even the fierce Nebraska wind rushing through bare tree limbs. Silence, I discover, is not fun if you are lost in it.

When Jack asks me about the group, I try to explain how weird I felt. But, I'm unable to convey the isolation I experienced, and my fear that Amy will feel this way much of her life as a Deaf person in a hearing world.

"You can't change the world, Rebecca," Jack says.

"I know, but it was awful to feel so, uh, so alone in a room full of people. I don't want Amy to feel like that." For the rest of the day, my thoughts dwell on how uncomfortable I felt at the gathering. I was there, but not involved. On the fringe of what was happening. Not so much ignored as invisible.

After many sleepless hours that night, I vow to include Amy in all our conversations. If she asks, "What did you say?" instead of responding, "Oh, nothing. It wasn't important," I will explain what I said; because if I tell Amy "It wasn't important," that will convey to her that she is not important and she doesn't need to know what happens in the hearing world. My thoughts jump to Kay Darnall. *If Kay's in the room, I will keep my mouth shut unless I can include her in our conversation.* The knot in my stomach loosens its grasp on me. As I drift toward sleep, I know I will not be able to keep either promise, but I hope God knows I made these vows with the best of intentions.

Today, instead of waiting for John to finish his session at Humpty Dumpty, Amy and I go inside for a parent-teacher conference with Mrs. Prescott.

"John's never been a problem," Mrs. Prescott says. "There was a little incident one day, but I quickly resolved it. We were working on numbers. I set three blocks on the table and asked the children how many there were. One of the children said 'three' and raised his hand with his three middle fingers upright. John told the child, 'That's not three, that's six. This is three.' He held up his thumb and his first two fingers. John and the other child expressed strong opinions on which fingers should be used to represent the number three. Then I remembered John's sister is deaf, and I thought he might be using sign language, so I said, 'John knows a language we don't know. Both ways are correct,' and the matter was resolved."

"Hmm." I'm at a loss for words. Will John be branded "different" because of his sister? How did he feel about this encounter? He never mentioned it to me. I'm pleased he knows some sign language and proud he defended his knowledge, but at what cost? Amy's deafness impacts all of us.

Several times in the past month, Kay and I have been the only people in the observation room, which has given me the opportunity to practice my sign language. We talk about the normal things most young wives and mothers discuss: our husbands, housework, children, yard work, but in our case deafness is a major topic.

"Where did you meet your husband?" I struggle to recall signs, and finger spell "husband." Kay is patient, showing me the sign to use, but I feel stupid knowing I will forget the sign within a few minutes, unless I use it right away.

"At the Nebraska School for the Deaf," Kay signs.

"I suppose that is where Amy will go to school. I have never been there." My signing is slow and jerky, not fluid, and smooth like Kay's.

"It's a good school. They have a summer camp for prospective students and their parents in June."

I sign the words that are a vital part of every sign conversation I have. "What? Slower."

Kay repeats her sentence, leaving a gap between each sign so I can process it. The sign "prospective" stumps me, so she spells the word. I watch each letter form, and struggle to keep track of them. "Pr-osp-ect, I've." I shake my head, unable to see the letters forming words as she does. After several attempts, my eyes widen with recognition. "Ah ha! Prospective. Yes, the summer camp. Marge mentioned it some months ago. She recommended that Amy and I attend this summer, so we're planning to go."

"Not going this year." Her signs dance off long fingers, with perfect fingernails.

"Amy won't be old enough to go there for three years, but I'd like to see the school." My hands, with bitten fingernails, stumble and cramp trying to speak.

"Next year, when Daniel is three and Linsay Jr. is five, I'll take both my boys."

Two deaf sons. I don't think I could cope with two deaf children. Dr. Zimmer thinks Amy's deafness is genetic. Because of this, Jack and I decided not to have more children, even though we wanted more. Our next child could be hearing, but I'm not willing to take that risk. In addition, I'm not sure I'd have enough time or energy to cope with a baby.

We sit in silence for a few minutes, watching Marge and the children. Kay brushes the silence away when she signs, "Why is Amy deaf? Was she born that way?"

"Yes. The doctors don't know why. Genetic probably. No one in my family is deaf. Before we were married, Jack told me some cousins in his family were born with cleft palates. I knew that might happen, but I never expected deafness."

"Neither did I," Kay signs.

"After Amy was diagnosed as deaf, my mother-in-law told me some of her great aunts and uncles were deaf." I bite my tongue and don't disclose that in spite of deafness in Esther's family, she blames me for Amy's deafness.

"I wasn't born deaf." Kay signs. "But I don't remember hearing."

"When did you lose your hearing?"

"When I was eighteen months old, my older sister, younger brother, and I all had the German measles at the same time. They recovered and were fine, but I had a high fever, which caused my hearing loss."

"Is anyone else in your family deaf?"

"No, just me. When I was pregnant with Linsay Jr., I never dreamed he would be deaf. My mother-in-law told me my husband, Linsay Sr., fell off a farm wagon when he was two and became unresponsive to sounds after that. I didn't think we would have deaf children since neither of us were born deaf . . ." The dim light in the room seems to darken Kay's face; her eyes cloud with memories.

Not wanting to intrude in her thoughts, I pick my cuticles. *Having deaf children is probably easier for her than it is for me since she and her husband are deaf. They know sign language. They know what it is like to be deaf. They can prepare their children much better for school and life than I can.*

Kay lifts her head, and turns toward me. The eyes I thought were full of memories are brimming with tears. "When the doctor told me Linsay Jr. and Daniel were deaf," her signs sag, a visual image of what she feels, "my heart broke."

Neither words nor signs are adequate. The pain of giving birth to a child with special needs is universal to all mothers, hearing or deaf. Tears run down my cheeks in sync with hers.

Kay continues. "I think their loss might be genetic, as Linsay Jr. had hearing but lost it at about age two like his father. Daniel was born deaf."

I'm at a loss for words or signs. "But you know sign language, at least you can communicate easily with your boys."

She nods her fist up and down, the sign for yes. "I know they will do fine, but I remember how some hearing people weren't kind to me. I hope my boys never have to experience that."

I hope they won't either, but I know they probably will. Human nature being what it is, anyone who is different is fair game for ridicule.

23

Summer Workshop Times Two

Rebecca

Yesterday, Amy completed her first year of therapy with Marge and can now speak, lipread, and sign many words. Her spoken vocabulary has more than one hundred words, far less than a hearing child her age, who would speak approximately nine hundred words. For a child born profoundly deaf, however, one hundred spoken words are a major accomplishment. Of course, many of her spoken words can only be understood by Jack, John, or me.

Lipreading is difficult for Amy, as it is for most deaf and hard of hearing people, because many English letters, such as P/B and T/D, have the same lip movements when spoken. Last week I looked in a mirror and said "papa" and "bye-bye." My lip movements looked identical. I marvel that Amy can lipread and understand any words. Another obstacle to lipreading is that many words and letters are formed inside the mouth. From what I've read, only 30 to 40 percent of the English language can be recognized visually.

I thought sign language would be the solution to our communication problem, but I've discovered there are different ways to sign. One method is signing in English word order, using a method like Signing Exact English (SEE), and the other is signing American Sign Language (ASL). My use of signs has been limited to individual words, but now that Amy has enough vocabulary to form simple sentences, I must choose to use either SEE or ASL. Everything concerning Amy involves decisions, and with no definitive answers available, I often feel that making the right choice is akin to playing darts in the dark. I hope I make the right decision; I only have one chance to do this right.

SEE is an accurate representation of the English language, which enables me to sign exactly what I'm speaking, when I'm saying it. SEE would allow Amy to observe the use of prepositions, articles, verb tenses, and proper English sentence structure. SEE is easy for me, because I don't have to translate my thoughts into a different language.

ASL is the true language of the Deaf community; a language with its own sentence structure. If I use ASL, Amy will have to learn English grammar and sentence structure later. Using ASL is hard for me, because I can't speak one thing and sign something else at the same time. I'm worried that using ASL will confuse Amy, since what she might hear and lipread will not be in sync with what I am signing. ASL is best used without speech, but if I quit speaking, I fear Amy will lose her ability to speak and lipread.

Without an instructor, learning either method is difficult. Kay shows me new ASL signs weekly, but I only see her for two hours, not long enough to become proficient, and I forget more signs than I remember. I don't think I can teach myself ASL, so I've decided to use SEE, which is a bit easier to learn. Maybe I should consider Amy in my decision, but how can I expect a three-year-old to make a decision I can't?

In June, John stays with my parents while Amy and I go to the Nebraska School for the Deaf Summer Workshop in Omaha. When Amy and I drive someplace alone, I really feel her deafness. I'm unable to communicate with her when she sits in the back seat except with simple signs I do above my head. Amy seems to know she must speak if she wants a response from me, but today we make the two-hour drive from Beatrice to Omaha in silence.

I wish I knew what Amy was thinking. For weeks I've told her we're going to NSD. Does she understand this? As I drive past wheat field turning golden, my thoughts swirl. *Am I doing the right thing? Of course you are, Rebecca. You're only visiting the school, not enrolling her. We could move to Omaha. Jack has a marketing degree; he could get a job there. Are you nuts? He'd never leave his family's business. He might.*

The buildings at NSD are scattered throughout an immaculate campus, which is surrounded by chain link fence. After we register, the secretary directs us to the primary dorm. Kathy Becker, the housemother fingerspells her name, and points to her name tag. I nod that I understand.

Kathy's auburn hair has natural blonde highlights. Freckle-covered arms, like those of my mother-in-law, Esther, beckon us to enter. I know Kathy's freckled arms will be more accepting to Amy than Esther's, because Kathy is deaf. In the large open dorm, she waves her arm over small beds and wardrobes, reminding me of the women on *The Price Is Right* who prance around showing items up for bids. The dorm is flooded with natural light from a row of windows along one wall. Kathy stops by two small beds and points to Amy and me. "You'll sleep here," she signs. Other signs follow at a rapid pace. I don't understand every sign, but I catch enough to determine supper is at five. A mother and daughter approach us. Kathy smiles and introduces herself to them.

Amy pulls open a wardrobe door and stands inside the large closet. "House for Dopey," she signs. I smile at her comparison of the small beds and chairs to those in *Snow White and the Seven Dwarfs.*

"Amy, let's get our clothes from the car." I close the wardrobe door, which has no lock.

Kathy taps me on the shoulder as we pass. Pointing to Amy she signs, "She may stay here with this girl and play while you bring in the suitcases."

The other woman's face reflects my weariness and concerns. We nod and walk outside.

"Hi, I'm Rebecca Willman. Have you ever been here before?"

"Nope, this is my first time to lay eyes on the place."

"Me too. I live in Grand Island. Where do you live?"

"I'm sorry. I didn't introduce myself. I've been running around like a chicken with my head cut off all day. I'm about half nuts now."

"I know what you mean."

"I'm Karen Thomas from Norfolk. Kelli's our oldest child. My husband took vacation to stay home with our other kids. It won't be much of a vacation for him chasing after them."

"It's nice your husband can do that. My husband owns a grocery store. He never has time off, or at least it seems that way. Our son John is with my folks in Beatrice."

"How old is your daughter?" Karen asks.

"Amy's three. She'll be four on January 23."

"What a coincidence. Kelli will be four January 22." Karen grabs her suitcases.

"I didn't know if I should come to the workshop this year or not. Kids can't enroll here unless they are five by October 1, and that's two years from now for Amy, but I wanted to see the school. If I don't like it, I'll have time to check out other options." I lift our suitcases from the trunk.

"What other options are there beside this school?" Karen closes her car trunk.

"None in this state, but I've read about a school in St. Louis and one in Massachusetts."

A discussion I had with Jack last week flashes through my mind. I had requested information from the Clarke School for the Deaf in Massachusetts and Central Institute for the Deaf in St. Louis. I asked Jack to read it, but felt certain he didn't since the material remained neatly stacked on the coffee table. After I had read it several times I asked him where he thought Amy should go to school. His response was typical, "I don't know. Whatever is best." But I don't know what's best, I pleaded. He replied, "Amy's not old enough to go to school for a couple of years. We can decide something then."

I recalled the old joke about a couple who had lived happily for forty years. When asked for the secret to long marriage, the husband said I let my wife make all the small decisions, like how to spend our money, raise the children, where to live, what job I should have, etc. I make the major decisions like U.S. foreign policy and how to achieve world peace.

Unlike that wife, I feel overwhelmed. I do not want to make this decision without his input and support. But, I fear this decision will be mine, and mine alone.

"Those are too far away. I don't like the idea of sending Kelli to a school eighty miles from home."

"Neither do I, but I'm hoping to move . . ." Karen opens the door to the dorm and my sentence is lost in the excitement of Kelli and Amy seeing us.

As I unpack our clothes, warped déjà vu engulfs me. I remember moving into Piper Hall as a university freshman, but now I feel like Alice in Wonderland. Nothing is right; everything is askew. The bed is low and too short for my five-foot, two-inch frame. The closet rod is so low my clothes rest on the floor, but Amy's hang perfectly. This space is designed for children.

That night, eighteen children ranging from age three to twelve, their parents, and NSD staff pass through the cafeteria line and sit at round tables. I'm surprised to see older children, and then I remember some parents send their child to a local school before accepting their deaf child needs specialized education. Our NSD host, Jill Ramsey, introduces herself and signs her name to the three kids and four parents at our table.

"How do the little kids manage here?" A mother's voice quavers. "I carried Robert's tray to the table. He won't be able to do this alone by fall without spilling half of his food." Her pained expression tells me she's afraid her son will starve to death if he can't carry his tray, a thought that never crossed my mind. I'm anxious to hear Jill's answer.

"Several high school students work in the cafeteria to earn spending money," Jill says. "They carry trays for the younger children and supervise their eating. No one goes hungry."

I'm glad Jill didn't preface her response with "Don't worry." She knows we're all worried.

After supper, George Thompson, the school superintendent, an older gentleman with well-groomed salt-and-pepper hair welcomes us. "This week will be educational and entertaining for the parents and kids. While the parents attend seminars on deaf education, tour our facility, and meet the staff, your kids will receive nonverbal intelligence assessments, an auditory exam, and speech assessment.

Wednesday, we'll all spend the day at the zoo. On Friday, parents will have individual conferences with the audiologist and the school counselor."

The next day, our first seminar is a panel presentation: Choosing the Best School for My Child. After opening remarks, the moderator allows us to ask questions. Silence spreads over the room like thick blanket. If the other parents are like me, they have so many questions they don't know what to ask first. How can you know which school is best? How will Amy cope without me? How will I cope without her? No, I don't want to ask that question.

A cough breaks the silence. "My son is eight. He's gone to public school for three years. He did all right in kindergarten, but he's taken first grade twice and still isn't ready for second grade. I don't want him held back again, but I really don't know . . ." Her voice fades away.

A woman panelist speaks. "Should you send your son to NSD? Is that what you want to know?" The mother nods. "Right now your son is struggling. He's falling behind, which will only worsen as he gets older. You sound worried about him having social problems too, right?"

"Yes. It hurts me when kids say he's stupid and make fun of his hearing aids."

"I don't know your child, but I know about deaf children. A deaf child in a regular public school may be able to keep up with other students for a few years with extra help, but despite all your effort, they will fall behind. The situation is progressive. If your child does poorly in third grade, he'll do worse in fourth, and so on. Deaf children educated with hearing children will be lucky to have a fifth grade education when they graduate, but if that same deaf child attends a school for the deaf, I guarantee he'll excel. Our teaching methods, in fact the entire NSD campus, are designed for deaf students. Why let your child struggle, when he can excel?"

"Yes, but I love my daughter too much to send her so far away," another parent says. Several others nod in agreement.

"Is your love enough?" A panelist pauses, waiting for our reactions.

"What do you mean?" someone asks.

"Is the love you give your child enough to take away the pain they feel when hearing students make fun of them? How many of your hugs are needed to remove the pain your child feels when they aren't invited to social events or selected for the sports team? Is the love and comfort you give your child at home enough to erase the hours of pain they feel at school?"

Her words confirm what I know, but don't want to accept: Amy must attend NSD. "The thought of sending Amy here when she's five is unimaginable. Do all the students live here or do some go home at night?"

"Most live here," a male panelist replies. "About 20 percent of our students live in Omaha. The younger ones usually go home, but the teenagers would rather live in the dorm with their friends than go home to a neighborhood where they have no friends. I'm sure —"

So, it would be possible for Amy to come home every night if we lived in Omaha.

"—many of you are thinking, 'great, we'll move to Omaha.' But, before you sell your house and uproot your family, remember, your deaf child is only a fraction of your family. Will moving to Omaha be good for the entire family? Will your other children like changing schools, losing their friends, moving to an unfamiliar neighborhood? Can you find employment here?"

He pauses. The room is silent, filled, I think, with suffocated dreams.

The speaker continues, "Don't let your deaf child control your decision. You must do what is best for your entire family."

The air seeps from my dream. I slump in my chair, realizing Jack will never leave his family-owned business and move to Omaha. The rest of my morning I wallow in self-pity.

That night, after the children are in bed, Karen and I talk in the hall outside of the dorm. While Amy has received speech and language therapy several times a week for two years, Kelli hasn't been as fortunate. Norfolk has no preschool program, so Karen pays a therapist to see Kelli once a week.

On Tuesday, the seminars focus on methods to teach your deaf child sentence structure and language. Labeling items is not new to me, but using photos is. "Show your child a picture of the grocery store, church or library, as you say and sign, 'We're going to swim.' This will help your child know what's happening."The speaker holds up a photo of a child under an umbrella. Underneath the photo is printed, "I <u>have</u> an umbrella."

"Why are some of the words underlined?" one parent asks.

"Underlining the verb is one way we teach parts of speech," Jill Ramsey replies. "You don't have to do that, but since we use that method, you may want to. I suggest you install a bulletin board at your child's level. Write 'yesterday,' 'today,' and 'tomorrow' on cards." She writes the words on a whiteboard and tapes a photo of a child riding a bike by 'today.' "Tell your child what you will be doing today. Put a photo of something you will do tomorrow by that word." She tapes another photo on the board. "The next day, move today's photo to yesterday, and so forth. It helps kids learn the concept of time."

"Whatever you do," a deaf panelist signs, "talk to your child." An interpreter speaks his signed comments. "My parents didn't know sign and made no effort to learn it. I felt very alone. Include your child in everything you do."

"I can't stress that enough," says the nurse on the panel. "The suicide rate among deaf people is higher than for most other disabilities, because a deaf person may feel isolated."

A high suicide rate. Ye gods! What next?

"Many disabilities are visible," the nurse continues. "If a person is blind or in a wheelchair, people will often offer assistance, but deafness isn't visible. Someone trying to talk to a deaf person often assumes the deaf person is retarded or mentally disturbed, because they don't answer. The helper may shy away, instead of realizing the person is deaf."

As the nurse talks, the deaf panel member constantly waves in an effort to interrupt.

"Yes, that's true, for some deaf people," the deaf man signs, "but not for most Deaf. We are very independent." He stands, his gestures become bolder. "Deaf can take care of ourselves. I do just fine. So do my friends. I've traveled all over the world." His stance relaxes, he signs in my direction. "Don't worry. Your child will be fine. Encourage them to be independent. Talk to them. Include them in everything you do." He signs "fine" in my direction before sitting.

I watch him sign "fine" again. He smiles; I smile out of politeness. I hope he's right. It's almost four. Time to quit. The moderator stands. "If you don't have a camera, take one of these disposable ones. You and your child will take pictures at the zoo tomorrow. We'll have the film developed overnight, and on Thursday you'll make a memory book."

While others reach for cameras, I leave. My camera is in the dorm. Since arriving I've taken photos of the buildings (inside and out) and the NSD campus to show Jack and my parents. I'll offer to show them to Esther, but I know what her answer will be: "No thanks."

The Henry Doorly Zoo is huge. By mid-afternoon, exhaustion has changed the excited children into crabby kids who refuse to take another step. Although equally tired and sweaty, I have no choice but to carry Amy to the waiting buses.

Once again when the children are in bed, the mothers gather in the hall to chat. We agree the workshop and NSD are great, but our positive comments often conclude with ". . . but I wish the school wasn't so far from where we live."

Several parents have decided to send their child to NSD this fall. I'm glad Amy's not eligible to enroll for two years. Hearing their worries and watching them hold back tears twists my intestines into a spasm. I hurry toward the bathroom.

"Stomach problems, I bet," a mother says.

"For me it's migraines," another says.

After a few minutes in the bathroom, I return to the group, and am greeted by a chorus of voices. "Are you all right? Do you feel better?"

"Yes," I reply. "I've got a nervous stomach."

"What do you have to be nervous about?" Karen says.

We all laugh.

Thursday after assembling our photo journals, we all enjoy the NSD indoor swimming pool. The P.E. teacher explains that the children have swimming lessons, and most are excellent swimmers by age seven. That night as I lie awake in the mini-twin bed, I recall one of Mr. Thompson's opening remarks. "When your child is on our campus, we're responsible for them twenty-four hours a day. I think we're the only school in the state that can boast none of our girls have ever become pregnant nor do any of our kids sneak a smoke. They're always supervised."

The main thrust of NSD is academic education. We've met the primary teachers and toured their classrooms. No class ever has more than eight students, so the teacher can have eye contact with each child. The rooms have a closed antenna system, like Connell, which amplifies sound into the auditory trainers (super magnifying hearing devices) the primary students wear. High school students take college prep courses as well as vocational classes. Drivers' education, drama, competitive sports, cheerleading, Girl Scouts, Boy Scouts, and a variety of other clubs give the students a well-rounded education. The buildings have lights to warn of fire, and a closed circuit teletypewriter system allows the teenage boys and girls to stay in contact after hours. The dietician said the children receive balanced meals as well as instruction on proper table manners. The physical development of the children is encouraged through daily P.E. classes and school athletics. The infirmary has four private rooms. A nurse tends to minor aches and pains, and doctors and dentists make regular visits to the school. Nearby Catholic and Lutheran churches have services in sign language, and children will be taken to Sunday worship if the parents desire. The school has thought of everything.

Four feet away from me, in a bed that is just her size, Amy kicks off the sheet and rolls to face me. Her hands flutter, appearing to make a sign. *Do deaf people sign or speak in their dreams? Will anyone check on Amy at night? Kathy's wonderful, but she's deaf. How will she know if Amy's crying or sick? Who will hug Amy when she's sad? Calm down, Rebecca. Amy can't go to school here for two more years. Two years. Two years.* Amy moans. I leap from my bed. She's asleep. I place her pink cat pillow in her arms. She pops her fingers into her mouth. My throat becomes tight with the familiar lump. No matter how well-equipped NSD is, there's one thing they can't provide: a mother's love.

Friday after breakfast, as we await our appointments, Karen and I pack our suitcases. "Will you and Amy be here for the workshop next year?" Karen asks. "We will."

"I will if my mother can keep John," I say.

"It's nice your mom helps out." Karen's voice warns of a touchy subject.

"Yeah, it is." I contemplate adding my mother-in-law doesn't accept Amy is deaf and despite Esther's belief that Amy is normal, she wanted to take her to a faith healer this spring. But, I'm not comfortable sharing this information. Thinking about it makes my temples twitch. Jack agreed that Amy should not be subjected to public scrutiny and possible embarrassment at a revival, but he refused to tell his mother this. I was left to deal with the sticky situation. I asked our pastor for guidance. Later I told my mother-in-law, "You can't take Amy to a faith healer." When pressed for a reason, I said, "If God wants to heal Amy, he can do it in the privacy of our home." I did not add, "We like her just as she is. I feel blessed she's my child." Esther was not happy with my decision, but said no more.

Karen has an early appointment, so we say goodbye, with a promise to see each other next year. At five minutes to eleven, I leave to meet the audiologist.

"Mrs. Willman?" A slender man with dark hair extends his hand. "I'm Dr. Force."

Dr. Force appears to be thirty-five, has a sincere smile, and a firm handshake. In a seminar we were told Dr. Force, who tests NASA astronauts, would test our children, so I expected an older man. "Nice to meet you," Dr. Force says. "Amy's quite a charmer." He motions to a chair and waits for me to sit before returning to his desk.

Dr. Zimmer never offered me a seat or even called Amy by name.

"Amy was easy to test, very cooperative." Dr. Force opens a folder.

"That's good to hear. She screamed like a banshee during her first hearing test. Of course she was only thirteen months old." I realize I'm babbling, but continue. "She's spent hours with therapists and audiologists in the past two years, so she's accustomed to people examining her. I'm sure your audiogram of Amy's hearing won't be much different from Dr. Zimmer's."

"I haven't seen his tests, so I can't comment on them, but here are my results." He places a single sheet of paper in front of me.

I stare at three graphs; right ear, left ear, and acoustic immittance. Dr. Zimmer would not let me see Amy's actual audiogram, keeping it in her file as if it were a secret document. He only gave me a sketch. Even though I do not understand the graphs, I ask, "May I keep this?"

"Of course."

I rub my fingers over the graphs. Nothing will erase the downward pointing arrows that indicate Amy's limited hearing is off the chart on most frequencies.

"Amy has a profound bilateral sensorineural hearing loss. In laymen's language this means she has a very severe hearing loss in both ears due to the inability of her auditory nerve to process sound." He picks up his copy of the audiogram. "Her right ear is slightly better than her left. I tested Amy with tones from 500 Hz, which is about one octave above middle C, up to 8,000 Hz, increasing the volume until she responded. All of Amy's values are off the chart except in the 500 Hz range where she acknowledged sound at 90 to 100 decibels, which is quite loud. Similar to the volume of a chain saw."

My palms are cool and dry; no surprises so far. "Yes, that's what Dr. Zimmer told me."

"The chart on the right details the acoustic immittance test, which measures the integrity of the eardrum and determines the anatomy of the middle ear. Amy's results were normal."

Dr. Force closes Amy's folder. I expect him to usher me out the door; instead he leans forward. "Amy really amazed me. Her speech is quite good. Most children born profoundly deaf say few, if any, words. The volume, pitch, and tone of many deaf people are poor, but Amy's speech is appropriate. A child with her loss shouldn't say anything, and yet she does." He shakes his head, as if trying to jar loose an explanation.

I swallow; the news is good. "I know another child who has a similar hearing loss and she doesn't say anything. Why do you think Amy speaks, and that child doesn't?"

"Well, first of all, Amy's intelligent, that's obvious. And second, she's been motivated to speak, probably by you."

"I have worked with her a lot." I offer as an explanation.

"That's good, but determining what motivates a person is difficult. I don't know what you did to motivate Amy, but the same effort applied to another child might yield no results. Amy speaks as well as she does because she's personally motivated to do it."

We sit in silence. He offers no further explanation; I wish I knew what I had done.

"Do you have any other questions?" he asks.

"No. I can't think of any."

He opens the door. I wander into the hall. The old cliché "as different as night and day" springs to mind as I compare Dr. Force to Dr. Zimmer, but the phrase is inadequate. I felt hopeless and helpless after seeing Dr. Zimmer, but Dr. Force gave me praise and encouragement. This moment alone makes my week at the summer workshop worthwhile.

I think Amy is bright, quick to learn like her brother, and I hope Amy's intelligence tests will confirm that. I knock on the door of Marian Phillips, the school counselor.

"Come in. Sit down." Mrs. Phillips remains in her chair behind her desk. "You must be Amy's mother; I see a resemblance. It's nice to meet you."

"Thank you." I sit on the edge of my chair. Dr. Zimmer's comment that Amy could be retarded screams in my head, muting Dr. Force's positive comments.

"Ah, here it is." She opens a folder and scans pages before speaking. "Amy was very cooperative. She actually seemed to enjoy the tests. We gave her two nonverbal tests, the Weschler and Hiskey. How old is she?" She shuffles papers in the folder.

"Three years and four months."

"She's right on target. Scored at the three-year level on one test, and at three years and six months on the other."

"Great. A doctor we saw when Amy was younger said she might be retarded."

"Amy's intelligence is normal or a bit above normal."

"You're sure?" I ask.

"Absolutely. The tests don't lie. A child can score lower than their actual intelligence, but it's not possible to do better than you are capable of doing."

I hurry from her office, retrieve Amy from the playroom and drive to Beatrice. One of Dr. Zimmer's curses was lifted today. Amy has normal intelligence.

Mother asks about the workshop and Daddy listens while I describe the events of the past week. My father is an excellent amateur photographer. On Saturday he takes many photos of John, Amy, my mother, and me and promises to send prints so I can make an album for Amy like we did at NSD. Before leaving, Mother hands me a heavy box. "For the albums." Inside are 200 sheets of oak tag paper, glue, and several marking pens.

Once home, my camera becomes an extension of my body. I snap pictures everywhere we go. In September, I take photos of John's first day of school. He attends morning kindergarten, which means he no longer has to go to Connell with Amy. I'll miss his company, but I'm struggling to learn sign language, and can now devote myself to Kay's sign instruction twice a week. I hope that will increase my vocabulary.

In what seems to be only a moment, John and Amy have finished another year of school. Knowing John will be in first grade in three months has a bittersweet effect on my thoughts. In September, Amy and I will have the day together while John is in school. She'll have therapy in the morning, but in the afternoons Amy and I can do special things together. I know I must make the most of our time together next year, because the following fall she'll go to NSD in Omaha.

I asked Jack about moving to Omaha, and he dismissed the idea as "impossible," so I've decided to attend the NSD workshop again this June to learn more about the school. As for the other children at Connell, Teena and Bernice Eaton will be in the primary dorm with us. Kay Darnall and her two sons will be housed in the boys' dorm. Kay's familiar with the school since she and her husband graduated from it, but her boys have never been there. Norma Wruble doesn't plan to attend with Jeannie until next year. I look forward to having my Grand Island friends with me, renewing friendships from last year, and meeting new people.

The workshop has the same format as last year. Even though Amy won't be enrolled here for another year, I take pictures of the primary teachers, the house parents, and the dining room staff so Amy will recognize them. On Friday, Dr. Force and I have a nice chat. He tells me Amy's hearing is unchanged and he's impressed with her speech and growing vocabulary.

Since Amy's intelligence was measured at normal or slightly above last year, apprehension does not accompany me to Mrs. Philips' office. She scans several pages, and then she takes off her glasses. "Even though Amy's only four, her IQ was measured well above the five-year level on both nonverbal tests. Here are the results."

I take the folder she extends. The numbers mean little to me, but a section titled "recommendations" at the bottom of the page captures my attention. "Enrollment in Prep 1, September 1973." That's this fall, less than three months from now. This must be a mistake; Amy won't be five by October 1 as the law requires. But no.

"The psychologists recommended Amy start school this fall. I agree. There's no reason to wait until she's five. She's mature enough and ready to learn now." She smiles, pleased to report good news.

My mouth would gape, but it's so dry I can't pry my lips apart. I'm sure Mrs. Phillips wonders how I have an intelligent daughter when I sit opposite her, staring and speechless. I close the folder, obscuring the recommendation. My thoughts and emotions tumble like clothes in a dryer. Next year was supposed to my year with Amy. I can't send her to school this fall. I'm not ready. Wow! This is great. Since the kids at NSD attend two years of preparatory classes before first grade, Amy will be eighteen when she graduates from high school, just like hearing kids. I wonder what Jack will want to do? I suppose she ought to start next year, but . . .

"I spoke to Kathy Becker, the primary house parent," Mrs. Phillips continues. "She said Amy's toilet-trained and gets along well with other children. She believes Amy will adjust well to dorm life."

How ironic. I worried I'd never have Amy toilet-trained by five, and she wouldn't be able to go to school, and now they want her to start *before* she's five.

"Mr. Thompson approved her admission for this fall." Mrs. Phillips leans forward as if to impart a secret. "Amy would be the first child we've enrolled at NSD before they were five."

I don't need this kind of first. I pull my lips into my mouth and rub my tongue over them.

"We can't force you to enroll Amy now. Nebraska law doesn't require children to attend school until they're six, but it would be in her best interest to start this fall. Do you want to begin the enrollment process?"

My mouth makes a dry click as I open it. "I suppose . . . I'm not really sure . . . I guess she ought to start, but I wasn't expecting this. Can I think about it? Ask my husband?"

"Sure. Talk it over and let me know as soon as possible what you decide."

When I stand, she hands me a large envelope. "Take this. It's for parents of new students. Inside are forms and the school handbook, which covers everything from medical emergencies to what clothes the children are required to bring to school and where to buy clothing labels."

I return to the primary dorm for Amy. When I see her, I hug her so tight she squirms to free herself. *Oh Amy, don't push me away. Let me hold you.*

I drive to Beatrice dry-eyed, stunned, my mind racing. When I arrive at my parents, John rushes to greet me. "Mommy! Amy! I'm glad you're here. I missed you."

"I missed you too, John."

"Are you all right?" Mother's eyes narrow; her forehead wrinkles. "Do you feel okay? You looked tired or something."

"'Or something' describes it. Guess what? You'll never guess, so I might as well tell you. NSD wants Amy to start this fall." Mother and Daddy listen as I tell about the past week. Their response is silence. They're as surprised as I am. Jack has no comment that night either.

The next morning, Mother pulls me aside. "Your father asked me if you were sure about this school for Amy. He's concerned they might mistreat the children." Her hesitant speech tells me this is her concern also. "I told him I'm sure you checked the place out, and it wasn't like those orphanages Dickens wrote about."

"No, it's not like that at all." I have many concerns about sending Amy to NSD when she's so young, but I'm not worried about her being abused and neglected. The school is perfect in every way but one: it's too far away from our home.

Since Jack's never been to NSD, he can't offer much advice on whether Amy should begin this fall or wait another year. "Whatever you decide will be fine with me," he says.

The phrases "caught between a rock and a hard place," "between the devil and the deep blue sea," and "damned if you do and damned if you don't" all apply. The decision is mine. I consider my options. The Grand Island schools have no suitable education for Amy. The Omaha public schools offer a day program for deaf students, which would allow Amy to live at home if we moved to Omaha, but Jack refuses to move. The private schools I read about in other states are too far away, and they only use oral communication, which I know is not the best or easiest way for Amy to learn. I don't want Amy any further away from me than necessary, so Dr. Zimmer was right: NSD is Amy's only option.

Two weeks later, per the requirements of the NSD laundry, I order three hundred cloth nametags printed with "Amy Willman" to sew on all her clothes.

24

Emptying the Nest

Rebecca

On August 27, John started first grade. Amy and I dropped him off at 8:15 a.m. with the promise we'd return at 3:30 p.m. Jack and I decided to have him attend Trinity Lutheran, which is across town, rather than the public school two blocks from our home because of the quality education he will receive at Trinity. Soon I'll be spending my days alone, but today I still have Amy with me.

As we drive home, chores nag at me. I need to call Mother to see if she's finished sewing labels on Amy's underwear. I'm glad she volunteered to do this tedious work. I'd go nuts if I had to sew labels on ten pairs of socks. *Good grief, I still have to sew four pairs of pajamas for Amy.*

The crossing arm drops as we approach railroad tracks. I turn to the back seat and say, "Look, Amy, a train." The whistle blares as the train passes. Amy signs "train."

Three massive engines chug by pulling hopper cars filled with coal. Amy signs "big, loud." I wonder if she heard the whistle or drew her conclusion from the ground vibrating. Minutes later, we bounce across the uneven tracks. Amy's flips her head from side to side to accentuate the bumpy ride; an earpiece is jarred loose, filling the car with its squeal. I wave my hand, but Amy ignores my frantic gesture. At a red light, I reach over the seat, tap her shoe to get her attention, and point to her ear. She searches for the earpiece by pulling on the slender cord. I shudder, knowing the cord will not tolerate such abuse. She inserts the earpiece. The squealing continues.

I better call Laverne and have new ear molds made before Amy goes to school. School. In less than two weeks, Amy will be in Omaha, and then I'll be home alone. All alone.

Sunday, September 9. After church and an early lunch, Jack lugs a blue foot locker I have filled with Amy's clothes to the car. John and Amy climb into their car seats clutching their stuffed animal pillows, while Jack and I latch our seatbelts for the three-hour drive to Omaha. The fields fly by my window at warp speed. Jack must be speeding. I check the speedometer. He's a mile under the limit.

Amy is sucking her fingers and hugging her cat pillow. For weeks I've shown her pictures of NSD, saying "This is where you'll go to school." I've explained that Mommy, Daddy, and John will take her there, but we'll go home and she'll stay. Can she fathom this separation? I don't know. I know I can't. One minute here, the next gone. There's no way to slide into good-bye.

At two-thirty we drive through the gates of NSD. Since this is Jack and John's first time here, I point out the buildings as we drive pass them. The door to the primary dorm is propped open. A colorful sign says, "Welcome parents and students." I do not feel welcome; I'm anxious. I want this wrenching separation over, but I want Amy with me as long as possible.

As Jack parks the car, I watch a couple hug a girl about eight years old; they turn and walk toward their car without looking back. Their faces remind me of the stern couple in the painting by Grant Wood I studied in art history. Their daughter bites her lips and stares at her shoes. Like a mother hen gathering her chicks, other girls surround the girl, hiding her from view. Their fingers flash words too fast for me to understand. Before the couple enters their car, they turn toward their daughter, but her back is to them. One of the girls signs something, and the eight-year-old girl turns and waves. Her parents wave and enter their car. The girls close their huddle, shielding her from the disappearing car.

Does parting ever become easier for the child? Or the parents? Our car parked, I open the door. I grasp Amy's hand, never wanting to let go. Her skin is smooth, her palms fleshy compared to my bony hand. My fingers caress hers, which are wet with her saliva. When I let go of her hand, I will not be able to touch it for thirteen days. NSD requires all the children to stay on campus the first weekend to become accustomed to their new routine. After that they are allowed to go home every weekend. Thirteen days. I can't let go. Amy struggles against my grasp. I loosen my hold but do not let go. Her hand relaxes in mine.

"Let me go inside first," I call to Jack who has already opened the car trunk. "I don't know where we're supposed to take Amy's stuff. I'll ask her house parent."

"Can I come with you?" John runs toward me. "I want to see Amy's school."

"I don't know. It's a girls' dorm." Jack closes the trunk lid and stands by the car, unsure what to do. He furrows his brow; his face wears a nervous smile.

"Men can go inside," one of the parents shouts. "On moving day, everyone is in and out of all the dorms."

We walk toward the welcome sign. The door looms before us like a giant maw. What's on the other side of the threshold will be Amy's world for most of the next nine months.

"This is where Amy and I stayed during summer camp. The classrooms are upstairs and the playroom is in the basement. They have lots of tricycles and bicycles for the kids."

"Can I ride one of the bikes?" John asks.

"No, they're for the children who live here." *Live here. This is it. Amy is really going to live here, not with us.* The door is four feet away. Kathy Becker walks toward us, waving. "Here comes Kathy. Her husband, Bruce, is the house parent for the high school boys. They both are deaf. They live at the school year round and spend their summers traveling."

Kathy signs "Hello. Welcome. Amy, how are you?"

Amy nods. I nudge her, "Say hello."

"Hello." Amy's voice has a hollow sound, but her pitch and volume are appropriate.

"She's so cute," Kathy signs. "I love her dress. Did you make it?" Kathy points to the large blue cat appliquéd on Amy red gingham dress, and signs "cat" to Amy.

Amy pulls her hand free from my grasp and smooths her skirt so the entire cat can be seen. "Kitty," she says.

"I remembered you liked cats. Come see what I put on your closet door," Kathy signs.

I recognize the signs for "cat."

"What did she say?" Jack asks.

"I'm not sure. She signs fast, and I'm not used to her signs." I hope I have not missed vital information. "What . . . did . . . you . . . say?" My halting speech gives me time to recall each sign and form it as I speak.

Kathy nods before I finish. Her fingers repeat their dance. This time they do a waltz, not a jitterbug; nonetheless, I'm not sure what she said. I nod yes, but my frown betrays me.

"Come," Kathy signs. Even a sign language dunce like I can understand this universal gesture. Kathy stops by a wardrobe. A-M-Y in blue letters and pictures of cats cover the doors.

Amy points to a gray tabby, "Kitty."

Through sign language I convey to Kathy that Amy has a cat like this named Kitty.

Kathy pulls open the wardrobe door. She indicates which shelves, drawers, and hangers are for Amy's clothes, and then she leaves to greet more students.

I sit on Amy's bed staring at the empty wardrobe. A lump forms in my throat, large enough to choke me, but I swallow it, forcing my tears into submission. I must not cry. The staff at the NSD summer camp said crying will upset your child.

Jack looks out the window in Amy's cubicle. "It's nice. And she's close to the bathroom."

"Amy has six toilets," John exclaims. "We only have one." He and Amy check out the dorm. I hear wardrobe doors opening nearby. "This one has clothes in it," John shouts.

"Do you know the girl who will sleep in this bed?" Jack points to the name on the wardrobe opposite Amy's.

His words are an annoying buzz to my thoughts. How will Amy react when we leave? Will she think we abandoned her? That's she been banished, never to see us or her cat again.

"Rebecca?" Jack's urgent voice interrupts my thoughts. "Do you know Kelli?'"

"Yes. I met her and her mom this summer. They live in Norfolk."

He pulls open the wardrobe door, creating a small draft. Dresses and slacks sway on their hanger. "She must be here already. We better get Amy's things," Jack says.

Kathy reappears and taps John and Amy on the shoulder. "No running! Do you want to go to the playroom? Is it all right if they go with me?" She signs.

"Yes." I nod my fist up and down. This is an easy sign. I'm sure I got it right.

Jack points at John, Amy, and Kathy, and then to himself, and then gestures toward the door, his questioning eyes wait for a response. Kathy understands he wants to join them. She signs, "yes, come."

"After I see the playroom, I'll bring in Amy's stuff," Jack says.

I gaze out the window at the academic buildings sprinkled across the school's manicured lawn. I watch as a teenage girl bounds out of a car and runs to join a group of girls by their dorm. Her hands flutter words. The girls respond with nodding heads and finger pointing. I follow their outstretched arms and see several teenage boys approaching. The girls clump together, their signs hidden from my view, but their furtive glances tell me they're talking about boys, a topic common to all teenage girls. When the boys arrive, the girls open their huddle, forming a wide circle.

Something moves in my field of vision: a hand waving. I focus on the woman. It's Vodis Dahlke. Calvin is pulling boxes and suitcases from their car. The teenage girl I was watching is their daughter, Julie; I've never met her. I wave and turn away from the window. Julie is fifteen. She's been attending school here ten years. *Ye gods, in ten years how many zillion miles will I have driven? How many good-byes will I have said?* Numbers, constant, reliable, infinite, and stable permit me escape from my pain. I rub my stomach, but kneading the knot does no good. I rush to the calf-high toilets and sit to do my calculations.

Let's see; Amy has nine months of school. Figure an average of four weekends a month, that's thirty-six trips to and from Omaha. Each trip is about three hundred miles, so three times six is . . . Wait, I have to make two round trips each week, so that's seventy-two trips a year. Seventy-two times three hundred is . . . That's not right either. After Amy turns five in January, Frontier Airlines will let her fly unaccompanied, so she'll fly home on Friday, which will reduce the number of trips I make second semester, so thirty-six plus . . .

The comfort of numbers is gone. They've betrayed me, becoming unreliable, unstable, and confusing. I wash my hands and return to Amy's cubicle. Her blue trunk is on her bed. Jack is walking toward me with her small suitcase. He tosses Amy's shoes in the wardrobe and sits on the small chair, silent, as I unpack her trunk and suitcase. In less than twenty minutes, I've hung all her clothes and filled her dresser with pajamas, play clothes, and underwear. I arrange her comb and brush, put her toothbrush in a glass, and place her pink cat pillow on her bed. I align her shoes on the closet floor. There is nothing more for me to do, but tell Amy good-bye.

"You done?" Jack stands. "It's after three-thirty. I have to work on the grocery ad tonight. We need to leave."

We go to the playroom. Kathy and an assistant house parent sit on chairs near the middle of the room, keeping a watchful eye on the activity of fifteen girls under age ten. Several of the older girls are signing to Kathy. I can tell they are asking questions. Kathy points to a child and spells "K-E-L-L-I." She points to a dark-haired child in a rocking chair and spells, "C-L-A-R-A." I realize she's telling the older girls the names of the new students.

"John, come on," Jack shouts. Only one head turns at the sound of his voice, but when Jack signals with his arm "come here," several heads turn to see who's being summoned.

I tug Amy away from her play stove. "John, tell your sister good-bye."

"Good-bye, Amy." John waves.

Jack stoops to hug Amy. "Be good. See you soon."

I kneel and face Amy. Separation is nothing new to us, but for therapy it was brief, a hangnail compared to this separation, which is an amputation. My lungs clamp shut as I hug Amy, refusing to inhale the pain of good-bye. I see Kathy sign, "She'll be fine."

Yes, I suppose she will, but what about me?

I kiss Amy's cheek, "Good-bye, Amy." I sign, "I love you. See you in two weeks."

Let me out of here. I hurry to the door, and turn to see if Amy's watching. She isn't. Her back is to me; Kathy's signing to her.

As we drive away I think, in thirteen days I'll see Amy. I wipe away my tears, but they return. I ignore the knot in my stomach and concentrate on my friend, numbers. *How long will it be before I see Amy? Hmmm. There are twenty-four hours in a day. Thirteen times twenty-four is . . .*

25
The Year with Few Memories
Rebecca

Sept. 9, 3:47 p.m.   Jack, John, and I leave Amy at NSD. Each mile we drive west takes me further from her. At 6:22 p.m. we're home. Amy is 152.6 miles away from me.

Sept 10–20.   I functioned in a stupor, either numb or full of gut-wrenching pain waiting for the first two week to pass so I could bring Amy home for the weekend.

Sept. 21, 3:30 p.m.   I peeked through the window of the Prep 1 class and saw Amy. My pain of missing her is replaced by smothering her with hugs and kisses. Fifteen minutes later we're driving toward home.

Sept. 23, 3:30 p.m.   John and I returned Amy to NSD. Neither Amy nor I cried. I wonder if she cries after I'm gone. Jack stayed home to work on the grocery ad.

Sept. 28, 3:50 p.m.   Arrived late at NSD due to traffic. I met Amy in the dorm, grabbed her suitcase, and drove home. Arriving at 7:00 p.m. Supper was rushed.

Sept. 30, 3:15 p.m.   Returned Amy to NSD. She cried. I waited until I was in the car to cry. Separation is not getting easier.

October.   A repeat of September. I drive to Omaha every Friday afternoon and back again on Sunday.

November.   More of the same. Thanksgiving? I guess we went to Esther's as usual.

Amy's fifth birthday party in her Prep 1 class, her first birthday celebrated away from home. From left to right, Cynthia Smith, Kyle Miers, a class aid, Clyde Brack, Mrs. Hosfelt, Amy Willman, and Clara Perales.

Dec. 19.   I brought Amy home for Christmas. She'll be with us for seventeen days! Did we celebrate Christmas? I don't remember. I'm sure we did.

Jan. 6.   Taking Amy back to school was difficult after she was home for two weeks. Gut wrenching, like last September. How will I endure five more months of this?

Jan. 23.   Wednesday. Today was Amy's fifth birthday. She's in Omaha. I'm in Grand Island. The roads are icy. I can't see my baby on her birthday. Did she have a party? I miss her.

Jan. 24.   Per Frontier Airline regulations, Amy may now fly unaccompanied. I bought a handful of one-way airplane tickets today. NSD staff will take her to the airport on Friday, but will not pick her up on Sunday, so I still have to drive to Omaha on Sunday, but one three-hundred mile round trip every weekend is much better than two

Jan. 25, 4:20 p.m.   Amy arrived at the Grand Island airport on her first flight home alone. I give her a book titled, "My Book About Me." The pages have places for the child to fill in blanks or check boxes about their life. On page 4, "How I Go to School," Amy checks off the box by a car and an airplane. I smile.

May 20.   The school year is almost over; it's been a blur of vague, isolated memories. I have functioned on autopilot for nine months. Today I told Jack: "In two weeks Amy will be home for the summer. I never thought I'd live this long." These words are my most vivid memory of the last nine months. Since September my life has been an endless rerun of taking Amy to school on Sunday and waiting for Friday when I could bring her home.

Kathy had Amy's blue trunk packed. At 1:15 p.m. John, Amy, and I left NSD for home. No more driving to Omaha for three months. Amy is home for the summer. Hurrah! We are a family again.

26

Residential Life in the Primary Dorm

Amy

Mother and I attended the NSD Summer Workshop for parents and deaf children when I was three, and again when I was four years old, but I don't remember that. Nor do I remember my first day of school at NSD, when I was only four-and-one-half years old, or even my first year or two. My first memory of NSD was seeing so many deaf girls who I would live with all week, and also my house parent, Kathy Becker, who was deaf. This memory is from when I was seven or eight years old.

The primary dorm where I lived as a young child was for students in Prep 1 through fourth grade. The boys and girls each had their own wing. The dorm had wardrobe closets, dressers, a big living room, bathroom, and playrooms so the deaf children would feel like it was a home.

I was one of the many deaf children who had to live in a dormitory because my family's home was so far away. It was not possible for me to go home daily, but I went home on Fridays and came back on Sunday afternoons. Staying at school all week and coming home for the weekend and for vacations was my early childhood routine.

I saw the staff and students of NSD daily in the dormitory, classes, and the dining room. We all knew each other. The students were a big family of sisters and brothers who were from ages four to twenty-one years old.

On the first day of school when I entered second grade, I remember opening the door to the primary dorm and seeing a long hallway down the middle of a large room. When I turned my head to the right, I saw three beds, each with their own individual closet and dresser. On the left side it was the same, but only two beds instead of three. I walked a little further, and there was another divided area with the same design as the first area.

Kathy Becker, our house mother, had put our names on the closet doors. I looked around to find my name, so I would know what area I would live in for the school year. Finally, I found "Amy" on a closet. It was near the front entrance on the right side. My bed was the first of the three beds in this area. I was curious. I peeked at the second closet to see whose name was there, "Jeannie." I knew Jeannie Wruble from when we were in therapy together in Grand Island several years ago. Then I saw that the third closet had no name. I only had one roommate, not two.

Mother put my big blue trunk on the bed and started to unpack my clothes, placing them into the drawers and the closet. Another school year had begun.

Many people might think that attending a residential school for the Deaf is not a good place to be. They may think residential schools are filled with many rules, and the staff does not provide love and care. Well, in a child's private home, there are rules and some parents provide love and good care and some don't. So residential schools and private homes are alike in many ways.

However, the rules and feelings are a bit different at a residential school. For example, if a person spilled a soda on the carpet in the living room of the dorm, everyone might be punished and no one could have any drinks in the living room. That would not have happened at my home. At the dorm we had to be in bed at a specific time, and children living at home might not have to do that. We also ate at specific times and were not allowed to roam freely outside to play without house parents present. We usually had the same routine daily.

In the morning, we woke up at 6:30 a.m., dressed, and brushed our teeth. Next we walked to the cafeteria to have breakfast. After thirty minutes of eating breakfast, we returned to the dorm to do light cleaning, such as sweeping the floor, vacuuming the living room, and cleaning the bathroom sinks. When we saw the clock hands showed 8:10 a.m., we lined up and walked upstairs to the primary school. There we spent all day learning many different subjects. When the clock hit 3:30 p.m., school was over. We walked downstairs to our dorm and changed our clothes if we wore a dress that day. After putting on comfortable play clothes, at 4 p.m., we went outside to play for thirty minutes to one hour.

When school ended, I was thrilled to remove my hearing aids. In the dorm, there was a lot of noise, because of kids yelling, playing, dragging tables, or moving chairs. Since we were all deaf, and so was our house parent, we did not need hearing aids. We all communicated through sign, because we could not understand each other's voices even with hearing aids. Without my aids, I was more comfortable; the silence was less annoying to my ears. Too much noise hurts my head. Also, I could play like a hearing child. I did not have to worry about catching my hand or a toy in the hearing aid cord and breaking it.

After supper, we spent the rest of our evening indoors. Either watching TV, playing with dolls and other toys, or riding bikes in the playroom. Thirty minutes before bedtime, we all took showers and hit the hay at 8:30 p.m. Ten hours later, here comes the next morning. In general it was the same routine over and over.

The only thing I did not like about this routine was that I had to clean. Daily cleaning was mandatory in the dorms except on weekends. Every week the cleaning chart changed, so I didn't clean the same thing every week. Sometimes I worked alone; other times I worked with two or three girls. When cleaning the bathroom, there were usually three girls. One did the sinks, one did the toilets, and the other did the shower stalls and floor. One girl vacuumed the whole living room. I understood why we had to clean daily. There were many girls living in the dorm and cleaning it would prevent us from getting sick due to germs. One good thing about cleaning every day was that it gave us some responsibility and in the long run, we developed the habit of keeping things clean. As an adult, I've discovered that most deaf people who attended deaf schools usually keep their homes cleaner than deaf people who were mainstreamed and did not have to clean daily.

At the dorm, everyone's space was similar, so I missed my bedroom at home. Nothing really suited my personality at school, unless I decorated my room. But even then it was not the same as my bedroom at home, which had a canopy bed and my cat figurines on the dresser and many more stuffed animals, mostly cats.

I didn't bring many of my things from home to school, because I would have to show and share them with the other girls, which I did not want to do. So in general, the only things I had at school that expressed my personality were my clothes, a few figurines, stuffed animals, and framed photos. The towels, bedspread, bedroom furniture, and curtains all belong to school and were very plain.

I will never forget the time I brought a poster to the dorm to put on the wall. When I showed it to Kathy, who was very strict and close-minded, she was shocked to see the poster was of a man. I was only eight years old and had a poster of a man. It was John Travolta dressed in a white suit from the movie *Saturday Night Fever.* Kathy refused to let me post it.

I said, "It is a gift from home. John gave it to me for my birthday." When she learned the poster was from my family, she said, "Okay." I wanted it right next to my bed, so I could look at him every night. John Travolta is still my favorite actor.

I don't think Kathy really appreciated it, but there was nothing she can do about it. Even when she asked me if I wanted to post an animal or cat poster, I declined. I wanted John Travolta. All the other girls posted horses, flowers, and such on their walls, except me. I had my man poster.

As for love and care at a residential school, it depended on which house parent I had. Some would give me a hug, a kiss on the cheek, or check to see how I was doing to be sure I was happy and safe. Others did not, but my fellow students always comforted me. Of course the feelings of love in my family were different from the love I received at school.

Was my life great living in a dormitory? Instead of saying yes or no, I will say "laughter" and "homesick." I had much laugher and great joy because I could communicate and socialize with the other students easily through sign language without being frustrated, like I would have been if I went to public school and had to speak and lipread. At NSD all my classmates communicated through ASL. It was a blessing that Mother allowed me to learn and communicate through sign language. Otherwise, I would have remained a frustrated child, like the wild little girl Helen Keller.

Yes, there was laughter in the dormitory, because of having a deaf house parent during my elementary level and having other deaf children to play with. Kathy gave each of us a doll with doll clothes. Every summer, she and her husband, Bruce, traveled to many places, even foreign countries. When September came, I looked forward to seeing what gift she would give to me and the other girls. The oddest gift I ever received was a green plastic necklace with a Buddha.

Of course I missed my family and, most of all, my cat, when I was away at school. We had no pets at school. The only thing I could bring to NSD so I would feel like I had a cat was stuffed cats. I had plenty of those with me. I just love cats! I missed my family, because I enjoyed playing with my brother and Mother. We played many different card games and board games, and went different places, like stores, museums, and the library.

Mostly I was homesick on Sunday, because that was when Mother dropped me off for the week at school. What a blessing it was to have Kathy as a housemother. Even though strict, she brought laughter to me when I was hurt or sad. She comforted me after my family left me at the dormitory and went home. My sad emotions did not last long, because Kathy would hug me and say, "It will be all right. Now go play with the other girls." And then the other girls in my dorm would come to me and say, "Do not worry. You be fine. Go home Friday." We gave each other pats on the back or hugs, and then we signed, "Let's go play doctor or go swing."

That gave me some comfort, and I would forget that Mother and John had just left. I did the same for the other girls who arrived in the dorm after me. The girls became my second family. Within ten minutes, I was laughing with the other deaf children, playing, or talking with them in sign language about what we had done at home on the past weekend.

During the week, I had good care and was busy at school and in the dorm, so I did not really feel homesick; I just looked forward to Friday. If I was homesick during the week, it was generally because I was really sick, not homesick. Staying in the infirmary was very lonely; no other children were there to sign with me. Nothing in the infirmary made me feel calm and comfortable, and the nurse did not come as often as I wished. I was blessed, because I rarely spent time in the infirmary. I think I was only there twice during my years at NSD.

At home, when I was sick, I felt calm and comfortable, because Mother would be around often, and my cat would be beside me. Plus John would bother me or play with me. Even though I was sick, I was comfortable. Maybe it was because I was at home with my family in my own space.

Mother told me that once I put on a good act and convinced the NSD nurse I was sick. Mother brought me home Monday afternoon and took me to the doctor. The doctor examined me and said, "She is not sick."

Mother asked, "What is wrong, Amy?"

I told her, "My ears hurt."

Mother said, "The doctor says your ears are fine."

"My throat hurts some."

Mother shook her head. "It's fine, Amy. The doctor said you are not sick."

We left the doctor and went home. Mother had no idea why I wanted to be home, until supper that night.

"Tomorrow is John's birthday," I said. "I want to be here."

Then Mother knew I was homesick and wanted to be with John for his birthday. She let me stay home all that week, but told me never to do that again.

At school I felt I was not with my family enough. Of course, the best days for laughter were on Friday when I went home. I rarely spent weekends at the dorm when I was in the primary dorm. When I was with my family, I did not want the weekend to end. The weekends at home seemed too short. At school when I had to stay for a weekend, the weekend seemed too long. Odd, both were only two days.

At home I enjoyed eating peanut butter and jelly sandwiches. I love the creamy peanut butter with any kind of red jelly. Mother usually bought "JIF" peanut butter. One day, when I was about eight, I asked my mother, "What does 'J-I-F' stand for?

She said, "I do not know."

I told her, "I know what it means. J-I-F means John is funny."

Mother and I laughed.

As an adult, I still enjoy eating PBJ sandwiches and when I look at "JIF," I think how funny my brother can be.

John did many funny things to make me laugh when I was home. For example, he had ragweed allergy and could not breathe well through his nose because of the pollen. His eyes were red and his nose was swollen. He had a funny idea about how to prevent the pollen from bothering him. He took a snorkel mask, removed the glass part, and put tissues where the glass used to be. He thought it would help him breathe better, but he could not see, and he just looked funny.

Other times he would pretend to act like an old man. He would pull his slacks up under his armpits, and walk in a weird manner and make a silly face. He was so funny. I would tell these family events to my second family, the girls in my dorm, when I returned to school.

Of course, sometimes I brought my family laughter. One year I thought karate was great because of the movie *Teenage Mutant Ninja Turtles*. Late one afternoon, I walked into the kitchen where my mother and brother were. I did not have on shoes, only socks.

I said, "I know how to do karate chops. You want to see it? "

They nodded.

Our kitchen was big, room enough for me do my karate chop. I gave them my best performance, almost! I jumped and kicked out my right leg and my arms and hands chopped the air. When I tried to land, my socks slipped on the floor. My body went straight downward on the hard kitchen floor. Splat! I landed flat on my back.

Mother and John stared down at me. I stood really fast to show my pride even though inside I was in so much pain. I told them, "I need some more practice."

They agreed by nodding. Afterward, I never tried doing the karate chop in the air. Even though it was many years ago, I still laugh to myself, and so does my family. I thought I could show off to them, but I only gave them laughter.

After years of staying at NSD, I became used to it. As I became older, I was less homesick. For the rest of my school years, I expected to live in a dormitory. At home were all my possessions, and I missed them, but I knew they would be safer there. And yes, I missed my family and my beloved cat, but where else could I have gone for my education?

The Nebraska School for the Deaf, a residential school, was the best place for me. There I learned academics and to appreciate being Deaf. I knew, once I stepped onto the NSD campus, I was in my own little world where everyone was just like me: Deaf and using sign language!

27

Smooth Roads

Rebecca

Preparing Amy for school her second year was emotionally more difficult than her first, because we both knew what packing the blue trunk meant. After Amy returned to NSD, I return to my monotonous routine. For the past six weeks, after driving John to school, I come home and return to bed. Sometimes I sleep, but today I lie awake, staring, but not focusing on anything. I feel empty, numb, disoriented. Maybe this is what it's like to be dead. My life is the same, day after day, week after week, month after month, and now year after year. I'm twenty-nine, but feel much older.

I'm too young to have an empty nest; John and Amy are still fledglings. None of my friends understand my life. The house is empty all day and the silence is nerve-wracking. Never a slave to television, I escape into books, but after hours of reading, even that bores me. I miss Amy and wonder what she's doing. Does she miss me? Or John, or her father, or her cat? I chuckle at my last thought. I must be alive; dead people don't laugh. I know Amy misses her cat; she grabs Kitty as soon as she comes in the house. A vision of Amy in her rocking chair, hugging her cat and singing "Oh baby Kitty" brings tears to my eyes. I stare at the framed snapshot Daddy took of Amy singing to her cat. I rub my fingers over her face; the glass is cool to my touch, keeping me distant from her even in this photo.

I stare at my reflection in the mirror. Dull blue eyes peer back at me from a youthful face. How can I look so young when I feel so old? Kübler-Ross's book on death and dying springs to mind. Ah, this must be depression, an overwhelming sense of blah. I fall back on the bed and gaze at the ceiling.

At 11:30 a.m., I hear the mailman and rush outside. Among the envelopes is a letter from Amy. NSD has the children write home once a quarter. "Dear Mother and Father, How are you? We are learning about the seasons. Love, Amy." Even though it's a form letter that all her classmates copied, knowing Amy touched the paper and wrote these words comforts me. Inside the envelope is a notice about Amy's parent-teacher conference.

When Jack arrives for lunch, I show him Amy's letter. "Her printing looks better this year, don't you think so?"

"Uh-huh." Jack mumbles, his mouth full of a BLT.

"Her parent-teacher conference is Friday. Will you take time off so you—"

"You know I can't take off on Friday. I have to unload the truck, and we're super busy."

"I know, but I thought you might come once."

"Why do they always have these conferences on Friday?"

"Because parents come to Omaha that day to pick up their kids."

"Well, that makes sense." Jack gulps his drink.

Disgusted that Jack spends so little time with the children or takes an interest in what they do, I ask, "What difference does it make what day it is? If it was on Monday, would you take off?"

Jack glances at the kitchen clock. "It's almost one. I have to go back to work."

I pick up the phone and punch in the number of my best friend. "Pat, you busy?"

"Nope. Come over. I'll make some spiced tea, and we can play cribbage."

The tea is excellent, the company great, and the cribbage games lousy. After I lose three in a row, Pat says, "You're not paying attention. What's wrong?"

"I really miss Amy." I fold my paper napkin into a small hat.

"Why don't you call her and talk to her?"

"How can I do that? She's deaf." My voice is filled with frustration, not sarcasm.

"I'm sorry." Pat reaches for my hand. "I wasn't thinking."

"It's all right. Nobody understands." I tightened my face into an angry scowl. "When I hear people whining about sending their eighteen-year-old kid to college, I want to scream 'Shut up! You can call your child anytime and write them letters. Try sending a five-year-old away without any way to communicate with them, then you'll have something to whine about!'"

"I wish I could help. Hey, I know what I'll do. Next time I'll let you win." She smiles.

"Ha! That will be the day." I shuffle the cards and deal. I lose again.

On Friday as I drive to Omaha, I remember last year's parent-teacher conference. Amy's academic and dorm reports were excellent, but the PE teacher said, "Amy always wants to be first. She should let others lead." I wonder what she'll say this year.

Amy's Prep II teacher had a glowing report, and the PE teacher's report was the same as last year's. On the drive home, as Amy dozes in the back seat, I replay the PE teacher's criticism of Amy. *I'm not going to encourage Amy to be less aggressive. Life's tough for everyone, but harder for someone with a disability. If Amy can rise to the top, good for her.*

To move out of my blah zone, I become John's room mother and his assistant Cub Scout leader. I join a garden club, composed primarily of older ladies. They know I have a deaf daughter, as I often mention Amy. Several of the women belong to organizations that need speakers, so without any effort on my part, I'm soon in demand to speak to groups on deafness. I explain the need for infant hearing tests (which are now readily available), the effect of high fevers on the inner ear, the best way to gain the attention of a deaf person, how to speak to a hard of hearing child or adult, and answer their questions, some of which are painful.

This week I am speaking to a book club in the home of one of Grand Island's most prominent citizens. Jack was home for lunch when she called to confirm the time. "Who was that?" He asked.

"Mrs. Steinmeyer."

He nods, wide-eyed, impressed. Although Jack is not very perceptive of my moods, my scowl and the fact I stuck out my tongue during the telephone conversation tell him I'm upset.

"What's the matter? What did she say?"

"She said, 'When you come to my house, enter through the back door and wait in the kitchen until I call you.' How rude is that? Why did she ask me speak if she doesn't think I'm good enough to come in her front door?" In my anger, I knock over my iced tea. "Damn it!"

"Don't go then." Jack, like most men, supplied a simple solution.

"No, I said I'd go, so I'm going." I toss a paper towel on the spilled tea.

"If she upset you, why bother?"

"I'm not going for me. I am going to inform ignorant hearing people about deafness. Amy and other deaf people put up with ill-mannered stares and hurtful comments every day; the least I can do is to try to educate a few people on their behalf."

"It was just a suggestion." Jack scooted his chair from the table and returned to work.

I enjoy a good novel, but prefer to read nonfiction. This afternoon I'm reading a book by a psychologist on the impact a disabled child has on the entire family. The author wrote: "The divorce rate is higher for couples with a disabled child, primarily because the parents can't agree on how the child should be educated and disciplined. The disabled child requires extra time and attention, leaving other family members shortchanged. The additional financial and emotional burden often leaves little time and money for the family to enjoy each other. Stress and growing resentments erode the marriage."

I lay the open book on my chest and contemplate what I've read. John seems fine, well-adjusted, no behavioral problems. He doesn't seem resentful that I give most of my time to Amy on the weekends when she is home; after all, he has me all week long. Jack and I never disagree on how to raise Amy. Well, that's not entirely true. When I wouldn't give Amy her supper until she vocalized, Jack thought I was terrible, but later he admitted it was the right thing to do. All the same, our marriage is floundering, but Amy is not the reason.

Married life, or at least my marriage, is not what I expected. Three nights a week Jack doesn't come home until after 10 p.m. Then all he does is watch the news and collapse into bed. The other nights he's home by 6 p.m., but those nights aren't much different. I ask him to spend time with John and me, but he'd rather read the paper or watch TV. Quarrels or a stony silence occur far too often.

We have no marriage in the true sense of the word. We live separate lives. Mine is devoted to the house, my garden club, activities with John, and carpooling Amy to school. Jack's life is work. The grocery store is his mistress; she demands and receives his quality time. I feel more like a single parent than a wife.

A few weeks after Amy's seventh birthday, the telephone interrupts my reading. "Hello?" I slip a paper clip on the page to mark my place.

An unfamiliar female voice speaks. "This is Joyce Garrison, the nurse at NSD."

My heart skips a beat. I inhale, holding my breath, expecting . . . I don't know what.

"Amy's in the infirmary with the flu. No fever, just stomach cramps and diarrhea. She can stay here, but when the younger children are sick, I think it's best for them to go home."

"I'll be there in about three hours."

"No rush, she's not going any place, except to the toilet." She chuckles, which calms me.

After making arrangements with Jack to pick up John from school, I leave. It's Tuesday, the traffic should be light, but every Sunday driver who failed to creep along the highway this weekend chose to go someplace today. The trip, which always is long and boring, is more so today because I am on an errand of mercy.

I haven't been in the infirmary since I toured the facility two summers ago, but I easily find it. The nurse, points to a door that's ajar. "Amy's in that room."

Through the open door I see Amy seated on the toilet doubled over with cramps. Her position reminds me of the numerous times I've sat like that, not suffering with the flu, but with a tension-filled gut. Amy cries, "Mommy come here. Mommy come here."

I push open the door. On seeing me, Amy smiles. I wipe her tear-streaked cheeks and blink my tears away.

Amy idolizes her first grade teacher, Mrs. Hosfelt. On weekends, many of her sentences start with "Mrs. Hosfelt says . . ." With constant exposure to ASL, Amy's sign language vocabulary has increased dramatically. So far I'm able to keep pace, but I wonder how long it will be before she's fluent in a language I struggle to use.

Several Sundays this year, Amy cried when I returned her to NSD. Kathy always signs, "She'll be fine."

But, my sigh and worried face convey another message. "Are you sure?"

"Yes." Kathy's fist nods yes with gusto. She signs. "Ten minutes before Amy arrived, Kelli's parents left her here. She cried, but look at her now, she's mothering Amy. The girls are like sisters, very close to one another."

I realize Amy has another family, one that empathizes and provides comfort, something I can't do for her now, because I must leave, and my leaving is the source of her pain.

For me, no amount of creature comforts can replace having a caring father for John and Amy and an attentive husband for me. While Jack says he cares about us, and I expect he does in his own way, his emotional and physical distance is taking a toll on me. I live with constant expectations that the situation will change, and despite Jack's many promises that he will spend more time with us, he never does. Neither counseling, tears, nor prayers can save our marriage. In February Jack and I divorce.

The lack of Jack in the house bothers John at first. He often tells me he misses his dad. We talk about how his dad was gone most of his waking hours and did not spend much time with him. John agrees that he never saw his father very much. Jack could visit the children any time, but his work comes first. I make a habit of stopping at the grocery store often when John is with me so he can be with his father, if only for the thirty minutes while I shop for groceries.

Amy seems unmoved by the divorce. She had even less contact with her father than John, since she lives in Omaha during the week. She accepts without comment that we have divorced.

For the past year, I've been drowning in unhappy childhood memories, coping with my failing marriage, and dealing with Amy being in Omaha. My usual energy is gone. I drag around the house as if treading water. I'm suffering many of the classic symptoms of depression: sadness, feeling worthless, fatigue, trouble concentrating, and no appetite. One morning I acknowledge I can't snap out of this funk, and my gloomy mood is not beneficial for John. I seek professional help. Five minutes into my first sessions I'm sobbing. "I miss Amy. I hate leaving her, but the school staff says I shouldn't cry in front of her."

"Why not?" The counselor hands me a box of tissues. "You're sad. Crying is a normal expression of sadness. Does Amy ever cry when you leave her?"

"Yes, sometimes." I wipe my eyes.

"You have the right to express your sadness about the situation. If Amy cries when you leave, if you feel like crying, do it. If she's sad, and you smile, your stoic appearance will confuse her. She'll wonder about her feeling. You both should express your true feelings."

I'm relieved to hear that shedding a few tears will not scar Amy for life.

Continued visits with the counselor give my life perspective.

During a parent-teacher conference, Jill Ramsey, the speech therapist for the primary school, tells me, "If I'm introducing a new subject and the children aren't interested, all I need to do is convince Amy we should do it. If I do, she'll tell the other kids in the class, 'this is what we are going to do,' and they all follow her."

"I hope Amy is not too bossy. She does like to give orders."

"Not at all. She's a good leader." Jill hands me Amy's report card.

I'm glad she recognizes Amy is a leader. I walk toward the gym, preparing to hear the PE teachers's usual comments. The PE teacher rises when I enter her small office, shakes my hand, and invites me to sit. "Amy is a good athlete and a natural leader."

Hurrah! I wonder why it took her three years to arrive at that conclusion. Anyone in a room with Amy for more than thirty minutes can see she's a "take charge" type.

In third grade, my parent-teacher conference with Amy's teacher, Patti Reitz, is difficult because she's Deaf, and my signing ability is that of a six-year-old. In addition, my decision to use Signing Exact English (SEE) as opposed to American Sign Language (ASL) was not a wise choice. The Deaf community uses ASL. SEE gives Amy a better understanding of English sentence structure, but Amy's desire to communicate with her classmates is more important, so she uses ASL. Despite our communication difficulties, Patti is patient and explains that Amy is at the top of her class.

Brian, a hard of hearing child, moved into our neighborhood this summer. He's two years younger than Amy. With only a moderate hearing loss, he's developed understandable speech and can follow conversations if only one person is talking, but in group situations he's lost.

Amy's severe hearing loss left her with one educational option, a school for the deaf, but Brian's 50 percent loss made the decision about his education more difficult. His parents enrolled him in a local school, which I think is a mistake, since he has already spent two years in first grade.

Brian's learning to ride a bike. I've seen him wobbling past our house, paying no attention to the traffic, and without adult supervision. Amy has ridden a bike for two years and knows to watch for traffic, and yet I'm still not comfortable letting her bike alone. John or I always accompany her. Yesterday Brian had a close encounter with a car; he only received minor injuries, but his bike was a total loss.

This morning, before brutal heat smothers the day, I decide to weed my rock garden. Amy and John are shooting baskets, at a lower than a normal basketball hoop on our driveway.

A shadow moves across the area I'm weeding. "I've wanted to visit you for some time. I'm Claire, Brian's mother."

"Nice to meet you." I rise, pushing hair from my eyes with the back of my dirty hand.

"Someone told me you had a deaf daughter. Is that Amy?"

Will I ever be known as Rebecca? I'm always labeled as "the mother of the deaf child." "Yes." The basketball bounces toward us. I deflect it with my foot, sending it up the driveway.

"Thank, Mom," John says.

Amy tussles with John for possession of the ball and loses. He shoots and misses. "Too bad for you," Amy calls. She grabs the rebound and makes a basket. "I win."

"She's a good athlete," Claire comments.

"Yes. The School for the Deaf has a great PE program. The kids play the same sports hearing kids do, because their coach can communicate with them. NSD also has a huge indoor pool. Amy already knows how to swim. Last year she joined the Brownie troop the school sponsors." I sound like a commercial for NSD, but I'm pleased with the well-rounded education Amy receives there.

"I'm sure NSD is good, but my husband and I would never send Brian there. He's not deaf, like Amy, he's only hard of hearing," Claire says.

Well, la-de-dah. I clench my teeth, biting my tongue in the process. *First she labeled me, and now Amy.* "I'm sure deciding where to send Brian to school was a difficult choice." As I kneel to resume my weeding, I recall the speakers at the NSD Summer Camp explaining why the Deaf community at NSD is important for your child's education and social development.

Remembering my grandmother's words of wisdom, "you can tell people, but you can't tell them much," I refrain from telling Claire what NSD staff might say about her decision to send Brian to a local school.

"We aren't like you. We'd never send Brian away. We love him too much," Claire says.

Thank God my eyes are focused on the weeds. What does she think I am, some monster who doesn't care about her daughter? Leaving Amy at NSD when she was four was the worst day of my life, but I did it because I loved her enough to put my feelings aside and do what was best for her. I inhale, holding my breath for a moment to calm my anger. "So, what brought you to this end of the block?"

"Brian was hit by a car the other day."

"Yes, I know. I'm glad he wasn't seriously hurt." I pull a stubborn pigweed from the rock garden and stand.

"That's why I'm here." Claire adjusts her sunglasses. "The driver honked, but Brian didn't hear it. I think signs should be posted to warn drivers there are kids in the neighborhood who have hearing problems."

I think you ought to watch your child and teach him not to play in the street.

"I've seen signs in other towns that say 'Caution Deaf Children,'" Clair says. "I'd like you to come to the city council meeting with me next week and ask them to post similar signs in our neighborhood." Claire stoops to pull out a small weed I missed.

Amy is nine. Five years ago she learned not to play in the street, a lesson Brian has yet to learn at age eight. I don't want Brian's future injuries on my conscience, so I say, "Sure. I'd be glad to go."

Four weeks later the signs are installed. As we drive by them Amy points to one and says, "Those signs are for Brian, not me."

I chuckle. *Out of the mouths of babes.*

28

Education, the Primary Years

Amy

I have many fond memories of my classmates and teachers from the primary years. As I look back I remember the joy I had from being able to learn and receive an education.

When I was in Prep II, which is similar to kindergarten, I had the sweetest teacher named Mrs. Kathleen. She was so caring and taught my class many funny and interesting things. She used total communication, a teaching method that uses signing and speaking at the same time. Many of the students, including me, wore body hearing aids. I heard Mrs. Kathleen's voice but could not understand every word she spoke. Still, I was required to use my body aids.

In class, Mrs. Kathleen taught us well by providing plenty of visual aids, since Deaf students learn visually rather than by auditory instruction. She put many posters and pictures with text on them in the classroom, which made it easier for me and the six other students in my class to understand what she was teaching us. At NSD there were never more than eight students in a classroom so we all could have eye contact with the teacher.

Every Friday, we always had snack time before we went home for the weekend. Sometimes, we had peanut butter on crackers, other times graham crackers and milk, or juice and cookies. On Friday afternoon we always took our little chair from our desk to the corner of the room where there was a sink and mini-refrigerator. We set our chairs in a semicircle facing Mrs. Kathleen; again so we could all see her.

"What will we eat for a snack today?' Mrs. Kathleen asked.

We looked at a calendar chart and signed, "Today—popcorn—Hawaiian punch."

She asked us several questions about the process of making popcorn.

We signed, "Pour oil—popcorn seeds. Not touch—popcorn machine—hot."

She always asked us those questions to be sure we knew the safety of cooking. Before she put the lid on the popcorn machine, a teacher from another classroom needed to talk to Mrs. Kathleen. "You children stay in your chairs, and be quiet," she said. She went to the hall outside our room.

We sat quietly and stared at the popcorn machine without a lid for a minute. All of a sudden one or two kernels popped out and lay on the floor. Then two or three more popped. We started to giggle.

Mrs. Kathleen heard us and flicked the lights off and on to get our attention. We turned toward her. "I told you all to be quiet," she said.

We said nothing, but more and more corn was popping all over the floor. We could not stop giggling.

She flicked the light again and signed with an angry face, "Stop it." And then she saw the popcorn all over the floor. She laughed so hard and signed and said, "Why didn't you put the lid on it?"

"You say stay chair," I said.

"Machine hot," said Kelli.

She signed, "You are all good children."

Of course, we thought we were angelic Prep II students, even when the corn was all over the floor.

Three years later, we learned how candles were made in the old days. Sure enough, I had to make a candle starting with a string. It took forever. I dipped the string three times into a bucket of wax. Next I walked around the classroom to let the wax dry, and then I dipped it and walked again. I did this over and over. Finally, it formed into a skinny candle. I also made a doll out of dried corn leaves one year when we learned about pioneers. Mother kept that doll and still uses it as an ornament on her Christmas tree. I loved the hands-on activities; they were very visual for me and other Deaf students. It was fun, and at same time I was getting an education.

In primary school we did an annual school play either at Christmas or Easter. I remember my first play, *The Night Before Christmas*. I was dressed as a mouse and was so cute. All my classmates were mice. On the stage, there were many props and decorations. The backgrounds on the stage were usually made by students and art teachers. NSD provided the props and made the costumes, or sometime they rented costumes. In third grade, I had a leading role in the Christmas play, which was about Toyland. I was a winter wonderland fairy. I wore a silver sparkling outfit and carried a snowflake wand. I signed and acted in the play. At the end of the Christmas play, every student came on the stage and signed various Christmas songs, such as *I'm Dreaming of a White Christmas, Silent Night*, and *We Wish You a Merry Christmas*.

Yes, Deaf people can sing in sign. During speech class, my classmates and I all sang many different songs or short poems at the same time. We spent fifty minutes once or twice a week in speech class. All primary students participated in a speech training to learn how to pronounce words accurately. The school also provided individual speech training for students, but I never did that. Mrs. Jill Ramsey worked to correct our speech and trained us to make new sounds. It seems funny to think that a deaf person can sing, but we did. I really enjoyed learning many songs, but not the speech skills.

In speech class, there was a piano and we stood behind it while Mrs. Ramsey played the piano and lip-synched the song. That way, we could follow the song at the same time as singing in ASL. How did we learn the song? Mrs. Ramsey either handed out the song sheets or wrote the words on posters. She spoke the songs and signed them in ASL at the same time. We spoke the words, but the main focus was on learning the words to the songs, not accurate speech.

When Jill taught songs, she showed us signs for the songs, but sometimes my classmates and I would suggest a better way to sign the words for the song. In the song, *Kum Ba Ya* there is a verse saying, "Someone's praying, Lord." We suggested that we sign "pray" and bend down our head instead of just signing "pray" and facing straight into the audience.

In the song, *America the Beautiful,* the last line includes, "from sea to shining sea." We signed to Jill, "Why not sign 'sea' at one side of our body and other 'sea' on other side of our body to symbolize two seas on either side of United States?" Jill was open to our suggestions about expressing ASL in songs. That's why I enjoyed learning songs because my classmates and I could create signs for some of the lines so our signs looked accurate in ASL.

Jill took our choir to government meetings or nursing homes to sign our songs to them. We were the Deaf Choir Signers. If it were not for Jill Ramsey, I would never know any songs.

When I entered the seventh grade, I was no longer part of Deaf Choir Signers, because I moved to a different schoolhouse. But I still sang to myself for fun, and I remember the songs I learned.

After school during my primary years, I was in a Deaf Brownie troop. Teachers from the school were our leaders. We did some crafts and took a few field trips to earn badges. I enjoyed earning badges.

I rarely stayed at NSD over the weekend when in primary school, but when I did, I went to Bethlehem Lutheran Church on Sunday, a Deaf church. Also, I attended classes there on Wednesday afternoons to learn about God and stories from the Bible. I learned from either Deaf or hearing church members who explained the words and meanings from the Bible by signing to me and other students.

My best experience in primary school was having Patti Reitz for my third grade teacher. Why? Patti Reitz was my first Deaf teacher. She was a great role model. In her class, when I was just eight years old, I realized a Deaf person can be whatever a Deaf person wants to be in life.

In third grade I still wore my body hearing aids, but I soon realized they were no longer useful in the classroom, because my teacher SIGNED! Really signed. ASL was her first language, not English like my other teachers. The only noises I heard in class were kids banging on the table or dragging the chairs. From Prep I through second grade, I heard the voice of my teachers, but I didn't understand them. In third grade, with a Deaf teacher who only used ASL, I stopped wearing my hearing aids. It was the best feeling in the world not to wear my body hearing aids for a full day then or ever again.

I wanted a reason to stop wearing the aids because of the bothersome noise, and now I could since I had a Deaf teacher. Oh yeah, it was completely different having a Deaf teacher rather than a hearing teacher. With a Deaf teacher, I was able to communicate and express myself better. Not only that, Patti could understand what my classmates and I were signing. She could catch our conversations and be part of it.

When I had hearing teachers, sometimes when I signed a sentence or question, the teacher could not understand and the teacher had to ask me more questions to clarify what I was signing. Why? Because ASL not only involves signs but body language and facial expressions. Deaf people can easily understand what these movements mean, but hearing people often don't, because hearing people are used to hearing emotions in the voice.

Having Patti Reitz for a teacher showed me that Deaf people can have the same jobs as hearing people, not just be a cook or janitor or houseparent, which were the only Deaf adults I had seen at NSD. I did not have many Deaf teachers during my years at NSD, so it was a nice feeling to have a teacher with my same background, one who could understand me: a Deaf person.

After third grade, I had hearing teachers again, but I never wore my hearing aids anymore. I heard no sound for the rest of my school years. Silence. It's a beautiful sound, really!

29

Moving into Deaf Culture

Rebecca and Amy

In June, Amy is ready to come home when I arrive at her dorm. She hugs her friends good-bye with promises of "see you next fall." Amy's almost as tall as I am. In the past two years her wispy hair has become thicker, but what really amazes me is that her straight hair is now curly! I look at her golden locks and wish that my straight hair would have such a transformation. As we lug her blue trunk to the car, I ask, "Where are your hearing aids?"

Amy nods her head toward the trunk. "Inside."

"Why aren't you wearing them?" We hoist the blue trunk into the car.

"No help. Too much noise. Not work good," she signs.

Even though I know Amy does not wear her aids at school, she always wears them when she comes home. "I'll call Laverne when we get home and buy new ones for you."

"No. I don't want them." She fastens her seat belt.

I knew the day would come that Amy wouldn't want hearing aids. Vodis told me many years ago to expect this, but I am not ready for Amy to shut out the hearing world.

"No. I don't need any. I am just fine." Amy stares out the window at the passing fields.

"The new aids are more powerful. The sound would be better." Silence has its place, but I can't imagine living in a hearing world without being aware of at least sirens and warning shouts.

"No. I don't like noise. It bothers me." She pulls the visor down to block the sun. "Older deaf people don't like hearing aids."

"Jeannie still wears her aids," I argue.

"She's still in primary dorm. Kids in primary dorm have to wear aids. I don't want them anymore. They are not for me." She closes her eyes against the sun and my moving lips.

We drive home with little communication. Amy happy in her silent world, and me lonely in a world that is never without sound—passing cars and trucks, birds, the wind, radios, TVs—the noise is constant and endless.

❧

When I stopped wearing my hearing aids at the age of ten, Mother asked me if I wanted a behind-the-ear aid as it is less visible than my two body aids. I told her, "NO. I don't want aids ever again for the rest of my life." Years later when new technology made cochlear implants possible, Mother asked if I wanted this, and she offered to pay for it. Again I said, "No." I love the sound of silence.

Am I against wearing hearing aids? Basically, no. Hearing aids didn't suit me well, but they might suit some people with a hearing loss. Aids did not work well for me since I have such a severe hearing loss, more than 100 decibels, but people with a moderate hearing loss of 60 decibels or less would probably find aids helpful.

There are different levels of hearing loss, from mild to profoundly deaf. Not everyone can benefit from hearing devices. What device will work depends on what kind of hearing loss a person has. As I have mentioned, I am profoundly deaf. My last hearing audiogram said the loss in my right ear was 110 decibels and 115 decibels in my left ear. This means I do not hear sounds until they have a volume of 110–115 decibels. I can hear very loud noises like chainsaws, rock concerts, or motorcycles, if I am near the noise source. I am not sure if I actually hear it ... maybe it is just loud vibrations toward my body so I think I heard a noise. Normal hearing people have a threshold of about 10 decibels, which allows them to hear whispers and even quieter noises.

Hearing requires volume and clarity. I need loud volume to hear, but even then I do not hear sounds like hearing people do, because

my ears do not hear certain frequencies. The sounds I hear are garbled since higher sounds are missing. Most of my life, all I've heard
is silence.

Since I have never heard most sounds, when I hear one, I am
not sure what it is unless I see something near me that could make
the noise. For example, I went on a cruise with my family. We were
seated on an upper deck outside and the ship's huge horn was aimed
right at us. It sounded four times to tell passengers to return to the
ship, because we would soon sail away. My family was startled and
jerked. They asked me, "Did you hear that? Do you know what it
was?" I said, "Oh, yes. It was the horn." But if I had not seen the horn,
I might not have known what the noise was.

There are three kinds of modern hearing devices: inner ear aids,
outer ear aids, and cochlear implants. The two body aids I wore as
a child are not used anymore because of cosmetic reasons. The last
time I ever wore my body aids was at the age of ten. I don't know
what Mother did with my old body aids; probably gave them away
to some needy people who needed hearing aids. I did not care.

The inner ear aids fit inside the ear canal and are good for people
who do not want the aid to show in public. It's a very small object
and not noticeable. The outer ear hearing aids are more noticeable.
An outer ear aid fits into the ear with an ear mold, or may hang on
the back part of the ear with an earpiece going into the ear canal.
Both the inner and outer ear hearing aids can be worn in one or
both ears.

Who would benefit from using the inner and outer ear hearing
aids? Not me, but persons with a hearing loss from 30 decibels to
80 decibels might hear and benefit from them. Hearing aids only
amplify sounds; they can't restore hearing that has been totally lost
or improve the clarity of sound, so even when wearing an aid, the
hearing is not really normal.

Some of my deaf friends who have more hearing than I do still
wear aids, because it helps them understand more of the hearing
world or because they have young children and want to hear if their
children cry. Others Deaf friends enjoy hearing some noises, even if
they cannot understand all of them. As for me, I don't understand
sound, because I've never heard a true sound in my entire life.

Cochlear implants are not hearing aids. It is surgery. Cochlear implants are more expensive than aids and involve risk because surgery and hospitalization are required. The implant is inserted inside the ear, and a device is attached on the outside of the head, which then goes to the ear. In the past, cochlear implants were only done on one ear, but now they can be done on both. Many doctors do not recommend having two cochlear implants, because removing the implant causes total hearing loss, unlike inner and outer hearing aids which can be taken off and on anytime without destroying residual hearing. There is no guarantee that an implant will work for everyone. Consider also that a cochlear transplant is not always 100 percent successful. Sometimes after the surgery, the device fails. Even if it works, the quality of sound is not perfect, and not everyone can learn to interpret the sounds they are hearing. For some, all the noise is confusing.

Do I support any kind of hearing aids? As for the inner and outer ear aids, I don't care about them since surgery is not involved. But, when it comes to cochlear implants, I say, "No." Especially not for children. To have a cochlear implant, a doctor inserts the device inside a deaf baby's head. Yes, this is done at an early age, often before age one. Even with a cochlear implant, the child must still have much speech and sound training, as it is a struggle for a deaf child to learn how to speak.

I have seen parents decide to have a cochlear implant on their baby, hoping their child will hear. I wonder, "Why can't the parents accept their child and let the child grow up Deaf?" Look at me. Mother started taking me to speech classes when I was sixteen months old. I could not understand voices and did not learn to communicate well vocally. At last, Mother communicated with me through sign language. I finally began to understand and was much happier. I know how hard it would be for a child with a cochlear implant to attend so many speech and sound training classes, because I went to them for many years. No child deserves to struggle trying to communicate through speech. A frustrated child is not a happy child.

In my opinion, I don't believe cochlear implants should be used on a child born deaf, because the child has never heard any sounds, ever. How can a child understand the meaning of sound if they have never heard it? I think it is better to let a child be Deaf, than to transform them into a "cyborg." Parents and family members should not force a Deaf child to be involved in the hearing world. Instead, the parents should become involved in the Deaf world, which usually is much easier on both the child and the parents. Deaf children and their parents can learn sign language easily, and then they would be able to communicate, just like my mother and my brother did.

American Sign Language is a beautiful language, and by learning it a Deaf child can "hear." I quote George Veditz, a deaf person living in the late 1800s, "Sign language is God's noblest gift to the Deaf."

I know deaf adults who have cochlear implants. Some had it done when a child, others when they were an adult. If they lost their hearing later in life, they tend to be happy with the implant, because they were used to hearing and interpreting sounds. If they were born deaf and had the implant as a child, many quit using the implant when they are older, because it really does not help them.

As for hearing people who become deaf later in life due to illness or accidents, a cochlear implant might be fine for them, since they have already learned how to speak and understand sounds, and they are already part of the hearing culture.

As for me, when I wore aids, all that banging, scratching, and yelling bothered my ears. Silence is a perfect noise for me. As an adult, I have three deaf cats and they are happy even though they can't hear. So why shouldn't I be happy with no sound just like my cats!

30

Caution, Speed Bumps Ahead
Rebecca

Amy considers herself a big girl now, since she's in the fourth grade, her last year in the primary dorm. All the children who had therapy with her at Connell are now at NSD. Teena's in third grade, Linsay's in fourth grade with Amy, Jeannie's in second, and Daniel is in first.

Amy flew home for Christmas vacation. On December 23, 1978, our white Christmas arrived early, all twenty-four inches of it. John, Amy, and I take turns shoveling the driveway and a path to the mailbox. The postman won't deliver mail to curbside mailboxes if he can't access the box from the street. After three hours of backbreaking work, we finished, and the snow plow passed, pushing a four-foot wall of snow over our mailbox. Now all the neighbors are busy digging out their mailboxes, again.

My back is aching when the postman extends his arm from the mail truck and hands me my mail. In it are the gas bill, which will be high since we've had below freezing weather for several weeks, and a letter from the Grand Island School Board. *What are they sending me now?* Since Amy can't attend school in our district, the school board reimburses me for the miles I drive to and from Omaha, but that check does not arrive until February. I've already paid for the gas by the time I'm reimbursed, so I sock that money into our vacation fund.

I rip open the envelope, pull out a sheet of paper, and read unfamiliar terms and phrases. PL 94-142. Section 504. Compliance required. Least restrictive environment. Mainstreaming. Regulations. Mandated. I read the last paragraph aloud. "To comply with this legislation, Amy Willman will be enrolled in special education classes in Grand Island in the fall of 1979." *What! There's no deaf education here.* The letter ends with the sentence, "Concerns and questions will be addressed March 12 at the Grand Island School Board meeting."

What is this? Why can't Amy continue attending school in Omaha? She's happy there and receiving a good education. The schools here wouldn't even consider enrolling Amy six years ago, and now they do? What's going on?

After supper, I telephone Vodis Dahlke. "Did you get a letter from the Grand Island school board today?"

"No, we're not in that school district," Vodis replies. "I wondered when you would call."

"I've already heard from several other parents from the hearing support group. I think you all received the same letter. Something about mainstreaming, right?"

"Yeah. But how did you luck out?"

"We didn't. Our letter came from the Hall County Superintendent of Schools. It's similar to yours. Julie only has two more years at NSD; I see no sense in disrupting her education now."

"What are you going to do?"

"I don't know."

"Neither do I."

Within days I discover that parents whose children attend the Nebraska School for the Blind have received similar letters. They're as upset as I am. I contact Jack. He rarely sees the children, but I keep him informed of what they are doing. He surprises me by suggesting we hire an attorney and fight this.

Several weeks later, Jack and I, along with a dozen other confused and angry parents meet with an attorney, Howard Allen. We file into his conference room. After introductions, Mr. Allen clears his throat. "Let me give you a little history first. Public Law 94-142 was passed by Congress in 1975. Regulations implementing the law were published in 1977. The law states that an appropriate free public education will be available for all handicapped children between the ages of three and twenty-one no later than September 1, 1980."

"So why did we all get these letters?" I drum my fingers on the table, smudging the polished surface. "The schools for the deaf and the blind are state-operated public schools. We don't pay to send our children there. That should fulfill the law's requirements."

"There's more." Mr. Allen continues. "The law also states that children must be educated in the least restrictive environment to the maximum extent appropriate."

I nudge Jack. "Huh? What does that mean?" Other parents echo my question.

Mr. Allen rests his elbows on the table. "Least restrictive environment is the key phrase. This means your child is to be educated with kids who are not handicapped. And that special classes, separate schools, or sending them to schools out of their district will not occur unless the severity of the handicap is such that they can't be educated in a regular class in their hometown."

In an instant, our silent shock is replaced by a barrage of questions.

"Does the law say anything about the quality of education?" Vodis asks.

"The federal government shouldn't tell us how to educate our kids," the father of a blind child says.

"My child is doing well at school. He's popular, plays sports, and is on the honor roll. If he's forced to attend school here, he won't have any friends. If his teachers don't know ASL, he'll get a third-rate education and probably won't be able to play sports either," another parent adds.

"We just started our daughter, Angie, at NSD a couple of years ago," Mrs. Walz says. "She went to public school here for several years. She was falling behind. The principal recommended she go to NSD. Angie's excelling there, and now they want to bring her back to a school here. It doesn't make sense."

"It's not fair. How can they do this?" another woman asks.

"Who's the president of the school board?" I ask, hoping the person might be a family friend of Jack's, and he can beg a favor, at least for Amy.

"Rod Diller," Mr. Allen says. "He's an attorney, so he's aware of the law."

"Doesn't someone in his family have a disability?" I scratch my head, trying to remember what I've heard. "Autism. That's it. His granddaughter is autistic. Perhaps he'll be sympathetic to our plea."

"We can't count on that." Mr. Allen grabs a yellow legal pad. "What I need from each of you is the name and age of your child, where they go to school, and why they should continue their education in that location? Personal gripes won't help. I need facts."

Ninety minutes later we leave Mr. Allen's office. Outside, under a streetlight, we continue our conversation with rapid voices, full of fear. Small vapor clouds float from our mouths and dissipate in the cold air.

"Since you're the most vocal in the group," Vodis says to me, "if the school board asks questions, you should answer for the group." The others agree. I hesitate, and then nod my assent

I hope my answers will do our cause justice, not only for Amy, but for the other eleven children. Sleep teases me tonight, the darkness promises rest, but only provides bad dreams.

Two days later, Amy flies home from NSD with a newsletter highlighting how the curriculum and campus life of NSD provide the best education for a deaf child. NSD also sends a packet of information on PL 94-142 and offers to send staff to our school board to help us plead our case. Even though Amy's only ten, from discussions at school, she's aware of the ramifications of PL 94-142.

Sunday morning, we take our seats in the fourth pew from the pulpit. I've discovered if we sit near the front of the church, John and Amy can see what is happening at the altar and behave better. Amy can't hear the service, but she follows the liturgy and songs in the hymnal.[4]

---

4. In 1979, ASL interpreters were not common except in larger cities and used primarily in legal or medical situations. Currently, many churches have ASL interpreters for selected services.

After the first hymn is sung, in the stillness of the church as the last chord from the organ fades away, Amy says in a clear voice, loud enough for people in the surrounding pews to hear, "No want school in Grand Island."

Before I can mouth, "Shhh," she blurts again, louder, "No school here. School in Omaha." The pastor's sermon is a dull buzz; my thoughts are focused on what Amy just said.

31

Mainstreaming, Not for Me

Amy

You might wonder why I did not want to be mainstreamed at a public school in Grand Island. My parents sent me to NSD, a residential school, when I was four years old, which was the best thing for me. It is something I would have chosen for myself. Why? Because of the language used (ASL), the Deaf culture, and similar peers.

After I shouted out at church, "I no want school Grand Island. I want Omaha," Mother asked me why I felt that way. I said/signed, "At NSD I see deaf adults for role models. No language problem. I understand what is taught, because my teachers use sign in the classrooms. I talk through sign to all the other students. If I go to school here, I cannot sign to other students and teachers."

"Would you be happier if you could be home every night?" Mother asked.

"Well, sometimes yes and no," I said. "I like home with you, John, and Kitty, but have no friends here. All my friends at NSD. Who would talk to me at lunch? I do not want to be alone all the time, like in dance class. No one talked to me. Can I be Girl Scout here?"

"I don't know," Mother said. "I'm most worried about the quality of your education. Also the schools have no TTY telephones. You could not call me if you had an emergency."

"What if the building has fire? I will die. No lights for me to know there is fire. Do you want me dead?" I asked.

"Of course not." Mother shook her head because my question was stupid.

"NSD has flashing lights for fire alarm," I said.

"I know," Mother said.

"I will tell you a funny story. The school administration has random fire drills throughout the year, to make sure we all know what to do during an emergency. My teacher, who is hearing, was teaching basic anatomy on how body functions. All of a sudden, the room and the whole primary building had flashing strobe lights in the rooms and halls. My classmates and I knew what it was, but our teacher did not.

"She asked, 'What is that?'

"At that moment, it was like my classmates and I had telepathy. We decided to dance, and told her, 'It means play time.'

"Another teacher came by our room and said, 'Get out of the building. This is a fire drill.'

"We knew that of course, but our teacher didn't. Her face was so red like a dark apple, because she was embarrassed. Later she had the best laugh of her life. The next time, we had a fire alarm drill, our teacher smirked when we tried to dance and forced us out of the room toward the outside. Lights for alarms are part of Deaf culture. I will never know what is happening at public school here."

Mother said, "I'm not worried about a fire. I'm sure your teacher would tell you to leave, or you could follow the class, but I am worried about the quality of your teachers. I don't think any know sign. If they do, they are probably worse than me." Mother smiled.

"Oh, no. Worse than you. I never learn anything. I want to stay at NSD forever where friends are."

"I want you at NSD, too," Mother said, "but the law says you must go to school in Grand Island."

"I do not want law. I stay at NSD with friends and teachers who sign. Law is crazy for me. Just tell them no." I snapped my index and middle fingers against my thumb several times. "No, no, no."

"I will try, Amy," Mother said.

She looked worried.

32

The Decision

Rebecca

Mr. Allen and two dozen parents attend the March school board meeting. The board members sit around a table in padded chairs, while we parents sit in wooden chairs that line the walls. Mr. Diller, the school board president, calls the meeting to order and announces that mainstreaming handicapped children will be discussed first. Mr. Diller is professional, all business. His face shows no emotion, not even a hint of a smile or frown. Perhaps the clients he defends in court every day have made him callous. I hope he'll at least listen to our plea. To support our cause and explain the benefits of NSD, Jill Ramsey from NSD has come to the meeting.

Mr. Diller recaps the law, stressing that the Grand Island School System is obligated to educate handicapped students living in the school district in the least restrictive manner. "Are there any questions or comments?"

I raise my hand, feeling like a schoolgirl asking for permission to speak. "I'm Rebecca Willman." I stand; my palms are sweaty, the room stuffy. For a moment I feel lightheaded. "My daughter, Amy, attends the Nebraska School for the Deaf in Omaha, as do the children of several other people here tonight. Other parents here send their children to the State School for the Blind in Nebraska City. We've had our children in these schools from three to ten years. We're pleased with the specialized education they are receiving at their schools. How do you plan to educate our children locally?"

Mr. Diller scans the board members, waiting for one to respond; they avert his eyes. "I thought Mr. Carstens would be here tonight. He's more familiar with the special education programs than I am, but I understand there's a special education class in every school now. Your kids would be put in that class, and would participate with kids in regular classes when possible."

"So all handicapped children, regardless of their age or disability, would be put in the same room?" I meant this to be a statement, but my voice conveys an astonished question. "How can one teacher educate a room with deaf, blind, retarded, emotionally, and physically disabled children? Each of these children needs to be taught in a specific manner. Will the teacher know Braille as well as sign language?"

Mr. Diller stares at me. I feel as if I'm being visually cross-examined. "I'm not a teacher; I can't say how it will be done, but the law requires these children be educated in the least restrictive manner, which in most cases means in their home community. What the Grand Island Schools will provide may not be perfect, but it will comply with the law."

Jill Ramsey asks if she may speak. I sit and she explains the educational, athletic, and social programs provided at NSD. She stresses the need for the deaf children to receive the specialized education that NSD offers.

After she sits, I stand. "I don't think our children's education should suffer because of this law. Our kids are receiving quality education at their residential schools. At NSD, as Jill explained, all the teachers know sign language, the rooms are equipped with flashing lights to warn of fire or other emergencies, the PE teachers and coaches know sign, the children can participate in sports. Can the Grand Island schools offer this?"

"Obviously the answer is no." Mr. Diller responds. Several board members fidget in their chairs.

"No parent should be expected to remove their child from a quality program and enroll them in one that can offer little in the way of education. We want our children to continue their education at the schools they currently attend." I sit down, not knowing what else to say.

"Thank you for your comments, Mrs. Willman. You too, Mrs. Ramsey." Mr. Diller scans the parents. "Does anyone else want to speak?"

"May I address the Board?" Mr. Allen asks. Mr. Diller nods his approval. Mr. Allen sums up our pleas, reinforced by letters from additional staff from the residential schools, statements from the parents, and from the older children at NSD.

"Give me a copy of your report. The Board will take it under advisement and give you our decision next month." Mr. Diller consults his agenda. "The next item is equip . . ."

After the meeting, I confront Mr. Diller in the hall. "Why are you being so hard on us? Your granddaughter is autistic. You know how difficult it is to obtain decent education for special kids. Why can't we leave our children where they are? They're happy, and we're happy."

"I understand your concerns, but when I'm presiding at the school board, the fact that I have an autistic granddaughter is not relevant," he replies. "I must be impartial."

"Yes, but you're trying so hard to be impartial that you're not being fair."

Several board members approach with questions for Mr. Diller, rescuing him from further conversation with me. Outside, Mr. Allen says, "I'd tell you all not to worry, but I know you will. I think we made some good points tonight. All we can do now is wait and see."

Wait and see. That's easy for you to say.

By conversing with other parents at NSD, I discover that students from small school districts, like Kelli Thomas, Tricia Tighe, Teena, Jeannie, Linsay, and Daniel are not facing a struggle with their school board, like we are. The smaller school districts cannot afford to implement education for their special needs children as required by law, so allowing them to attend the residential schools is the best option for these school districts.

If I lived in a smaller town, I wouldn't be faced with another hurdle to jump so Amy can receive a good education. Whoever said "life is not fair" was right.

Two weeks before Amy finishes the fourth grade, Mr. Allen and the parents are once again at the school board meeting. Seated against the wall, we look like a group of children waiting to be lectured by the school principal for misconduct.

After calling the meeting to order, and dispensing with the minutes, Mr. Diller says, "First on the agenda is Public Law 94-142. After an extended review of the information provided to us by Mr. Allen, the Board has decided it is in the best interest of the children currently attending schools outside of the Grand Island school district to continue their education there." My shoulders relax. "But, from this point forward, no more children from this school district will be allowed to attend those residential schools."

Hurrah! A victory for Amy, but I ponder the long-term effect of the Board's decision. Amy can finish her education at NSD, but I wonder what quality of education young deaf and blind children will receive in the future, when all school districts mainstream their special needs children into classrooms designed for "normal" children. How can any teacher provide extensive individual attention to a special needs child, when teachers are already challenged to spend individual time with twenty "normal" students? I think we have won the battle but lost the war.

Amy receives the news with her usual positive attitude, "I knew I would win."

I envy her confidence.

By August, Amy is anxious to return to school and her friends. This year she'll live in the girls' dorm, which is similar to a college dorm, except there is a small room downstairs with a teletypewriter, which allows after-hours contact between the girls' and boys' dorms. Deaf teenagers are not unlike hearing kids; nothing is more important than gossip, sports, and young love.

John helps Amy tote her blue trunk upstairs, while I follow behind carrying a box of pillows, stuffed toys, and miscellaneous items. I open the trunk to unpack her clothes. Amy nudges me toward the door, saying, "I can do it myself."

Forcing Amy to become independent has drawbacks. My sigh is filled with joy and sorrow. Happy, because I won my battle with the school board and that Amy is becoming independent, but sad because she's growing up so fast. After a long hug, from which she struggles to free herself, Amy walks us outside.

Several high school students are seated on the steps. Their fingers fly, talking so fast I only catch a few words, not enough to know what they are saying. Kelli and Tricia, two of Amy's classmates, rush up the sidewalk to greet her. Amy signs something, and points to a window on the second floor. Kelli and Tricia ask in sign, "Where my room?"

"Show you," Amy signs. Before she escapes, I give her a final hug. Amy signs, "I love you." Without looking back, she hurries into the dorm with her friends.

"Well John, looks like we're not needed here anymore." I slip behind the steering wheel.

"Yeah. All I'm good for is lugging her two-ton suitcase upstairs."

As I drive out the NSD gate, knowing I'm facing nine months of weekly trips to Omaha gives me a dull headache. I look forward to the day John can drive, so we can share this chore. "Just think, John, in four years you'll be old enough to drive."

"I don't want to learn to drive." He slumps against the car door.

I think he suspects my plan.

33

Deaf Child in a
Hearing World

Amy

Since I was athletic as a child and liked to do stunts and dance, Mother enrolled me in a dance class on Friday evening. After she picked me up from school or the airport, I hurried to change my clothes and put on my purple dance leotard. I was the only deaf child in the class.

Mother told me at first the teacher was not sure about letting me be in the class, because she had a bad experience a few years ago with a hard of hearing child named Melissa. Melissa's parents expected the teacher to give Melissa special attention, and she caused problems in class. Mother told my teacher, "I don't think Amy will be a problem. All I ask is that you let Amy be in the first row so she can see what you are doing. She will learn by watching, not by what you say." The teacher agreed to let me try the class.

At first I did not care that I was the only deaf person in the class, since I wanted to learn how to dance. The class was a mix of dance and gymnastics. At the beginning of dancing class, the instructor lined us up and talked to all girls, telling them what to do. I basically followed the movements of the girls in front of me. When I saw the girls hop and skip, I did the same. Then, the next move, a cartwheel. I learned to stand on my head and make a tripod. Once I took my purple leotard to Grandma and Grandpa's house to show them what I learned in class. Grandpa took my picture doing a tripod.

The instructor never really talked to me. I think the other girls attended additional classes during the week, because when I came on Fridays, I noticed they did new movements or were placed into a different group with more experience.

After a year or two, I felt like I was falling behind and could not catch up. I did not understand the instructor, and she never put in any effort to teach me compared to the other girls. That was when I decided it was not worth attending if the other girls practiced more than I did. Since I could not communicate with the other girls or the instructor, I was often uncomfortable. Sometime the instructor had me sit out and do nothing. I quit the class because of this and time conflicts.

I always looked forward to June when the school year ended. Off I went to home for three whole months with my family and cat. That was the best. I had many fun moments, since I could spend time playing with my brother or cat.

During several summers, I went to the week-long YMCA day camp. I was the only Deaf girl and not able to communicate. John went with me. Sue did one summer also. At camp, Sue and I hung around a lot together. If she was not there, I focused on doing my own things, making crafts, or doing other activities.

One summer, when my brother and I were at the YMCA camp, we had a sleepover for one night at the camp. Everyone slept in tents. John was in the boys' tent while I was in the girls' tent. In the middle of the night a thunderstorm started. There were so much lightning. A camp counselor woke me and my brother and said, "You two will have to move into the cabin to sleep." I do not know why we had to leave our tent; none of the hearing children had to move, except John. Maybe they thought I would be scared of the storm, but how could thunder scare me? I can't hear it.

I liked the YMCA camp. There were many things to do. I made a sand candle. We went swimming, and I shot a bow and arrow and a BB gun. The first time I shot the BB gun, I fell backward after I shot it. I did not know what to expect, because I could not hear the explanation about holding the butt close to my shoulder to lessen the recoil of the gun. I am sure someone laughed at me, but I don't remember.

~

In fourth grade and higher, I was in a Girl Scout troop at NSD. One summer I attended Girl Scout camp in Grand Island. It was not too bad, but a little boring since I could not talk to any of the girls, but I enjoyed making many crafts. My goal was to get more Girl Scout patches on my vest, since at NSD I could not earn many patches compared to what the hearing scouts did.

Mother arranged for me to attend the local Girl Scout camp, because NSD did not have activities in the summer. She told me at first the leader of the Girl Scout camp was hesitant to let me attend, but once gain Mother explained to the camp leader, "If no one is using sign, Amy learns primarily by watching others, so let her be near the leader or the front of the group. Amy's attended school since she was thirteen months old. She's accustomed to watching others for cues. I don't think she will cause any problems."

"All right, but the camp is by the river," the Girl Scout leader said to Mother.

"Amy knows how to swim. She loves the water," Mother said.

"But the children can't go in the river! How can I tell her that?"

The leader was very worried I would drown, I guess.

"Don't worry," my mother told the leader. "I'll tell Amy to stay away from the river before she goes to camp."

"Okay, but what if . . ." The leader had many other questions and Mother soon realized the leader did not know how to communicate with a Deaf person. Mother said, "Amy may be able to lipread what you say, but if you really want to be sure she understands, write it on a piece of paper. Amy just finished the fifth grade. She can read."

"Oooh. I never thought of that," the leader told my mother.

Mother shook her head when she told me this and said, "I can't believe the leader did not realize you could read and write."

Sometimes hearing people have a mental block on what to do with a person who has a disability. Deaf people don't call themselves disabled, but in the eyes of political groups and the ADA, Deaf are considered disabled. There is a funny joke about a Deaf and hearing person. They were sitting at separate tables in a restaurant. The hearing person asked the other person for the ketchup. When the hearing person realized the other person was Deaf, he wrote on a paper, "Can you read?" The Deaf person read it and wrote back, "Can you write?"

Duh! It's a folklore joke that has been passed along in the Deaf community for many years. Hearing people often don't realize that Deaf people are intelligent humans, just like most other people, except we don't hear.

In the summer John and I, and sometimes Mother too, would go to a movie. If there was a book about the movie, Mother would read it to me before we went so I could understand the movie.

When I was a little girl, I loved to watch *Snow White and the Seven Dwarfs*. Many little girls would pick Snow White as their favorite character, but not me. I chose Dopey. Remember, thirty years ago no movies had closed captions. Therefore I relied on visual actions to entertain me. Dopey gave me plenty of funny things to watch, so I could laugh while watching the movie.

It's ironic that Dopey doesn't talk, but he can hear. Some people thought I chose Dopey because he can't talk, just like me, but I said, "Dopey can hear, but he chooses not to talk."

In general, many Deaf people like a character that is funny based on their visual actions. One good example is Charlie Chaplin. In the 1920s, many Deaf people enjoyed his movies. He was a hearing person who did not talk in the movies, but did funny acting.

I liked cartoons for that reason also. When I was growing up, I usually watched Tom and Jerry cartoons. Without captions, I still could understand and laugh at the TV show.

I remember several times when I was older and went to the movie theater with Deaf friends. I do not remember the title of the movies, but in one, an actor made a funny facial expression, and my Deaf friends and I all laughed. All of sudden, hearing people stared at us. They were not laughing. Some gave us dirty looks. I thought to myself, maybe the actor said something sad, but his facial expression was so funny to Deaf. Again, I could not understand what the actors were saying, so I relied on visual expression, and when I saw something funny I would laugh.

Now that I can rent captioned movies and the TV is captioned, I can fully understand what is happening, but that was not always possible for Deaf people.

34

Tossed and Blown by Life

Rebecca

June 3, 1980. The day is hot and sultry. In three days Amy will be home for the summer. After supper, John and I grab tennis racquets and I drive to a nearby park. After three games, we are tired and sweaty. It's only 8:30 p.m., but dark clouds swirl above warning of an impending storm. We toss the tennis equipment in the car and sit on the bumper, scanning the skies. The air is stagnant, heavy with humidity and oppressive heat, making breathing difficult. A flash of lightning urges us into the car. As I drive home, I tune to KRGI-AM for a weather report. Static punctuates the broadcast as the National Weather Service reporter says, "Severe thunderstorms with possible tornadoes are expected from 9 p.m. until midnight in Central Nebraska."

Such reports are a weekly occurrence in the Great Plains states during the summer. John and I hurry home to our basement. Within minutes the lights flicker out and the tornado siren for our area blares. Jupiter, our latest cat, scurries over my feet in the darkness, howling to escape. The wailing siren is now muffled by the sound of a hundred lawnmowers. We huddle under a table as our home is assaulted by a tornado. Minutes later we crawl out and thank God we're alive, and that Amy's safe in Omaha. We look up the basement stairwell; where there was a light fixture, we see lighting flashing. Rain trickles into the basement, not a good sign.

John, Rebecca, and Jupiter the morning after the June 3, 1980, tornado destroyed their home. The remains of John and Amy's bedroom are in the background.

At first light, John and I see the extent of the damage to our home. The roof is entirely gone. So is the screened in porch, including part of the cement block foundation that had been under the ground. The only walls left standing are our interior hall walls. All the exterior walls have fallen into or away from the house. Without walls for support, the garage door has collapsed onto the car, but I think the car will be drivable if the door can be moved. The huge cottonwood trees in our yard are uprooted. Debris, from the size of nickels to chunks as big as logs are strewn in every direction. I see the remains of the Holiday Inn sign four blocks away. Homes once filled those four blocks, now there is nothing but rubble in every direction.

Since Jupiter, our cat, howled to be let out shortly before the storm hit, the first order of the day is to locate him. We find him scared but unharmed in the remains of Amy's closet. Hanging on the interior wall of our kitchen is my harvest gold telephone. I lift the receiver; there is a dial tone. I can't believe it. After my parents recover from the shock of our destruction, they agree to pick up Amy from school on Friday and keep her until I can find a place to live. Like the oo-bleck spread by the Cat in the Hat, our mess is so big and so tall and so deep and so wide, I don't know where to start. I focus on short-term goals: food, clothing, and water.

None of my family lives near me. My mother-in-law would have offered to let us stay with her, but she died last year from heart failure. Jack's house has minor damage, but he has a girlfriend who might not like his ex-wife and son moving in with him. In addition Jack's grocery store was destroyed, so he's busy dealing with insurance adjustors like I am. For the next month, Amy stays with my parents in Beatrice while John and I bunk with friends until we can move into a lovely FEMA trailer.

As a result of the tornado, we need a new house, and a houseful of furniture. Several months ago our parents' organization received information that the National Captioning Institute is now marketing a device through Sears that will display captions on TV sets. A new TV and that device are my first purchases. Few programs are captioned, but I'm sure more will be in the future. I discover that *The French Chef*, Julia Child, on PBS is captioned. What a relief! I can now watch the show without hearing Julia's irritating voice.

John and I have bedrooms at opposite ends of the trailer, and Amy's room is in the middle next to John's. In August, when a severe thunderstorm occurs in the middle of the night, I rise to check on John and Amy. I discover Amy in the living room.

"Why aren't you in bed, Amy?"

"Too noisy?" Amy says, backing up her words with energetic signs.

I'm puzzled, knowing she can't hear the thunder or driving rain, and then I realize she associates vibrations with noise. The trailer quivers in the strong winds. The tie-down straps hold the center portion of the trailer more stable than her bedroom; that's why she moved to the sofa.

The night-light in the hall makes the vinyl floor sparkle, as if moonlight were reflecting upon a river. Upon closer examination, I discover a small stream flowing down the hall. The wind has driven the rain through the shoddy window frames. The water runs into Amy's closet, soaking the only items I was able to save for her from our destroyed home.

I snap on the light in her room to access the damage. Awake, Amy charges after me. "Why you in my room?"

I pull a soggy box from her closet to see if anything is worth saving. Items I dried and cleaned two months ago are again in ruins.

"Why my things? Why not John's?" Amy pulls her pink cat pillow from the water-laden cardboard box. Tears of anger and frustration fall on her stuffed cats, puzzles, and books.

"I'm sorry, Amy." My words are not comforting.

"No good. No good." She tosses items from the box across the room and kicks the closet door, which bounces away from the door stop. She kicks it back into the wall several times.

I feel her pain, anger, and disappointment. Exhausted, she collapses on her bed. I pat her back. Soon she is asleep. I spend the rest of the night washing and drying stuffed animals and ironing pages in books.

The Morton Salt slogan is right on target, "When it rains, it pours." Life after the tornado brings a torrent of new challenges; I have endless decisions to make about rebuilding our home and settling the insurance claim. Any time there's wind or a sudden loud noise, John and I are edgy, fearing we'll be victims of another tornado.

Throughout the remainder of the summer, our FEMA trailer had one temperature: uncomfortable. The window air conditioner I bought keeps the living room tolerable, but the bedrooms were hot and stuffy. To escape the brutal heat we attended movies at the nearby mall often. I saw *Batman* four times. Now that winter is here, our trailer still has one temperature: uncomfortable. My bedroom, near the furnace, is like the Sahara, hot and dry; John's is Siberia, complete with wisps of snow sifting through gaps in the window frames.

When Amy comes home for Christmas, we cut red and green construction paper in strips and assemble a paper chain that stretches from one end of the trailer to the other. We loop the seventy-foot chain, ornaments fashioned out of colorful pipe cleaners, and a string of lights on a small tree. Our surroundings are sparse, but the joy of Christmas fills our hearts and home.

Christmas morning I awaken to the sound of vomiting. I rush to the bathroom and discover Amy clutching her stomach. Santa has brought her the flu bug.

"I'll get you salt water to rinse out your mouth." In the kitchen I grab a glass and turn on the faucet. Nothing. I rush to the bathroom; a lone drop falls from the faucet.

"The pipes must have frozen. I'll go to the Pump and Pantry to buy 7-Up." I help Amy to bed, tucking the blankets under her chin, and yell, "John, I'm leaving to buy Amy 7-Up. I'll be right back." As I hack the ice off the windshield, I pray Pump and Pantry will be open on Christmas morning. My prayer is answered; I return with 7-Up and call FEMA to thaw the pipes.

Three weeks later, when Amy is home, we celebrate her twelfth birthday with her favorite foods: macaroni and cheese, lobster, rainbow sherbet, and angel food cake. I bought several outfits for Amy. She is delighted with my choices, but I know my days of selecting clothes for a preteen girl are numbered. John's gift, however, surpasses mine.

After the first Kitty died several years ago, we adopted two kittens. A female cat Amy named Kitty and a male that John named Jupiter. A year later Kitty was killed by a speeding car; Amy was heartbroken. Jupiter became the family pet, even though he was John's cat. Jupiter was not partial to John, giving Amy as much petting time, and yet Amy wanted more. She wanted her own cat.

"Where's my present, John?" Amy asks. He hands her an envelope. "What's this?" She opens the envelope and reads a hand-printed cat ownership certificate. Amy makes no effort to hide her tears. "Jupiter is mine. John gave me Jupiter. I love you, John."

Jupiter, who was sleeping on a nearby chair, is unprepared for her assault. She clutches him to her chest, repeating, "Jupie, Jupie, Jupie. My kitty."

Sunday afternoon, I pack cupcakes for Amy to share with the girls in her dorm. "Are you ready?" I ask Amy. She signs, "yes." "Come on John, let's go."

"I think I have the chicken pox." John pulls up his sweatshirt, exposing his chest.

"Let me see." He points to three red bumps. He has no temperature and the welts don't itch. "I don't know what it is, but I don't think its chicken pox. Get your coat and get in the car."

"All right, but it might be chicken pox. Several kids in my room had them last week."

As I drive home from Omaha, John falls asleep. Perhaps he does have the chicken pox. His behavior isn't normal. Usually we play twenty questions or other mental games on the ride home. If he has chicken pox, Amy had plenty of exposure to them.

The next morning John still has his mysterious bumps. He says he feels fine, so he goes to school. Two weeks later, Amy flies home on Friday. On Saturday morning I have no doubt that Amy has the chicken pox. Her body is a mass of fluid-filled blisters that merge to form palm-sized welts. Her scalp has not escaped the virus.

"My knees hurt," Amy complains.

After a quick call to the doctor, I learn Amy's chicken pox are both external and internal. The internal ones are swelling her joints. "Give her Benadryl and watch her breathing. Her throat could swell shut." Soda baths give Amy little relief from the itching. Her skin is so tender I have to use a spray bottle to apply calamine lotion. For the next week she is the color of cotton candy.

35

Middle School
Amy

By the time I reached middle school, I started to enjoy my time at the dorm and my involvement in sports. I was less and less homesick. At home were all my possessions and I missed some of them, but I felt they were safer at home. I never gave much thought to the fact that John stayed home and I went away to school. I just thought hearing kids go to one school and Deaf kids go to a different one. That was just how my life was.

In middle school, I didn't have a deaf house parent, but a hearing one with a strange name: Verda. She was an old lady with reddish-white hair, and her clothes seem to have been frozen from the 1950s. She was not an excellent signer like my previous Deaf house parent, Kathy, but Verda would be my house parent for the next two years.

Naturally, I got into more mischief, because Verda could not understand what I was signing. I signed dirty words or insulted her. I laughed, and so did the other girls.

One winter, Verda had a cast on her leg, as she fell on the ice and broke it. I asked her, "May I draw a picture or sign something on your cast?" At first, she resisted, but later agreed. I took a brown marker and wrote "Lewob." She asked me what the word was.

I said, "It's my friend's pet's name." Actually, it was a word I had learned in science class several days ago, but I spelled it backward: Lewob meant bowel. I find that odd as Verda did not even bother to ask why I wrote friend's pet's name instead of my name or pet. After several days, the other house parents figured out what it meant and scolded me, but Verda still had no clue.

The girls on my wing decided to create a song called, "My Pet's Name Is Lewob." Tricia, one of my classmates, brought a recorder with a microphone from home. Tricia and I sang so loud we drove Verda nuts! It was so funny. Finally I was caught when Verda figured it out. I no longer could sing the song called, "My Pet's Name Is Lewob.

At school, I usually was on my best behavior, not acting like I did in the dormitory. During the fifth and sixth grades, my classes rotated among three different teachers. It was much different from my primary years when I only had one teacher. Having three teachers and getting a chance to walk to the next classroom was fun. All of my teachers were not excellent in sign language, but I understood them anyway.

I'll never forget Mrs. Flowers, who loved to assign an overload of homework each day. I am pretty sure she set the Guinness World Record for giving the most homework. My hand would cramp trying to finish all the homework she assigned that was due the next day. NSD usually finished the school year on the first Friday of June. Mrs. Flowers gave me and my classmates piles of homework the last week of school. It looked like a whole year of homework. I thought, there is no way I can finish this by tomorrow. The school year is almost over. Give me a break.

My classmates and I all complained. "We can't do it. It's way too much." We were so harsh with her, she ended in tears, and told us not to do the homework. Of course, I was jumping with joy, and so were my classmates.

In the seventh and eighth grades I moved to the opposite side of the hallway in the dormitory and had a different hearing house parent. Another old lady, this time one with dyed brown hair. Her name was Mrs. Jolly. She was funnier and less strict than Verda, but I still had mischief with her anyway.

One night I really shook her brain, making her very confused. I turned the light switch upside down in my room and changed the white light to a blue light bulb. Then I screamed on purpose, so

Mrs. Jolly would come to my room and ask what was wrong. Sure enough, she came and tried to figure out the light switch. When she finally did, her mouth hung open wide when she saw the blue light. I laughed so hard. She said I was crazy!

Another time, I wanted to move into a room further down the hall, so I unhooked the air conditioner in my room. It was spring time and the room was muggy and hot, so she allowed me to move. Later, a mechanic told Mrs. Jolly that somebody had unhooked the air conditioner on purpose. I was sure Mrs. Jolly knew I did it. Ha ha!

There were plenty of pranks I did, but I can't tell them all as there were too many. I would not do them at home, only in the dorm. I thought it was so funny to do pranks on the houseparent. I did not really think or intend to be a mean to them. Well, maybe the "lewob." Most of my pranks were when I was in middle school. What do you expected from a teenager! I just wanted to make dorm life filled with many fun memories.

I came to expect that I'd live at a residential school for the rest of my school years. Once in a while, I stayed at NSD for the weekend, but not too often, usually just one weekend a month. Was it different from staying in the dormitory during the week? Yes, because not many of the girls stayed there over the weekend. On the second floor, there might be eight girls on a weekend compared to thirty during the week. On the first floor, where the high school girls lived, more of the girls stayed over the weekend due to sports activities.

Since I was only in junior high, I did not have weekend athletic games. We played our sports on Tuesdays and Thursdays. Our weekends were boring, but once in a while the house parent would take me and the other girls who were staying in the dorm to a park or zoo if weather permitted. We went to the mall, watched our high school sports, and spent Saturday night watching open-captioned films. Some weekends the dormitory was filled with boredom.

Why did I stay in the dorm on weekends when I knew it would be so boring? I am not so sure, but my mother told me to stay there. Maybe it was a way to prepare me since in few years, I will be in high school. The high school sports were usually played on Fridays and Saturdays. Meaning, I would have to stay there over the weekends. In my whole primary years, I think I stayed once or twice on weekends.

During middle schools, I stayed at the dorm on weekends once a month, but in high school, I usually went home only once a month during sports season.

In seventh grade, my classes were held in a different building. This time, I rotated among eight different teachers. I had classes in the high school, vocational building, and gym. My schedule was much different from my previous years when I spent all my time in one building. I always enjoyed going to school more than staying in the dormitory.

In middle school I played many sports. Sports allowed me to get away from the dormitory, which was filled with many unnecessary rules, such as no food or drink in the living room. No playing outside without adult supervision, even though it was safe outside. Also, we had study hour at specific time, and even if I didn't have any homework, I had to go. These rules were broken many times. Sometimes we might be grounded and had to stay in our room for the evening. Usually, if one of us did something wrong, all of us would be punished. There was not usually punishment for just one person, unless it was serious misconduct.

From primary through middle school, we always had school plays two or three times per year where all students acted in front of the audiences. The audiences were usually NSD high school students, staff, teachers, and students' parents. The primary and middle school plays were performances by holidays. For example, at either Thanksgiving or Christmas, the primary students gave the performance, while in spring, for Easter, middle school students did theirs. Then next year, primary students did the spring play and middle school did the fall or winter plays. Being involved in the school plays was fun things to do. I enjoyed acting and learned to memorize the lines or new songs.

When I was in seventh grade, each class level had a performance about an international culture. As for my classmates, we did the Japanese culture. The boys in my class did judo for the play and the girls wore kimonos. I was thrilled wearing one and also shoes that had two pieces of wood on the bottom. It was difficult to walk with that kind of shoes. We sat on the floor on huge pillows drinking tea. When we practiced and practiced for the play, the tea pot was empty. But, the director told us just act like you were pouring. I gave an idea to the director. "Why not add a soda pop to pretend it was tea." We drank and drank a lot of soda pop during the play.

Each year, before the school year was finished, awards were given to outstanding students, sports awards and others. In junior high, I was honored by the Women's Chamber of Commerce in Omaha as an Outstanding Eighth Grade Girl. I also had many honor roll awards. Twice I earned awards as the Most Valuable Player—once for volleyball and once for track.

I was so excited when school ended knowing I will be home all summer long, but summer always seemed too short. I would feel like I just got home, and here would come August and my big blue suitcase would be brought out.

36

Gaining Independence

Rebecca

I want a close relationship with Amy, but our inability to communicate on an equal basis makes this difficult. One way we can share time together without communication being an issue is playing games. Amy enjoys both indoor and outdoor sports. In the summer, while I'm at work, John and Amy swim at a nearby pool, play croquet, badminton, or shoot baskets. In the evening, we play board games and card games. Amy's current game of choice is *Sorry*. Having had my fill of losing the past week, and hearing Amy say, "I win. Too bad for you," I suggest we walk to the Dairy Queen (DQ) since the summer evening is pleasant, less than ninety degrees. As we near the DQ, I ask Amy, "What are you going to buy?"

"Chocolate cone," she signs.

"What about you, John?" I ask.

"A Peanut Buster Bar." He kicks a stone off the sidewalk into the street.

"Here. This is for you to buy your treat." I hand them each two dollars.

Amy stuffs her money in the pocket of her shorts. "Mine. I have much money at home."

"That's because you never spend any," John grumbles. "She must have thirty dollars in her bank."

Amy's personality is competitive by nature. She wants to excel at everything; this applies to saving money too. She hoards her money, counting it each week to make certain neither John nor I have taken any, something we have assured her we would never do, but counting her money, locking her bank, and hiding the key are a ritual for her.

"The money I gave you is not for your bank. It's for your treat," I say. "Tonight you will buy your own treat."

"Oh." Amy pulls the money from her pocket and thrusts it toward me. "You do it."

"No, you keep it. You have to buy your own treat."

"Why me?" Amy replies.

"Because you need to do things by yourself."

Amy stares at me; her forehead wrinkles with confusion. Her eyes narrow as she processes what I have said. "I not buy it. I cannot talk."

"Then you'll have to figure out another way to tell them what you want. You have to buy your own treat tonight. I am not buying it for you." We are now less than a block from the DQ.

"Here, John." She extends her money toward John. "You buy it."

"No." I push Amy's hand away from John.

"Why not John?" Amy asks.

"Because John will not always be with you. You must learn to do things on your own." As we walk across the Dairy Queen parking lot, Amy shuffles her feet, lagging behind. She knows I am as obstinate as she is; whining will not change my mind. This lesson on independence is taking place in public. I pray I do not have to give in to avoid a scene.

John opens the Dairy Queen door and a rush of cool air greets us as we enter. Amy remains outside. I motion for her to come in. She shakes her head. Her blond curls swing across her face but do not dislodge her scowl. "No." She snaps her index and middle finger to her thumb several times.

While John and I stand in line, I keep a watchful eye on Amy. Darkness is approaching. She's upset and I do not want her to run home along poorly lit streets without us.

"John, after you buy your ice cream sit at a table outside." I let him order before me.

"Sure. I want a Buster Bar," he tells the clerk.

"Next!" The high school girl behind the counter wears a soiled uniform. Streaks on the front indicate it's been used for hand wiping.

"I'll have a Buster Bar, too." I wanted a parfait, but if I have to chase Amy, it will be easier to run with ice cream on a stick than in a plastic glass. John receives his ice cream and goes outside. I pay for my ice cream and join him. Amy shuffles toward us, kicking loose gravel that stings my legs. "Are you going to buy something?"

"I cannot do it." Amy's eyes beg for help.

"You have to try." I bite into the fudge and nut filling of my Buster Bar. The sweet concoction melts in my mouth, giving me no pleasure. Acid creeps into my throat, threatening to choke me. I watch a drop of melted ice cream drip onto the table. I place a napkin over the mess and rest my elbow on it to keep the napkin from blowing away. When I look up, Amy is gone.

"Where's Amy?" How did she get out my sight in less than ten seconds?

"She's inside." John uses his ice cream bar as a pointer.

I turn my chair so my back is to the window. I do not want to see what happens. The need to be a mother hen and protect my chick is strong, but I control myself. If I rescue her, she may be dependent on me, her brother, or another speaking person for the rest of her life.

"I did it!"

I'd recognize that unique voice anywhere. Amy sits beside me. Her smile is broad, filled with happiness, pride, and chocolate ice cream.

Tonight, before I drift to sleep, I feel time racing. I've been divorced more than six years. Two years have elapsed since our home was destroyed by the tornado. Last year we moved into our rebuilt home.

Shortly after we moved into our new home, Jack married Linda, who has two young children. John and Amy were part of the bridal party. The night of the wedding my best friend Pat and I spent the evening playing cribbage and drinking wine coolers. I did not care that Jack remarried; I wished him happiness, but I am often lonely. I would like a special someone, but I decided shortly after my divorce that if I had not remarried before my children were teenagers, I would wait until they finished high school. Biological parents find raising a teenager difficult, and I knew adding a step-parent to the family could make it worse. All the same, part of me was jealous that Jack had found happiness.

Change has been a constant in my life since the divorce. I became a working mother, first at the answering service, later at KGIN-TV, and for the past two years at the Nebraska Department of Labor. During a period of unemployment between the last two jobs, I decided to obtain my master of social work (MSW), which I had planned to do years ago, but having babies changed my plans. No colleges in the area offer an MSW, but the University of Nebraska campus in Kearney, fifty miles from Grand Island, offers a Master's degree in counseling and psychology. I began night classes; some in Kearney, others in Grand Island.

This December, after eighteen months of night classes while working full-time, I'll have my master's degree. Hopefully this will open the door to a better paying job or one that is more rewarding. This fall Amy will be in eighth grade and John will be a high-school sophomore. Three years from this summer, we plan to take a trip to Europe. Jack and I had talked about doing this for John and Amy, but now I'll be taking them alone. Ye gods, I better apply for passports. June 1984 will be here before I know it.

At age fourteen, Amy is eligible to detassel corn, hot sweaty work, but the only job available to kids under sixteen except for babysitting. Amy wants spending money, and I want her to have the experience of a summer job, so I speak to a field supervisor and she is hired. On Amy's first day of work, I wake her at 5:00 a.m. "Do you have your lunch?"

"Don't bother me." Amy is surly, disliking to rise early as much as I do.

"Is that all you are taking to eat?" She grabs a small paper bag and a can of soda from the refrigerator.

"I never eat much for lunch. I will be fat."

"This is hard work. You'll be hungry by noon." I back out of the garage.

Amy glares at me. "Leave me alone. I know what I am doing."

I shrug. Amy's independence often verges on pigheadedness. This is one battle not worth the fight. Amy will discover soon enough that walking through muddy corn fields, being slapped by corn leaves, and fighting all manner of vermin that fly and crawl will work up an appetite by noon.

By three in the afternoon Amy is home. I am not there when she arrives, but John tells me she looked like a swamp monster.

"She had mud splattered all over her." John points to Amy's tennis shoes, drying on the back steps. "Mud completely covered her shoes and socks. She hosed everything off, took a shower, and threw her clothes in the wash."

"Where is she now?" I ask.

"Stuffing her face with food in front of the TV."

Downstairs, Amy is watching a prerecorded *Wheel of Fortune* show, one of her favorites. Her fair skin is flushed, but unlike her brother who only sunburns, she will soon be a golden brown. Her blonde curly hair is still damp from her shower. A bag of chips and Fig Newtons are by her side.

"How was your first day?" I ask.

She grunts a noncommittal response. "Wearing the same clothes tomorrow. Not going to ruin everything I have."

I reach for reach for the chips and cookies. "Don't spoil your supper. We'll be eating in an hour."

After supper, Amy packs a larger sack lunch and announces, "I'm tired. I'm going to bed."

By the end of the week, she is packing a small Igloo cooler with drinks, sandwiches, and fruit for her lunch. Her surly, teenage-girl attitude has succumbed to eight hours of strenuous physical labor. By 8:00 p.m., she collapses into bed exhausted from hours of working outside in the sweltering heat or pouring rain. *Hmm*, I think, *work camps might be the solution to keep teenagers out of trouble.* Amy has neither the strength nor the inclination to challenge me.

Amy and I now have inverse language skills. I have a vast spoken vocabulary and a shrinking sign vocabulary; Amy has a huge sign vocabulary, but her speech is often difficult to understand except by John or me. When she comes home each summer, I see our communication gap widening. Our conversations are reduced to short spoken sentences, signs, and if all else fails, paper and pencil. Lipreading is not a solution for her or most deaf people. I'm frustrated. There are no sign language classes offered in our area. Since John spends more time with Amy than I do, their ability to communicate with each other is good, which strengthens their bond. I've bought several sign language books, but teaching myself is not easy.

People often ask me if Amy lipreads. If I say "yes," the person thinks Amy can converse like a hearing person, which she can't. If I say "No," they ignore her. I'm at a loss how to answer this question.

37

Do You Sign?

Amy

Mother told me that many people who discover she has a deaf daughter ask, "Does Amy read lips?" Mother asked me what she should tell these people, since I can read some lips.

I said, "You should reply, 'Do you know sign?' Duh!"

Do I use lipreading? Sometimes, but I try not to because I may misunderstand the communication. I only use lipreading during a conversation that does not require much communication or does not affect my life. When ordering food, I may use lipreading. If a server asks me, "Do you want cheese?" I can read their lips and reply back, "No." If the food I order is not accurate, I can remove the item I don't want from my plate. I can live with wrong lipreading on my food order.

However, if the conversation is about something that will affect my personal life, such as a discussion at the bank for a loan or a visit to a doctor, I do not use lipreading. These conversations are complicated and I don't want any confusion. I'd rather receive all the information accurately. In these situations, I use an interpreter or paper and pen. An interpreter is better when having a serious conversation. The business or medical office provides an interpreter if I request one. This is not my expense.

There is a law requiring interpreters to be provided the Deaf, but it does not have a very strong emphasis on some small businesses and companies. Businesses are supposed to provide an interpreter if a Deaf person attends or works at their place. The employer is to pay for it because it is their employee or client. Sometimes a Deaf person wanting an interpreter can stir up problems and the matter ends up in court. Or worse, a deaf person might have to quit their job or find a new doctor if they don't provided any interpreters.

Sometimes I lipread my relatives, but not all the time, as I cannot always understand them. For them I use pen and paper. On special occasions, if Mother is with me, she will hire an interpreter for me. This allows me to talk easily with my family since my relatives do not know sign.

When I meet hearing people for the first time, they often ask me, "Do you lipread?" I usually say, "No." I ask them to write, as it is easier and less confusing.

Is lipreading hard to learn? Yes. My lipreading ability is based on my knowledge of speech. Since I was sixteen months old, I had speech training and memorized the mouth movements. I can recognize many mouth movements and identify some words, but I can only do this if the hearing person speaks clearly and at a normal pace. Even then, I only recognize some of the words, never the whole sentence. I catch the mouth movements I know, and then try to figure out the possible meaning of the whole sentence. Lipreading involves a lot of guesswork.

If the hearing person speaks too fast, does not move their mouth much, is in a shadow, the sun is in my eyes, or if their mouth is covered by their hand or a thick mustache, I will not be able to lipread their words. I can lipread hearing people that I see often better than I can a stranger. If I have just met someone, I may be able to lipread their mouth movements if they speak normally, but if several people are speaking at the same time, it is impossible for me to follow the conversation. Lipreading really only works on a limited one-to-one conversations.

I prefer not to use lipreading. I think hearing people need to learn how to deal with Deaf people in the community. Why do I have to do lipreading? Why don't hearing people sign?

I find it funny when a hearing person asks me, "Do you lipread?" When I answer, "No," they reply, "Okay." How ironic, I can understand what they just asked and answer properly. That must be confusing to them, so I always have paper and pen to use, which is the best solution.

When I was a child, sometimes Mother's family gathered for Thanksgiving. One year when I was about ten, my mother hosted and cooked the turkey feast. Mother told me and my brother, "Set the table. Put on the place mats, dishes, glasses and silverware."

Naturally, I could not hear any sounds I made with the dishes and silverware. While John and I were in the dining room setting the table, my Aunt Helen from Chicago came into the room and said something I did not understand. I frowned. She put her finger on her mouth and acted out, "Sshhhhh!"

I thought to myself, what? I did not yell or make any noise. I looked at John. He just shrugged. In a few minutes, Aunt Helen came back and told me the same thing. She even scolded my brother since he was doing the same thing I was. I did not know what was wrong. Then my Aunt Susan came into the room and told me, "You are making too much noise." I did not know what noises I made, because I cannot hear myself.

Mother heard the discussion and came into the dining room. Of course my aunts knew I am deaf, but sometimes hearing people do not fully understand what that really means. Mother said, "Amy can't hear the noise she makes like moving chairs, dropping silverware, or clinking glasses. She hears NOTHING!"

My aunts said something to Mother and I asked John what they were talking about. John interpreted the conversation for me. He said, "Aunt Helen and Aunt Susan said to Mother, 'How can you bear all the noise that Amy makes?'" My Mother replied, "When I hear those noises, I know John and Amy are okay and nearby." I bet all the noise I made would drive my aunts crazy! Mother never seemed to care.

Sometimes my aunts called me by name. Of course, I never replied. I remembered one time when my Aunt Margaret called to me several times and wondered why I did not answer. Within a few seconds, she realized that of course I couldn't hear her because I'm deaf. Duh!

I know some deaf people can hear due to different degree of hearing loss. Well, that does not apply to me. I am "stone" Deaf, like a
rock that can't hear.

My aunts, uncles, and cousins, they don't sign to me at all. Sometime, they will try to write something down on a paper or speak to
me and I have to lipread, but most of the time I don't understand
them. Basically, I am left to myself at family gatherings or I ask my
brother or mother what they are saying, but that does not tell me
the whole conversation.

At a young age, I usually watched TV or read something when I
was with them. Now that I am an adult, I either stay with them for
a short time or do not go to family gatherings at all since I know I
will be BORED when they are talking and talking.

Grandma Schmierer, my mother's mother, was the one who would
put in effort to learn signs, so she can communicate with me, her only
granddaughter. I was named for her.

Every summer, when I was young, I spent one week with Grandma
and Grandpa Schmierer without my brother. I asked Grandma why
my brother could not come with me and she said Grandpa did not
want too much noise in the house. Also, Grandma wanted to spend
one to one time with each grandchild, so she could do what they
want. My brother spent time with them on a different week either
before or after I was with them.

What did I see in Grandma and Grandpa Schmierer? I always saw
Grandma as lovely and funny. She walks and walks since she never
learned how to drive. I had to walk with her to the food store and
other places. We did four main things together.

We played many games together. I will never forget the one week
I played the same game over and over, the Uncle Wriggly game. One
day, Grandma told me to pick a different game but I proudly refused.
All I wanted to play was Uncle Wriggly. One day, I decided, I was
bored with it and picked a different game.

Grandma said to me, "After playing 101 times, you finally got bored?"

I said "YES!" I bet Grandma would say it was about time to
change. Imagine it, I still have that Uncle Wriggly game.

Schmierer family reunion. Amy and her cousins goofing off. Front row: Tom Walthers, Richard Walthers, and David Soriente. Back row: Amy Willman, Tony Soriente, and John Willman, 2001.

Second we went to the library. I picked any books I wanted and I read to myself at night before going to bed.

One time we had a homemade sling shot. Grandma made the sling by finding a "y" wood stick. Then she used her old, torn panty hose for the strap. We used apples from the backyard and saw who could shoot the apples farther. Or sometime, we picked a target to see who shoot closest to the target. Years and years later, she finally brought a REAL sling shot.

Sometimes we had a tea party—usually just us or my cousins, Tony and David, who lived in the same town as Grandma and Grandpa Schmierer, joined us. They are younger than me. We just played together, games or at the park, I really did not communicate with them, just played as kids.

As for Grandpa, I saw him as an intelligent man, who always wore his fedora and was "tough" looking, a hard-working person. What we did together the most was going to his farm. There I would help him cut asparagus, which is my favorite vegetable. We watched baseball games on TV. I rode in his big, blue, old car around the town of Beatrice. Grandpa read the newspaper lot. I tried to imitate him. I read the comics or pretended to figure out the crosswords puzzles. He loved to do crosswords. Grandpa did not sign to me at all, but he would write on a paper to communicate with me while Grandma signed to me. The week I spent with Grandma and Grandpa Schmierer from age five to ten was a good fun week.

As for my grandma and grandpa Willman, my father's parents, my grandpa died when I was only one year old, so I don't remember him. Grandma Willman did not sign; she died when I was eight. I did visit their home for a day or several hours, but not often. She gave me a doll to play with. We lived in a same town, but I never spent a week at their home. I really never had much of chance to know her compared to Grandma and Grandpa Schmierer.

Sadly, but what is general true for many Deaf people is that their relatives don't sign. Or far worse for the Deaf person, even their parents and brothers and sisters don't sign. My brother and mother can sign, but what about my other relatives? Many deaf persons are left out when their hearing family gathers and everyone is talking through voice. Most deaf people don't rely on lipreading in a large group of people. It's hard to catch what they are speaking. In general, deaf people are left out, feel alone, and are not able to be part of the family conversations. Sometimes deaf people don't even know what has happened to a family member, such as who moved away, got married, divorced, or had a baby.

There is a term for when Deaf feel "less than" or invisible. It is called *audism*. Audism is prejudice. It occurs when a hearing person acts superior because of their ability to hear and speak over those who don't.

Do I feel that way with my family? Yes, but I know they don't really mean it, but it happens anyway. It is really very boring when I sit all myself and wonder what they are talking about. They don't learn how to sign, but once in a while they will use paper and pen to communicate with me. Still, most of the time, when they are having a conversation, I either read something or watch TV if I am home. If we're in a restaurant, I look at the surroundings while other relatives are chatting. Yes, I ask them sometimes what they are talking about, and they either give me simple sentences or say, "It's not important" or "I'll tell you later."

At a young age, my brother and mother learned how to communicate with me through sign language. My mother was a stay home mom, while my father worked many hours at the store that he owned. You could call him a workaholic. My father did not learn but a few signs. He did not communicate with me much like John and Mother did when I was young. At age seven my parents divorced. After that I usually visited my father at the grocery store or at his home once in a while if he was not working. We didn't use sign language to communicate. Then and now, I relied on my brother by asking, "What did father say?" Sometimes father and I wrote messages, and I tried to lipread him. If we were talking about something simple, I could understand him. Even now as an adult it is the same.

I know it's not possible to have ALL relatives learn how to sign, but the parents and siblings of a deaf person should learn how to sign because they live together daily. It's important to have family communication at home, so the deaf person can feel and be part of the family and know what is going on. Living with my mother and John, we talk a lot because they sign to me. And I either sign or use my voice to them. I am so glad that John and mother can sign even though they are not fluent in ASL. I don't care if we sign in Alien Sign Language or other odd sign languages, as long as we COMMUNICATE.

Growing up, I am very close to John because he is my only sibling. John now lives in same town as me and does many things for me. We communicate a lot. Sometime I sign and use my voice when I speak to him. Of course, he does not use voice back to me but signs only. He is the best brother you could ever ask for.

38

Driving Miss Daisy Crazy

Rebecca and Amy

On January 23, 1982, Amy joined millions of other kids as a teenager. We celebrate with homemade pizza and rented movies, selecting two with closed captions. Two weeks later, John is fifteen, old enough to obtain a learner's permit, but he has no desire to drive. For weeks after his birthday, I offer to take him to the licensing bureau to obtain his learner's permit, but he uses snow-packed streets as an excuse, which makes no sense since all that is required for the permit is a birth certificate and an eye exam.

In April, I insist he obtain his learner's permit, which he does. I would like him to have a driver's license so he can run errands for me. I'm planning a family vacation this summer and having him help with the driving would be great. On Friday, Amy flies home for spring break. The snow has melted. On Saturday, I will give John his first driving lesson. I remember how tense Daddy made me when he taught me to drive; I've vowed to remain calm.

Saturday afternoon, John is riding shotgun, and Amy is in the back seat. I drive to Fonner Park, a racetrack that has a huge parking lot and narrow abandoned streets between horse barns, a perfect place to practice driving skills. I turn off the ignition, and John and I switch positions.

"Okay, John. Start the car and drive around the parking lot." John turns the key. The engine springs to life. He continues holding the key in the start position; the starter grinds. "That's enough John." I'm still calm, but Amy is not.

Being a sibling to John, I feel it's my job to be wacky and to go batty on him. So today, while John is having his first driving lesson, I have a plan. Mother told John to check the mirrors and put on his seat belt before starting the car. When John starts the car, I lean over the seat and shout, "Go, John."

John waves his hand at me. Wanting me to shut up and not bother him.

Mother tells me, "Sit down, Amy. Be quiet."

I sit down, but am not quiet. John drives toward the horse barns. I shout, "Slow down. Too fast." Then I see a stop sign and yell, "Stop!"

Mother told me, "Amy, be quiet. John is driving not you."

Mother continued to give John instructions, like drive forward, turn left, and stop, to see how he can turn or stop properly, instead of making wide turn or quick stops. After several practices on the Fonner Park parking lot, Mother told John, "Drive home now." The distance was not far, maybe one mile.

John drove onto a real street. As he drove toward a traffic light I say, "The light is green, John. Keep driving."

John said something, I don't know what, but probably "shut up."

"Pay no attention to your sister," Mother told John.

"You make me crazy," John turns and signs.

"Watch the road," Mother yells.

At the next intersection the light was red, so I yelled, "Stop, John." John stopped fast and Mother and I were held tight by our seat belts.

All the way home I yelled orders. "Keep driving, John." "You almost hit that car, John." "Faster, John." "Slow down, John." I sure made my brother went batty and Mother, too.

Finally Mother told John to stop driving. She said to John, "Next time we'll practice during the week when your sister isn't home."

Mother started the car and drove smoothly onto the busy street. I poked John in the shoulder until he turned to me. "See John. Mother knows how to do it better."

John frowned and said, "Don't bother me."

Despite Amy's backseat driving, John learned to drive and obtained his license several weeks after he turned sixteen.

Two years from now, Amy will turn fifteen. Since she has a January birthday and I do not want to teach her to drive on icy roads, I will not have her apply for a learner's permit until she comes home for the summer. NSD teaches driver's education, but only to students after they have obtained their driver's license, which makes little sense to me.

Many fifteen-year-olds are thrilled to drive and some might be scared or don't care. I was one of those with the attitude "I don't care if I drive." Anyway, Mother told me we are going to Department of Motor Vehicles (DMV) to get my permit.

When we went into the DMV building, as usual, there was a long line of people coming to renewal their driver license, pay car taxes and apply for a learner's permit. There were many forms available in bins along the wall. I looked for a permit license form and found it. I filled out the form and handed it to one of the examiners, along with my birth certificate. He told me, "Look in the eye exam machine and write down what letters or numbers you see."

I looked in the machine and waited for letters or numbers to appear. I told Mother, "I see nothing."

Mother said, "Look again."

I told her the same thing, "I still see nothing."

That was when the examiner walked around from behind the table to see if the eye exam machine was working or not. I thought to myself maybe the machine is broken. But the examiner told Mother, "It works just fine."

Mother looked in the machine and said, "There are letters in there, Amy. Tell me what you see?"

I looked and finally saw a big F-O-Z with one eye and a big E with the other eye.

Mother told me the examiner said, "She needs glasses. She can't have a permit until she can read the chart. Get her glasses and then bring her back."

When my mother told me what the examiner said, all I could think was *Oh no, am I going blind?*

After my eye exam with the doctor, Mother took me to the glasses store to select frames. I was not thrilled to have something on my face. I had an idea on how not to get glasses. I would not try on any frames, and if I did, I told Mother, "I don't like them." And then Mother took me to another store and another again. I did the same thing.

A week later Mother offered to take me and my friend Angie Walz, who would be a senior at NSD next fall, to the mall for shopping and a movie. Angie lived on the other side of Grand Island, far from us, so I was excited to be able to spend the afternoon with a deaf friend. Mother told me, "There is an optical store at the mall. We will go there first. After you select frames, you and Angie can go to the movie."

I still did not want any glasses at all. At the Conestoga Mall with Angie, when Mother reached her last straw, she said, "Amy, pick a frame or I will pick one for you."

I did not look carefully at the frames, I just picked one. I choose the biggest and ugliest frame I saw. They were tan-colored plastic with big round lenses like an owl's eyes. The side pieces bent down like the letter "C." I thought, I don't give a damn what they look like because I am not going to wear them at all. Mother left and Angie and I had a good time at the movie and shopping.

A week later, Mother and I returned to the mall. After the clerk fitted the glasses on me, I took them off, put them in their case, and gave them to Mother.

Mother gave them back to me and said, "Amy, you need to wear these."

I refused to take them. I said, "Maybe later. Not now."

Mother yelled, "Amy! Wait!"

Later, when I got to home, I still refused to wear the glasses. Mother said, "You have to wear them Amy so you can see."

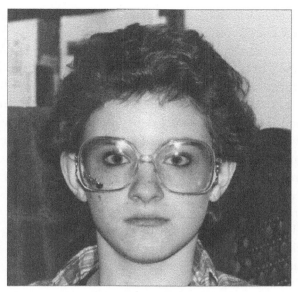

Amy with her first pair of glasses, which she disliked. Summer of 1984.

I kept saying, "No."

"Amy, wearing glasses is not a big deal." Mother said. "I was younger than you when I got my first pair of glasses. You'll still be beautiful with glasses."

"I don't want glasses." I started to cry.

Mother asked, "What's wrong, Amy?"

I said, "Maybe I am going blind."

Mother shook her head, "no," but still I would not wear the glasses.

Having sight is very important to me and every Deaf person. We rely on our eyes to see what is happening. Without eyes, a Deaf person would find it very difficult to survive since we have already lost one sense, our hearing. But being Deaf and blind, what would I do?

A few nights later when Mother and I were playing cards, I looked at my cards and said, "Wait!" Mother looked so puzzled. I ran to my bedroom. Guess what I went there for? I picked up and put on my big, ugly glasses. Why did I do that? I could not really read the cards without the glasses. At that moment, I felt so relieved that I could read and knew I was not going blind. Of course, I got rid of my "eeew" glasses in less than a year. The next glasses I had were preppie glasses. Very classy compared to my first ugly ones.

I find it ironic that when Helen Keller was asked, "Would you rather be deaf or blind?" she chose to be blind over deaf. I thought, gosh, she must be a nitwit. I would rather be Deaf than blind. Deafness does not limit my ability to do things such as riding a bike, driving cars, and seeing nature. I depend on my eyes for everything I need to live in a hearing society. Of course, Deaf people and hearing people don't receive equal information. Hearing people have access to radios, announcements at airports, and live news that Deaf don't, and yet, I and other Deaf people still find a way to receive this information, just not through our ears.

I have heard stories from hearing people that they are afraid of losing their hearing. They told me, "If I lost my hearing, I would not know what to do or how to live, because I depend on my ears to tell me what is happening."

Funny thing, I live without my ears and I am doing just fine. I understand their concern, because they have heard sounds and enjoy it. The same is true for me; I have seen the world around me and enjoy it. So, both of us, Deaf and hearing, can't imagined losing a valuable sense once we have experienced it.

Minutes later Amy draws a card from the deck, "Going down for three." She spreads her gin rummy cards on the table. "You lose. Too bad for you."

I may have lost the game, but I won the battle of the glasses, which was a bigger issue. I can only imagine how scared she was, thinking she was going blind. From this point on, Amy's glasses become part of her. They are the first thing she puts on in the morning, and the last thing she takes off at night. I should have known. When it comes to winning, Amy would utilize anything, including glasses, to sharpen her focus and have a competitive edge.

Wearing her glasses, Amy passes the eye exam and receives her learner's permit. I brace myself for teaching another child to drive. The next evening after she comes home from her summer job, I said, "After supper you will have your first driving lesson."

"I can do it. I know how," she says. "Driving is easy."

Amy said this before ever being behind the steering wheel. Her "I know everything attitude," a strong part of her personality, may be challenged this time. "Driving is not as easy as it looks," I reply.

John opts to stay home and play *Frogger*, so Amy and I depart for Fonner Park alone. Once there, we change seats. I put my hand on her arm. She turns toward me. "Amy, let's go. Shift into gear, and drive forward, slowly." As soon as I signed "go," Amy turned from me and stomped on the accelerator.

The engine whined to maximum RPMs. Once again I lay my hand on her arm, this time with gripping force. She turns toward me. "Why don't we go?"

"Because you have to shift the car into drive, first." I point to the "D" on dash.

"Oh." Amy's voice reflects her I-know-that attitude.

"Put the car in drive, and go slow . . ." Amy turns away from me and floors the accelerator again. The tires squeal; burnt rubber fills my nostrils. Amy turns toward me, frowning. "Take your foot off the brake," I say.

We charge forward. Amy clutches the steering wheel like a NASCAR driver. We zigzag through the lot. Yikes! Now what? If I tap her arm, she'll look at me and may hit one of the many light poles in the parking lot. If I do nothing, she'll shoot through the parking lot onto a busy street. "We're all gonna die," I murmur, a line I often say when a situation is perilous.

I wave my hand in her field of vision and sign, "stop." I'm thankful for seatbelts. I'm yanked back by my shoulder restraint to the point of pain. Amy turns, nods her head, and smiles with confidence.

"Watch me!" I sign and say through clenched teeth. "Don't go until I say so." I jerk the shoulder restraint to release it.

"Fine," Amy signs. "Now what."

"Drive in a straight line. See the lines on the parking lot? Drive on one of them. Go slow, and stop by each section marker." I point to large letters on the light poles.

"Okay." Amy takes her foot from the brake and accelerates.

"Go slow!" I scream to no avail.

After Amy completes several jackrabbit starts, and bone jarring stops, she turns to me while the car is still moving. "Now what?"

"Put the car in park. I'll drive home."

When we arrive home, John runs up from the basement. "I won the first level of *Frogger*. I got all five of my frogs home safely."

"Good," I reply. "We got home safely too. No thanks to Amy."

"I drove, John," Amy says. "I told you I knew how."

I roll my eyes up and shake my head. "She needs a few more lessons." I say to John behind Amy's back. I tap Amy's shoulder. "Tomorrow after work we'll drive again."

Amy shakes her head. "No. I don't need to. I know how." She walks toward the basement door. "John, you won *Frogger*. Let me see." Amy's voice is full of disbelief.

"Wait, I'll show you." John grabs Amy's shirt, but she twists away from him.

"I know how. I can do it." She runs down the basement steps.

Each afternoon, when I return from work, I ask Amy, "Do you want to drive tonight?"

Her response is always the same, "No. I know how. I can do it."

A year passes. The summer after her sophomore year I am determined she will learn to drive.

The next summer I was sixteen, Mother insisted I had to learn to drive. She said, "I don't care if you ever drive after you get your license, but you need to have a license for an ID." My learner's permit had expired, so we went to the DMV to get a new one.

This time my brother went with me when Mother gave me a driving lesson. John was excited, because he wanted revenge from all the screaming I had done to him two years ago. I slipped on my seat belt. In the rearview mirror I saw John's face. His eyes were filled with mischief. He was ready to drive me batty, but he couldn't, because Mother was signing to me what to do, and at the same time I was trying to watch the road. Eventually Mother said, "Watch the road."

John realized he could have no revenge, because he was in the back seat, and I could not turn to see his signs. He could scream "stop," "go," "red light and green light" all he wanted and I could not hear him, but he still wanted revenge. He knew I could feel vibrations, and that they are distracting to me, so he kicked the front seat where I was sitting.

I yelled, "Stop it, John. You bother me."

He kicked more. I didn't like the thump, thump, thump over and over on my seat. "Stop it," I yelled again, but he didn't. Good enough, he drove me batty.

Mother told John, "Quit that and be quiet."

I looked in the rear view mirror. John had a huge grin on his face.

In general, Deaf people are sensitive to pounding or vibrations; it can be distracting. One sensation Deaf people enjoy is a loud band or concert that makes the floor or table vibrate. We can sense the noise of the music that way and feel the beats. In Deaf culture, (our Deaf World) it's okay to pound the table or stomp the floor in a proper place (usually at home, dorm and school; not at library, church (unless it is deaf church), and restaurant) to get the attention of other Deaf people; this is proper, but making these vibrations for no reason is annoying.

So what John did to me was very distracting, similar to a hearing person tapping a table with a pencil. That action might be distracting to hearing people. My distraction to John when he was driving was to shout orders and make noise. John's distraction to me was making vibrations. So, we both had the perfect sibling revenge.

Many months after I passed my driver's test and had my license, I was going to run an errand while Mother was a work. We had a Monte Carlo with a dark red body and a white top. When I backed out from the garage, I scraped the driver's side along the garage structure. A hearing person would have known what was happening, because of the scraping noise, but I did not know it until I saw what I had done.

I thought to myself, "Oh no! What should I say to Mother?"

John said, "You will be in trouble."

I had a good idea. When Mother came home and saw the car she was not happy. She asked, "What happened?"

I said, "I backed straight out of the garage and all of a sudden the garage structure moved and bit the car. That's how it happened."

Mother tried not to laugh but she did. She said, "I've never heard of a garage biting a car." Afterward she told me I had to buy new wood trims for the garage.

39

More Audism

Rebecca and Amy

A major ramification of Amy's deafness is that she misses out on thousands of hours of peripheral conversations, not only the ones John and I have, but also most of the conversations in the hearing world. John has gained a lot of knowledge indirectly by overhearing conversations on filing income tax returns, mortgage rates, applying for a job, investing money, gardening, repairing a car, fixing a broken toilet, etc. While Amy has normal intelligence, her worldly knowledge is far below that of hearing kids her age because of her inability to hear casual conversations. To make matters worse, many hearing people do not make any effort to speak directly to her, assuming she can't understand, so why bother.

Mother told me I have a dentist appointment today. Basically, I don't want to go as my teeth are just fine and perfect! I don't have teeth like John had. He wore braces. He looked like a monster. I mocked at him. I gave him a monster facial expression with teeth wide open at the same time doing the Frankenstein walks!

John decided to do his monster face back to me. Saying that's what I looked like. Mother told us stop it or you will be late for dentist appointment. I told Mother that I want John to take me to the dentist. John agreed as he wants to drive around.

The dentist had a very small waiting room which was an an ugly light green. John told the front desk that I had an appointment today.

Mother had told me all the dentist would do is clean my teeth, but when I was in the small room with the dentist, he did other things to my teeth. I did not know what he was doing. He told me nothing. I was scared, confused, and crying by the time he finished. When I returned to the waiting room, John saw me crying and said, "What is the matter?"

I tried to tell John what the dentist had done, but he could not understand me. I kept saying, "The dentist hurt me. I don't know why."

John got mad. He told the lady at the desk, "I need to see the dentist now. I want to know what he did to make my sister cry."

When Dr. Blackburn came out in a few minutes, John asked him, "What did you do to Amy?"

The dentist said, "Nothing."

John said, "Amy doesn't cry about nothing. What did you do to her?"

The dentist then told John, "I found a small cavity in one of her upper molars, and I had time available, so I decided to fill it. When I was filling her tooth, Amy seemed upset, but I did not hurt her."

John told Dr. Blackburn, "I'm not happy how you treated Amy. You should have told her what you were doing. No wonder she was scared when you were jamming needles in her mouth and drilling her tooth."

The dentist mumbled, "I'm sorry."

When John knew I was not physically abused, he signed, "Get in the car, Amy, and stop crying. All you had was a cavity."

Ha! But at least he cared enough to ask the dentist.

Later, when John told Mother what happened, she was mad. She had chosen Dr. Blackburn for our dentist because he was used to working on disabled patients. Mother called Dr. Blackburn and said, "Why didn't you explain to Amy what you were going to do?"

Dr. Blackburn said, "I didn't think she would understand, so I didn't tell her anything."

Then Mother was really mad. She said, "Amy may not be able to read your lips, but she's deaf, not stupid. You could have written on a piece of paper what you were going to do. Or showed her the x-ray and gestured what you planned to do. You could have asked her brother to explain to her what was going to happen. I can't believe you did this. She was really scared."

"I'm sorry," Dr. Blackburn told Mother. "I've never had a deaf patient. I didn't know what to do."

Other deaf people have had medical procedures without knowing what they were, just like what happened to me at the dentist. I heard of a deaf couple who gave birth to a beautiful baby through C-section. The parents of the daughter told the doctor to sterilize their daughter because they did not want her to have more deaf children. This was done without their daughter's knowledge or consent. After several years, the deaf couple tried to have a second child but could not conceive. When they returned to their doctor, he told them, "You were sterilized at your parents' request." Imagine their shock.

Some hearing people think that Deaf people can't make a complex decision or understand the issues involved. That is what happened to me at the dentist's office. All I saw was a big needle and some odd tools. Gosh! I thought. What the heck is the dentist doing to my perfect teeth? The dentist should have told me or asked my brother to explain about the cavity to me.

40

Stateside Travel

Rebecca and Amy

Later this summer we took a vacation to Yellowstone and nearby sites. When driving someplace, John and I easily discuss what we want to eat, when to stop, and what we notice outside. It's difficult but not impossible to include Amy in our conversation. If she sits in the back seat, John can turn and speak/sign to her while I am driving, but she tires of riding in the back. When she's in the front seat, I can't sign and drive, and Amy gripes about having to turn her head around to see what John is signing. It's no better when John is driving. I can't win. Maybe it is just being fourteen.

Weeks before our departure, I spread maps and brochures on the table and told John and Amy, "Read about these places and select three you want to see, and then we'll vote. If we all agree, we'll go there. But, if we don't, each person has one 'ultimate choice' vote. When you cast that vote we will have to go to the place you select." We agreed on all our scenic destinations except one: Devil's Tower. Neither John nor I had any desire to see a big rock, plus it's sixty miles off my planned route. But, Amy loved *Close Encounters of the Third Kind* and was determined to see the "alien rock." She invoked her right of "ultimate choice."

I started to travel at very young age. Mother always took me and John to museums before we even started school. Later we drove to many states and flew to different countries. Today I enjoy traveling, not just because I grew up travelling (maybe that is part of it), but I enjoy seeing different cultures, how people live, historical things, and the architecture of buildings. Now I sometimes travel with my mother and her husband, Walt, with John, or with my Deaf friends.

When I was eight years old, I went to Hawaii and crossed the ocean for the first time by an airplane. I went with Mother, John and Grandma Schmierer. We stayed at a hotel on Waikiki Beach in Honolulu, Oahu, Hawaii. I saw firsthand what happened at Pearl Harbor and toured the Honolulu Zoo. One evening, we went to another town to visit the Polynesian Cultural Center where the different cultures of the South Pacific did a beautiful dance performance. The Hawaiians danced and drummed while we dined on a Hawaiian luau. I remember I ate from a real pineapple with the skin on. They cut off the top and ground up the pineapple inside and added ice cream to it. Yum, so good.

When I was fourteen we went on a road trip to Yellowstone Park and several other states around it. We drove and stopped and drove and stopped. When we stopped to sightsee, most of the time, we picked a self-guided tour instead of joining with a group and tour guides. Why? There are two main reasons. First Mother knew I will be bored with a tour guide, since I cannot understand what the tour guide is saying. Also, my mother and brother do not like to stand and wait for other people to arrive, and neither do I. This limits our time to explore new things, so we explore on our own, which give us more free time to choose what to see and how long to do it.

At Yellowstone Park, we walked around looked at amazing views, some with an awful smell from the sulfur in the geysers. The smell was like a rotten egg.

During this trip we also went to Montana and saw Custer's last stand, and on to South Dakota to see the Black Hills and Mount Rushmore. There were many signs that I could read. My brother and mother signed to me what they heard from the public speakers or tour guides. Some places I already knew about from studying it at school. Mother usually gave me information or books to read about our trip a month or so before we went. That way I was familiar with what I will see when we travel there. It's no different today. When I travel with Deaf friends, I still read information or books first. It's much easier that way and I can plan what I want to see most.

Mother decided where we would drive on the trip. She liked to stop early so she did not have to drive all day. Also if we were at our hotel early, we could swim, which I love. When going to Yellowstone, we stopped in a small town in Wyoming. There was nothing there but a Pizza Hut. We did have cable TV at the hotel, but that was all. Not even a pool. I bought a postcard for my friend Angie, who went to public school in Grand Island for several years but now is at NSD in two classes ahead of me.

The card was all black, with two white dots and small white letters that said: Some of the night life in Green River. I wrote on the card, "I am on vacation. We went to pit city." Later I sent her and my classmates Kelli and Tricia better cards.

This vacation was my first long trip with my family. We traveled through six states and saw many historical sites. Mt. Rushmore was so big that my eyes could not believe it. At NSD, I read about Mt. Rushmore and saw a picture of it in the book, but I did not realized how big it was. Devil's Tower was my choice of a place to visit, because I wanted to see if any aliens flew over it or landed there. I did not have any luck seeing one. Ha ha!

The trip was very interesting and I saw many new and different things, but did not learn as much about the places we visited as John and Mother did because they could hear the guides talking, and I couldn't. Mother or John tried to explain what the guide was saying sometimes, but at the same time I wanted to rely on eyes to see information at the historical sites so I did not care if they signed to me or not except when I asked them something.

Yellowstone was wonderful, despite having to warn Amy numerous times to stay on the trail, keep away from the geysers, and not approach the animals. Encouraging Amy to become independent has

John and Amy at Devil's Tower, Wyoming in the summer of 1983. This was one of Amy's "ultimate choices" for us to visit on our vacation.

drawbacks. Keeping track of her physical whereabouts is challenging, requiring a lot of quick steps on my part since I can't shout to locate her. When she was young, I kept a tight grip on her hand, but now that she's a teenager that's not possible. She often wanders off to explore other aisles in a store, a different display in a museum, or disappears when my back is turned. I become short-tempered when I have to retrace my steps and send John in another direction to find her. Under constant supervision at NSD, and feeling confined by their rules, Amy wants no restrictions at home and does not understand why I insist on knowing where she is or where she is going.

At Custer's Last Stand in Montana, explaining the historical events required more sign language skill than either John or I possessed. While the history lesson was important, keeping Amy out of the tall grass where rattlesnakes lurked was vital. She was more willing to obey the posted signs than my constant warnings.

During lunch, I tried to convince Amy to give up the trip to Devil's Tower with no luck. As John drove down the narrow winding road to Devil's Tower National Park, Amy rolled down her window and yelled, "There it is! Come on John. Hurry up, park the car."

Before John took the key from the ignition, Amy was out of the car. "John, lock the car doors!" I dashed down the path after Amy. While we saw no aliens, or even a hint that they had been there, Amy was thrilled to be at Devil's Tower. I must admit that for a big rock, it was rather impressive.

41

Plans in Turmoil

Rebecca and Amy

For years, Amy has spent more time at school than she does at home. I'm happy she does not cry or complain when her worn blue trunk is brought up from the basement each August. I loved going to school, so I understand why she's excited to return to her friends, but as her mother, I wish she showed a bit of regret when she leaves. Only Jupiter, her cat, gets a fond farewell complete with tears.

I was excited when I could move from the second floor of the girls' dorm to the first for my high school years. As Mother and John prepared to carry things into the dorm, I said to John, "Don't worry. You don't have to carry my rock of a suitcase upstairs this year." I don't recall what he said, but I am sure he felt relieved. But, he still had to haul all my stuff to my room anyway.

Inside the dorm, a house parent said, "This year things have changed. Ninth, tenth, and twelfth grade girls will all be in the hall to the right."

"Why?" I asked.

"Because there are so many eleventh-grade girls, about fifteen. They fill the entire left side."

"Wow! I get to be near the seniors."

In my freshman class there were only four girls, so in my hall there were only a total of eleven students: four freshman, three sophomores, and four senior girls. Since there were not as many girls in the dorm this year, or during any of my high school years, I had a room all to myself with two beds, two closets, and two dressers. What a blessing to have two closets and dressers. I had plenty of room for all my clothes. From the angry looks my freshman classmates and I received from the seniors, we knew they disliked hanging around with us, but for the most part, we had a blast living with the senior girls.

By April of 1984, our European trip plans are complete. I've booked a three-week tour; we've obtained passports, bought travel books, and purchased foreign money. Since we will be traveling for three weeks, I allow two "ultimate choice" votes. Amy invokes this right for the Little Mermaid statue in Copenhagen and Madame Tussaud's Wax Museum in London. John and I agree on visiting East Berlin, Postjana Cave in Yugoslavia, and the Vatican museums, specifically the Sistine Chapel. We will fly to London two days after John finishes his junior year. But, as often happens, the best laid plans of mice and men oft go astray; my scheduled life is thrown into confusion when Mrs. Ferguson, the NSD school secretary, calls me in the middle of May.

"Allegations of improprieties have been lodged against Superintendent George Collins and some of the NDS dorm staff," Mrs. Ferguson tells me.

"Why? What's happened?" I recall my father's concern that students at NSD might be treated like the orphans Dickens wrote about in his novels.

"I'm not at liberty to discuss that," she says.

A torrent of questions fills my mind. When did this start? Who's involved? Why hasn't Amy said anything? I ask the most important question. "Is Amy all right?"

"Yes, the children are fine. I called to inform you the school is being closed, pending a full investigation. All the children must go home tomorrow. They'll return to finish the school year the second

Monday in June." Her voice sounds weary and rote. Having to tele-phone one hundred and sixty parents has taken a toll on her usual pleasant demeanor.

"Return in two weeks! Amy can't do that. We're leaving for Eu-rope on May 29th. I can't change our plans." I pace the kitchen floor, gnawing on a fingernail.

"Don't worry about that." Mrs. Ferguson sighs. "Other children have similar problems. A trip to Europe is a great educational op-portunity, one few children have. None of our students have traveled abroad. Go to Europe, enjoy yourself. I'm sure her teachers will agree, but check with them tomorrow when you come to get Amy."

After hanging up, I mumble, "It's always something."

The next day, the NSD staff is silent, as confused about the investi-gation as the parents are. Perplexed by the situation, I search for Amy. She and her friends are having an animated conversation when I ar-rive at the dorm. Their fingers fly with determination. Their worried, angry expressions tell me they are as upset about the school closing and the allegations as I am. As her friends tote Amy's belongings to the car, I'm amazed that they can converse in sign while carrying boxes and clothes on hangers. Their faces portray a range of emotions that the best actors in the world would envy. After bidding a tearful good-bye to her friends, Amy sits in the front seat.

"It's not true what they said." Amy's voice is full of anger, almost to the point of hatred.

"Who? What did they say?" I ask. "What's going on?"

Before the school was closed, investigators asked me if I would like to be mainstreamed into a school in my hometown. I said, "NO! If I am mainstreamed, I would not be able to understand anything in the classes or participate in any school events such as drama, cheer-leading or sports."

Since I was already in the ninth grade, switching to a public school at that time would be the worst thing for me, like moving to a strange land. High school is supposed to create a student's best memories, and I doubted I would have any good memories if I were mainstreamed into a Grand Island school. Not only that, who could I talk to during lunch or recess?

"NSD," I said, "is a much better place for me to attend due to language communication through ASL."

Mother asked me, "What happened?" when we were driving home. I was upset. I signed, "They said Mr. Collins did something wrong, but I don't know what. He's never done anything wrong.[5] We all love Mr. Collins and think of him as "our father." He knows the names of all students. He would never hurt us."

Mother asked, "Who said he did something?"

"Some people from outside NSD. They come to the school to ask questions and interview to us kids. The investigators even asked the younger students to answer the questions. Some of the questions were off the point or nonsense. Basically, they just wanted us to answer the questions either "no" or "yes." They collected information from all students at NSD. They decided who was "good" or "bad" staff on the NSD campus. Then police arrested some of them. The worst part was they did it front of students in the cafeteria. All of us were so shocked that they would do that."

"Who were these people that started asking all these questions?" Mother asked.

"Different people came to school and asked about what happens in the dorms and school. They make problems for Mr. Collins and other staff. They say the school is not good. I don't like them." I would not say anymore. I did not like the people who made the trouble. The story was told through TV news and newspapers, too. It was a very dark moment for Deaf people in the Deaf community.

I was puzzled and wondered what will happen to NSD. I didn't know what was actually happening in Omaha. All I know was I received tons of homework from them. They mailed homework packages to every student.

The people in the Deaf community thought the state legislature and Lt. Governor were trying to destroy the deaf school. They tried

---

5. Mr. Collins had been the NSD superintendent for many years. He replaced Mr. Thompson when he retired. Mr. Collins had a wife and family.

to put all the NSD students into mainstreaming programs. I was told they had been trying to do that for several years, but were unsuccessful.

Amy crinkles her nose and snorts. I've seen her make this gesture many times. It's her final statement on a subject. The discussion is over. I try to pry more information from her, but she shuts me out by turning toward the passenger window, eliminating visual contact with me. We leave for Europe as planned not knowing the fate of NSD.

42

Europe and Beyond
Rebecca and Amy

The morning we arrive in London, Amy reminds me, "I want to see the wax people."

"Not today Amy, we have to join our tour group, but we'll be back in London before we fly home. We'll visit it then."

Armed with maps, guidebooks, cameras, and a calculator for determining the value of foreign currency, we are prepared for anything as we take out seats on the tour bus. John and Amy banked their spending money with me, and Amy keeps a meticulous record of what she's spent. When we arrive in Rome, she asks for money. I give her a 5,000-lira note.

"Wow! Five thousand dollars!" Amy's eyes gleam with the thought of having so much money. She pulls out the calculator, enters the rates of exchange and her smile is replaced by a scowl. "This is only two dollars and twenty cents."

John and I have a good laugh at her expense.

At fifteen I used my passport for the first time traveling to Europe. Basically, it was a cultural and historical experience, because it was different from what I saw or expected in the United States. WOW! I was surprised when I landed at Heathrow Airport in London. The first guy I saw working at the airport had colorful pointed hair. Ahh, the punks! A few years later, United States got the fad and I told my classmates, "It's old news. I saw it in London." In general, Europe was way ahead in fashions and fads. Not only that but also weird-looking cop uniforms and hats.

In Germany, we went to the Berlin Wall, both the free and communist side, and Nuremburg where Hitler gave his speech. In Rome, we saw Vatican City and the Coliseum. In Paris, we went to the top of the Eiffel Tower and to a huge castle, Versailles. It was interesting to see many different buildings, people, clothes, and designs that I would not see in America.

When we went to Europe, Mother did the same thing she did for our first big family vacation. We voted on places to visit. I chose to see the Little Mermaid statue in Copenhagen and Madame Tussaud's Wax Museum in London. I am not sure why I picked the Little Mermaid statue. Maybe for the same reason I picked Devil's Tower. Perhaps I wanted to see if the Mermaid was real and could swim in the sea. As for the wax museum, I thought it would be a very visual museum, good for me, so that is why I picked it.

In Copenhagen, I reminded Mother about the little mermaid statue that I voted as a place we must see. Our tour did not go there, so we had to find it on our own. We rode a bus and then walked and walked in a park until I spied the statue. "There it is," I said and smiled.

Mother said, "The statue is nice, but not worth the blisters on my feet."

In London, Mother did not want to go to the wax museum and suggested I pick something else, but I refused. I wanted to see the wax people. "Maybe we won't have to walk so much," I said, "like with the mermaid."

We didn't. We rode the subways, called the Tube, to the wax museum. When Mother saw the price, she gasped and tried to change my mind again, but I told her, "You promised me we would go." So in we went and had a grand time.

If you have not been to London, a must to see is Madame Tussaud's wax museum. There you see many wax figures of famous people from London and all over the world. The wax statues were set up in various scenes. We walked through an exhibit of Lord Nelson dying during a fight with the Spanish Armada and a Jack the Ripper scene of narrow streets filled dead wax bodies. I saw the royal family and famous actors, musicians and TV characters. John liked Dr. Who and his weird dog, K-9. It was a very fascinating place to visit. All I had to do was walk through the displays, look at the wax figures, and read a small sign saying who the person was and when the statue was made.

It was a very visual place. Sometimes I was not sure if that person was wax or real. My brother and I tried to freeze our body to see if people thought we were wax persons. Some of the people thought we were wax.

There was not much done by "voice" speaking at the museum, more like a self-guided tour, which is perfect for me and Deaf people. At the end of the museum, I asked Mother, "Did you enjoy it?" She said it was fun, and so did my brother. Much better than what they expected.

On the way to Big Ben, we talked about what we liked best. I liked the royal family. John thought Boy George and Dr. Who were best. Mother said, "Dr. Who and K-9 get my vote."

When we were in foreign lands where Mother and John did not always understand the language, they were confused. Now they could imagine how I live all the time in the hearing world. As for me, not understanding the language did not bother me, because I know what it's like to be not able to communicate with people around you. So, traveling to foreign lands does not bother me. I actual find it easier than hearing people do, because people in other countries understand many of the common gestures used in ASL.

The week after we returned from Europe, I started a new job as a federal agent. I liked my job at the Nebraska Depart of Labor, but it was not full time. John is a senior in high school this year and will be attending the university following graduation. I need the income of a full-time job.

Weeks later while putting our European photos in an album, I take a break and call Vodis to see if the issues at NSD were resolved.

"Yes and no," Vodis says.

"What does that mean?" I ask.

"The school reopened after several weeks without a superintendent and with a lot of new staff."

"What about this fall? Will the school be operating?" I worry Amy will be mainstreamed, something neither of us wants.

"Yes, but there will be a new superintendent."

"What happened to George Collins? I liked him. I can't believe he did anything wrong."

"Neither do I. The school board forced him to resign. I saw him once this summer. He was upset by the entire ordeal. He said, 'I'll always have a shadow hanging over my head since the board did not let me have my day in court where I could prove my innocence.'"

I agree with Vodis, the entire mess was a tempest in a teapot, stirred up by people who did not have children at the school. I'm at loss what to believe. I am sad that George Collins, a genuine, compassionate man whom I liked, and whom Amy and the other students considered a father figure, will no longer be at NSD.

After the 1984 incident, NSD lost some good staff. The next fall, after going to Europe, I came back and so did many other students. The number of students dwindled down a little bit but not enough to close the school, yet. Of course, it was a funny feeling when seeing new staff and they even created more rules. But I survived through my high school and am so glad that I graduated from NSD before it closed.

43

Making Memories, High School
Amy

During my four years in high school, I spent less and less time at the dormitory, because I was involved in many activities and sports. These activities gave me good reasons to get away from the house parents and their unnecessary rules. I kept busy by playing volleyball and basketball. I participated in track during my freshman year and disliked it, so I never did that again. Ironically, I was named the Most Improved Track Player, and yet I still did not return to be a part of the track team. When I stayed in the dorm over the weekend in my high school years, it was less boring due to attending home or away athletic games.

Volleyball was my best sport. Playing volleyball was fun for me, and it was a perfect getaway from the dormitory. We won fourth and fifth places at tournaments. When volleyball season ended, I thought, I have to participate in basketball, even though it is not my best sport, so I can stay away from the dormitory.

In the spring, I thought I would have to spend time after school in the dormitory, because I was not part of the track team, and I knew I would get into mischief, so I participated in the high school play during my junior and senior years, which were only in the spring. The junior play was mime with Ricky Smith. It was fun. The stage had

Amy with Ricky Smith, a renowned deaf mime who was an artist in residence at the Nebraska School for the Deaf one year. This photo was taken after the NSD mime performace.

black lights, and we wore neon colors and white faces. As for senior play, I was the "thief" who pretended to sew a robe for an emperor in the play *The Emperor's New Clothes*.

Mother and John were in the audience waving after the performance. For Deaf people, hand waving is part of our culture, a way to show our appreciation. Again, it based on the fact that Deaf use their vision to gather information and knowledge. When my classmates and I saw hands waving in the audiences, we knew they enjoyed the performance. You have to remember that Deaf people use eyes to see their world and hearing people use their ears.

My goal during my high school years was to keep busy and spend very little time in the dorm. I was a class vice president for two years, the pep club president for two years, and student council president one year. With the help of our adult sponsors, I learned how to conduct a meeting according to parliamentary rules, and how to organize fund raising events and parties. I was also involved with cheerleading and on the pom pom squad.

The pom pom squad was a drill team. Yes, there was music. Even though I didn't hear it, some of the girls did because they wore hearing aids. I memorized the order of our movements since I could not hear the music. We had a pom pom coach who sat in front of us counting to be keep us on the right pace.

I liked to be part of the sports team or a cheerleader or member of the pom pom squad, because we went on road trips, which were fun. It was nice to leave our campus and see other schools either hearing or deaf schools. Not only that, but I liked to represent our school and to show other school that Deaf people can do anything. Sometimes we beat the hearing teams in sports, which was great.

I wanted to be a cheerleader when I entered high school, so I learned the ASL signs for the "Star Spangled Banner" from the cheerleaders.

Changing a song from English into ASL is not done word for word, just like it's not done when translating a sentence from English into Spanish or any other language. An ASL user does not sign the exact same words a hearing person would sing because ASL grammar has a different word order than English. Also, one ASL sign can convey the same concept that requires several English words to express.

For example, in "The Star Spangled Banner," the words "at the twilight's last gleaming" are signed as "sunset dark," which means the same as "twilight's last gleaming." Also in the national anthem the line, "whose broad stripes and bright stars" is signed with facial expressions to express emotions and descriptions. The person signing this phrase uses the first finger of each hand to create a flag shape, and then signs "red-white stripes, blue (to show the area of blue in flag shape) bright stars (using a "claw" hand shape on the blue area to represent stars)."

My hands are very expressive, just like the voice of a vocal singer. I made the pom pom squad during my first two years in high school and cheerleader squad in the last two years of high school. Before the sports game started, the duty of three cheerleaders was to carry the United States and Nebraska flag before the crowd and another cheerleader signed the "Star Spangled Banner." Sometimes I just carried the flag, and other times I signed the song.

You might wonder how I knew when to start the song. Yes, there was music blasting the "Star Spangled Banner," because of the hearing teams or hearing people in the crowd. Usually a hearing staff sat by the stage. When I stood and was about ready to sign the song, I looked at the hearing staff's lips to know when to start. Once in a while, I would look at the hearing staff's lips to be sure I was on the right line of the song. While the music played, I sang away my beautiful ASL signs expressing the song.

During my fourteen years of living at NSD, I lived through many different house parents, roommates, and necessary and unnecessary rules, had my mischievous moments, received an excellent education, played with girls and boys on the playgrounds, participated in many sports and organizations and earned a number of awards.

In volleyball I was selected a Deaf All American, athlete of the year, Most Valuable Player, Midwest States School for the Deaf All Star, and Logan Valley Conference, All Conference player. I won awards in basketball for Most Valuable Player, the Logan Valley Conference, and All Conference. I was always on my best behavior in class and was the first Deaf person selected to attend the Hugh O'Brien Youth Foundation Leadership workshop for an outstanding sophomore. I was honored by the Exchange Club of Omaha for Sophomore Scholastic Achievement, was on the honor roll, and twice received the Mathematic Honors Awards. I was a class vice president, pep club president, and the student council president. In my senior year, I was chosen class valedictorian.

Do you think I could have done all this mainstreamed in public school? No. Do you think any deaf child could excel like I did if they were in mainstreamed classes? Probably not.

My classmates and I had our own little world on the NSD campus. All of my memories at the Nebraska School for the Deaf are full of laughter and homesickness. In my class, there were four girls and four boys. By our senior year, we had lived together for many years, shared plenty of laughter, and done many mischievous things to each other and our teachers. I formed many good memories with my classmates.

In our senior year, we had to choose a motto for our class. We decided on a perfect motto for us. "Today's precious moments are tomorrow's fond memories." I will never ever forget my classmates. They will always be in my eyes.

44

Last Chances

Rebecca

Amy's volleyball and basketball games are on Thursday night, not a good day for me to do six hours of driving after working all day, so I never saw her play a game. I feel guilty. NSD plays small schools in the Omaha area, as well as the residential deaf schools in Iowa, Missouri, Minnesota, Oklahoma, and Kansas. I know little about Amy's school activities, because she does not talk about school when she is home, and prying information from a teenager is difficult. In addition by the time she arrives home on Friday, she considers the past week ancient history.

While John was busy during his senior year with debate, band, and college preparation. Amy's sophomore year was filled with drill team, cheerleading, sports, and drama. John and I saw Amy perform in a theatrical production, *Silence Speaks Louder than Words*. We were not sure what we would see, but Amy assured us it would be wonderful. Ricky Smith,[6] an artist in residence at NSD, who is deaf, directed the students.

John and I found seats in the crowded NSD gym. Most functions with this many people present would be noisy, but it's strangely quiet

---

6. Ricky Smith has been a professional mime for more than thirty-eight years. He was a student of Marcel Marceau. His website is www.rickysmithmime.net.

here since most of the audience is deaf. An oral and a sign language narrator stand to one side of the stage. Their part of the production is minimal: introduce the title of the scene and make a brief comment at the end. The first scene is "The Tempest."

When the curtain rose, John and I searched the students for Amy. She was difficult to locate because all the students had faces covered with white grease paint. Their bodies were clothed in black, including black gloves. Ricky was also dressed in black, but wore white gloves. The children held aqua chiffon material above their head. Their bodies swayed in unison, a fluid motion that made them appear to be an ocean wave. They dipped and stretched like crashing waves as they moved across the stage. Ricky's white-gloved hands soared as a seagull above their waves. We were mesmerized.

A stage filled with Deaf people, who are accustomed to using their bodies to express emotions, makes mime every bit as volatile and passionate as a spoken play. Having acted in high school plays, I knew how exciting it was to hear the applause of an appreciative audience. After the one-hour performance composed of several vignettes, John and I clapped until we notice most of the audience was waving their hands in the air. We extended our arms and waved in rhythm with the crowd.

When Amy was a senior at NSD, at last I saw her play basketball. She's competitive and gave the sport her all. I was surprised when a personal foul was called on her for hitting an opponent in the stomach with her elbow. After the game I asked her about the incident.

"Number six on the other team fouled me many times," Amy said. "Ref and coach never saw it because she did it behind their backs."

"What did she do?" I asked.

"Stomped on my foot two times and shove her elbow in my back two times."

"Why didn't you tell the coach?"

"Would not help, so I hit her."

"What did the girl say when you hit her?"

"Oofh!" Amy did a great mime of her action and the response of the girl she hit. "After that she left me alone."

In spite of Amy's unsportsmanlike conduct, I chuckled. Amy has always refused to let anyone get the best of her for long. Her opponent learned a painful lesson that night.

45

The Big Question
Rebecca and Amy

I love movies, and like many other movie buffs, memorable dialogue is incorporated into my everyday speech. One of my favorite lines was spoken by the little rabbit, Thumper, in *Bambi*. "If ya can't say nothin' nice, don't say nothing at all." Long ago I adapted that sentence to reflect one of my personal philosophies: "If ya don't want to know the answer, don't ask the question." Repeating that sentence saved me needless pain when going through my divorce and in other stressful situations.

But this philosophy has kept me from asking Amy important questions: *How do you feel about being deaf? Do you feel cheated? Are you upset because I attended all of John's school activities but missed most of yours?*

How do you feel about that, Amy? I know how I feel: lousy and sad. *Do you feel deprived of a family life?* I tried to do all the special things when you came home on weekends; I hope that was enough for you. It wasn't for me. *Did you ever wish you could have lived at home and gone to school in Grand Island like John did?* I do; I missed you, but I knew NSD was your best option. *Are you angry about being deaf?* I'm not, but I'm concerned about your survival in a hearing world. You've missed out on so much.

I need to ask Amy these questions. I want to know her answers. I've rehearsed them a thousand times in my head, but fear of her responses has paralyzed my tongue for years. Before Amy entered high school, I reasoned she was not old enough, nor did she have a broad enough perspective of life to give me a thoughtful answer. I can no longer use that excuse. Amy is eighteen. In less than a month, she'll graduate from high school and will leave for college. Her perspective of life encompasses more than Grand Island and the Nebraska School for the Deaf in Omaha. In the past ten years, John, Amy, and I have traveled over half of the United States, visited Mexico, and toured Europe, including countries behind the Iron Curtain. She's seen enough of the world to give me a thoughtful answer, and yet, I'm still afraid to ask the question.   ·

How will I react? If her answer is "Yes, I feel cheated," I'll be heart-broken, and will try to explain the decisions I made for her years ago. Telling her how hard it was for me to send her to school in Omaha will not lessen her pain and anger if she feels cheated.

If her answer is "No," I'll be relieved she's not bitter and resent-ful, but her answer will not lessen my selfish pain. She may not have suffered, but I have. I feel cheated that I could not participate in her life on a daily basis.

Today, we're shopping for jewelry to match her aqua prom dress that I finished hemming last night. Next week she will wear it to her senior prom. I will take a picture of her tonight in her finery, but that's not the same as seeing her leave for the prom with her date.

As we drive toward the mall, I realize there is no perfect moment to ask the big question. Time is fleeting. Soon she'll be at college, distancing herself further from me emotionally and physically. Now is the time. We are alone, confined in the car. She cannot look to John for answers or avoid my question by escaping to her bedroom. Amy is staring out her window.

I wave my hand in her peripheral vision to get her attention. She turns toward me, her face a question, waiting for me to continue. I inhale, gathering the strength to continue. "Amy, do you feel cheated because you didn't get to live at home like John did?" My mouth is dry. I'm glad she can't hear my voice quaver. "Were you unhappy that you had to spend most of your life away from your family, living at school in Omaha?"

Her brow forms a soft wrinkle, her eyes narrow, and she turns her head away just enough so that I cannot look into her eyes. Seconds pass. She licks her lips, something she does when concentrating.

My eyes dart from her to the busy street, and then back. Waiting, hoping, anxious for her response. My knuckles turn white, so tight is my grasp on the steering wheel. I need something to steady myself when she responds.

"No." Her voice has an I-never-gave-it-much-thought tone.

I wait, lean toward her, hoping for more. I want to know if she is happy in her silent world, a world I can't fathom. I'd find the absence of music, the chirping of birds, human voices, and years of separation from my family devastating, does she?

Her mouth moves to explain. "I've never known anything else."

I relax in my seat, loosen my grip on the steering wheel; the color returns to my knuckles. Perhaps we can discuss this again. Maybe she will elaborate on her answer if she has time to think about it. But, I know this is all she will say. Amy's answer is typical of her: succinct and conclusive.

"I have never known anything else," is what I told Mother when she thought I might have felt cheated since I was gone from my family most of the time. I told her this, because that is what I thought and felt. If I had ever experienced being a mainstreamed student and going home daily, I would have had an entirely different experience, and yet my answer would probably still be, "I have never known anything else."

I grew up with one kind of experience by attending the Nebraska School for the Deaf. I was there since age four until the day I graduated. It was a good place for me, because it was filled with Deaf culture, Deaf language, Deaf education, and Deaf activities. But best of all, I spoke with my hands to my friends using American Sign Language. I knew that school was my place to get an education and I had to be raised there instead at home.

Of course, it would have been nice to be home with my beloved cat, family, and my surroundings, but what choice did I have? Deaf school was my only path to success and I don't regret it. If I was mainstreamed, I might not be writing this book. My life would be completely different.

46

Graduation and College Bound

Rebecca and Amy

After starting school at sixteen months, seventeen years later Amy is finally receiving recognition for all her hard work. Not only is she valedictorian of her class, but she also receives several special awards and scholarships. During the course of the ceremonies, as each graduate's name is called, their family and friends are asked to stand. Amy has the largest group in attendance. My three sisters and their families, Jack and Linda with her two children, John, Amy's godmother, Mrs. Beatty, and my father are present. I'm sad my mother isn't here; she'd be so proud of her namesake. Mother died two years ago after several grueling years of fighting bone cancer.

This fall Amy will attend Gallaudet University in Washington, D.C., and John will return to the University of Nebraska in Lincoln. Student loans for John, and scholarships, assistance from the Buffett Foundation, and my purse make it possible for her to attend Gallaudet.

As I prepare to endure the expense of having two children in college, my friend Pat brings me a small gift. I open the package and discover a mug filled with new pencils. On the mug is written, "Pencils 5 Cents." I chuckle as I pour her a glass of iced tea and we prepare to play cribbage.

Amy's NSD high school graduation. May 1987. Jack, Amy, John, and Rebecca Willman.

"Look at this." I show her a small silver dish with a cork liner.

"What is it?" Pat shuffles the cards.

"My sister Helen sent it to me. It's a fancy dish for a bottle of wine, but Helen said with two kids in college next year, I might want to use it as an offering plate."

"Looks like one, that's for sure." Pat searches her purse, retrieves a dime and places it in the silver plate.

"Thanks. I need all the help I can get."

All the activities I participated in at NSD added to my educational experience. At NSD I learned about Gallaudet University, the only deaf liberal arts university in the world.

I never really knew about Gallaudet until I was a seventh grader. One of my seven subjects was study hall. So, I spent fifty minutes daily at the library. Sometimes I studied and did my homework and other times I just explored the bookshelves. One shelf was filled with Gallaudet College *Tower Clock* books from the 1960s and 1970s. The *Tower Clock* is Gallaudet's college yearbook. I was curious, which led me to read the books. There were some funny pictures in the books. I wondered why the students did these things and my classmates and I discussed the photos and laughed about them.

Amy and Marge Beatty, her godmother and preschool Deaf teacher, at Amy's graduation, 1987.

One day I discovered some of my NSD teachers and staff were in the *Tower Clock* yearbook. I asked Bruce Becker, the houseparent for the high school boys, about the pictures.

He told me, "Go to Gallaudet when you graduate and find out for yourself."

Other graduates from Gallaudet at NSD told me, "Go to Gallaudet. You will love it for sure."

Ironically, graduates from Gallaudet told me to look up Phi Kappa Zeta and encouraged me to join that sorority. (Many years later I did, and joined it!)

As I read and looked through the pictures and stories from the yearbook, I thought to myself, why did the students dress up like that? There were photos of sororities and fraternities doing their probation with uniforms. Other photos were of rat funerals and naked streaking by students. The *Tower Clock* books made me really very, very curious. Teachers and staff at NSD encouraged me to attend there.

At that time, Gallaudet was the only Deaf liberal arts college in the world. I thought it was awesome. Later in high school, I learned there were other Deaf colleges combined with hearing colleges, but I continued to tell myself, I will apply to only one college: Gallaudet.

To be accepted, you must be fluent in sign, which is no problem for me, and capable of doing college-level courses. Many applicants must attend a year of preparatory classes before being admitted as a freshman, but I was accepted as a freshman. Assistance from the Buffett Foundation and Mother made it possible for me to attend Gallaudet.

John overdrew his bank account several times when he was a freshman at the university. To ensure this does not happen with Amy, I open a checking account for her in June so I will know she is capable of managing her finances at Gallaudet this fall. I explain to Amy that her account has no monthly fee, but she'll be charged ten cents for each check written. In July, Amy and her friend Angie, who graduated two years ago from NSD, arrange to meet at the mall to shop for clothes. Angie will return to the National Technical Institute for the Deaf in Rochester, New York, this fall to finish her degree. Amy grabs the car keys. "I'll be back in three or four hours."

Fifteen minutes later she stomps into the house, fuming.

"What is the matter, Amy?"

She pulls her bank book from her purse. "I went to money machine for $20 and the paper says I have $106.37 in the bank. My book says $106.97. Where is my sixty cents?"

"Let me see your checkbook." I examine her check register noting that she has failed to subtract the ten cent fee for checks she wrote. "Amy, you wrote six checks last month, so you need to sub . . ."

"What! The bank did nothing." Amy snatches the checkbook from my hand and scribbles something in it. "They're ripping me off."

I laugh, having felt the same way. "Well, Amy, I suggest you take a number and get in line. Thousands of people feel the same way."

As Amy backs the car down the driveway, I realize my concern that she'd overdraw her checking account was unfounded. This is the child who counted her money every week when she came home from NSD to make sure John and I had not taken so much as a penny from her mailbox bank.

Preparing Amy for college is not much different than preparing her for NSD. The main difference is the drive time, and the amount of paperwork to complete. John's college classes start two weeks after Amy's so I plan to make the journey to Washington a vacation. We'll visit the Amish country, Philadelphia, Atlantic City, and tour the monuments in Washington before taking Amy to Gallaudet.

In mid-July Gallaudet sends an envelope of forms: health insurance, roommate preference, arrival information, and a huge psychological evaluation. Some of the words in this form are unfamiliar to Amy, so I sit with her to explain words as she completes it.

While I have struggled most of my adult life with feelings of inadequacy by trying to achieve perfection, Amy's answers reveal she is more confident than I am, and probably better adjusted.

"How many more? We already do one hundred." Amy asks, impatient to be finished with the questionnaire.

"About fifteen." I inhale and read, "Have you ever contemplated suicide?" Knowing that the suicide rate is high among deaf people due to their isolation, I'm interested in Amy's response.

"No. Never. Why would I do that?" Her pen makes a slash through the "no" box.

My tense shoulders relax. I'd like to take the credit for raising a well-adjusted, confident daughter, but I'm not sure I had much to do with it. By the grace of God, Amy is becoming a woman who will accomplish much due to her positive attitude and determination.

That night at supper, Amy seems lost in thought. John and I try to engage her in conversation, but she is uninterested. When I serve dessert, I see tears in her eyes.

"Amy, what's the matter? Don't you feel well?"

"I'm fine."

"If you're fine, why are you crying?" John asks.

"I'm not crying." She brushes tears from her cheeks.

A list of Amy's possible concerns race through my head. Maybe she's worried about being so far away from home. No, I don't think so. She's boarded at school for years. She's accustomed to being away from her family. Perhaps she doesn't want to go to college. That can't be it; she's talked about attending Gallaudet for the last two years. None of her classmates are going there; maybe she's afraid of not having any friends.

"Something is bothering you. What is it?" I ask.

"What if I fail? Maybe I can't do the homework at Gallaudet?" Amy says.

I'm surprised. I did not think failure was in Amy's vocabulary, not an option for her. "Amy, I don't see how you could fail. You are a good student, used to getting As and Bs. The classes will be harder so you might have some Cs the first year, but I am sure you can do the work."

"I don't want to fail."

"Study hard; you will do fine."

Amy's freshman year at Gallaudet does not include failure—instead it is filled with more new experiences.

47

Gallaudet, New Horizons

Amy

After I graduated from high school, I went to Gallaudet as a freshman. My five years of being a Gallaudet student were some of my best times, and I am grateful that NSD teachers and staff told me to go there. Later in life I met deaf people who attended public school. They had never heard of Gallaudet, and thus missed their opportunity to attend a Deaf college.

When I enrolled at Gallaudet, I didn't know what major I wanted, as I was not sure what I want to do in the future. I decided that I should major in studio arts as I love to do house decorations and painting. Then I realized there might not be any jobs for me in that field, so I added elementary education to my major.

During my freshman year at Gallaudet, 1987 to 1988, there were big changes on the campus. First, Gallaudet changed from a college to a university at that time, so those of us who were freshman became the first university students. I was so proud to be a Gallaudet University student.

The biggest change that happened in my freshman year was the Deaf President Now movement in March of 1988. What caused this? A new president, Dr. Elisabeth Zinser, a hearing person who knew little about Deaf culture and was not familiar with American Sign Language, was selected to be the new president of Gallaudet. The Gallaudet students protested, because we wanted a Deaf president to run the university, someone who understood our needs and culture. Even though the Board of Trustees had selected the hearing person, we students protested and were on the national news.

When Mother saw the news, she was worried I might be arrested, because she remembered what happened to the Vietnam War protesters years ago, but that did not happen to us. The newsmen were on our side. It was a quite an experience for me when I marched to the U.S. Capitol. I was thrilled it happened during my first year. What a good start for my years at Gallaudet.

I strongly agreed with the protest and supporting it was worthwhile. Since Gallaudet University is the only Deaf university, I believe it needs to have a Deaf president that understands Deafness and our needs and culture. Gallaudet was established in 1864, and in 1988 Dr. I. King Jordan became our first Deaf president. He did an excellent job improving and serving Gallaudet during his years as president. He retired in 2006 and then Gallaudet had their second Deaf president, Dr. Robert Davila for several years. Now, Gallaudet has their third Deaf president, Dr. Alan Hurwitz.

At the Nebraska School for the Deaf, I was involved in many activities. When I entered Gallaudet, I was so glad I had learned so many basic skills from NSD. Naturally, I learned more at Gallaudet because it has bigger organizations and more people to manage at the meetings. There I enjoyed being an officer or chairperson of a committee. Today, I still do this when the opportunities are just right for me. I grab at the chance to serve Deaf community organizations.

At Gallaudet, I became a member of Phi Kappa Zeta in the fall of 1989, a social sorority. It is the oldest sorority on Gallaudet campus, founded 1892. Phi Kappa Zeta is only a local Greek organization; no other universities or colleges have this sorority. It was a really awesome experience to have sorority sisters. I loved being involved in rush parties, pledge programs, community events, and other activities where my sisters and I worked together. Some of the volunteer work I did with my sisters was similar to what I did for other organizations on campus.

What did I do during my five years at Gallaudet? I was very busy all the time. In my freshman year, basically, I was just a freshman, but I was on the Rock Festival committee in spring time. I signed up for the party cleaning committee. So, my duty was to clean the dock when Rock Festival ends. Picking up plastic cups and other garbage was not fun as my hands were so DIRTY! At least I did something during my freshman year.

In my sophomore year, I decided I needed to be more involved in any kind of organization. So I became a Volunteer Student Residential Advisor, volunteered at the *Tower Clock* and the Rock Festival (this time, I had a better job on the admission committee. I collected tickets). I also volunteered for the class of 1991 committees. We raised money for our class so we could have a senior trip and plant a tree on campus with a memorial slab in honor of our class. On these committees I had various duties from selling tickets, food, and tee shirts to decorating and cleaning up afterwards. During spring breaks in my college years, I went to Puerto Rico and Venezuela with my college friends.

My junior and senior years were similar. I was the layout editor of the *Tower Clock,* for two years. The yearbook is called the *Tower Clock,* because at the front entrance of the campus there is a large tower clock attached to Chapel Hall. It is a landmark on the campus. That building and the clock tower were some of the first buildings constructed on the campus in 1864. My duty as layout editor was to design each page and to insert the pictures and text. During these years I was involved a lot with my sorority and class of 1991 events. I joined intramural sports to keep in shape and was on a team with my sorority sisters. We were the intramural champions in both volleyball and basketball. I worked as residential advisor at Benson Hall during my junior year. During my senior year, I was in the play, *Circus in the Wind.* I acted as a clown. It was a fun and reminded me of the pleasure I had performing in plays at NSD. I wish I could have acted in more plays during my years at Gallaudet, but at least I did it once, better than nothing.

In my second year as a senior, I was a student development advisor. I did this on the Northwest Campus (NWC). The NWC is the preparatory school affiliated with Gallaudet located in another part of Washington, D.C. Their purpose is to assess a student's need and improve their knowledge in various subjects so they may be admitted to Gallaudet as a freshman. I was not a preparatory student at the

NWC, so I wanted to work at the NWC to experience what life was like on the other campus. While working at the NWC, I was also a sponsor for their yearbook.

To be active in events on the Gallaudet campus was a great experience, as well as fun. I learned how to be a leader and how to work on a team with other chairpersons or committees. Some of these experiences I had learned at NSD, but I expanded on them while at Gallaudet.

While doing all of these things, I found time to study and earned my bachelor's degree in elementary education and studio arts.

Then, I decided to earn a master's degree. Therefore, I went to Western Maryland College in Westminster, Maryland, now known as McDaniel College, to pursue a master's degree in Deaf Education. While doing this, I was as a teacher at Kendall Demonstration Elementary School (KDES), which is on the Gallaudet campus. It is an elementary school for Deaf children who live in the area surrounding Washington, D.C.

For two-and-a-half years, I taught at KDES during the daytime and at night attended graduate classes. One year during my postgraduate courses, I worked as a development educational specialist and conducted educational workshops for the preparatory students at the NWC. I developed workshops on how to study better in college, how to adapt to college life, and where to go if you have problems at your job or on campus. I did all of this to gain experience in different types of jobs and to work with the students and additional people in administration.

These years were some of the craziest moments in my life; being a teacher, working on the NWC, and attending graduate classes in the evening as a full-time student. It was a great experience to do so many tasks all at the same time. My life was really hectic during graduate school, but I accomplished it all, earned my master's degree, and added many new experiences to my life. I was now ready to step into a real world job because I had outstanding experiences during my Gallaudet years. I searched for an elementary teaching position.

48

No Choice,
Mainstreamed in 1994
Amy

I was not mainstreamed in my early school years, but I was when I was a student at Western Maryland College and at the University of Maryland. I attended these colleges while working on my master's degree. Both are regular colleges, primarily for hearing students, so I understand what it's like to be mainstreamed, as well as to attend classes just for Deaf students.

Was it easy for me to learn in classes with the help of interpreters? I will say it was an interesting experience for me. I was the only Deaf student in the entire hearing class at the University of Maryland, but I was so focused on my interpreter for the entire class, I often forgot there were other people in the classroom. Learning with an interpreter is difficult, because sometimes the interpreter's signs do not keep pace with what teacher and classmates are saying. Sometimes, I could not identify who was talking if two people were talking at the same time. I just got the information of what they were saying from the interpreter, but not who was talking. Also, shifting words from English to ASL is not always easy. By the end of first day of class, I felt my eyeballs would pop out from sockets due to staring at the interpreter for hours and hours. Focusing through an interpreter was difficult for me as an adult; I can only imagine how hard this would be for a child.

At Western Maryland College, some of the classes I took were taught by Deaf professors and others by hearing professors that required interpreters. That meant I could sign and not have to be 100 percent focused on interpreters. A nice break for my eyes!

I look back and wonder, if I had not attended NSD, but was mainstreamed into public schools in my home, which had big schools, I'm sure I would have felt so lost and lonely. As an adult, being mainstreamed, these feelings were not so strong, because I had many Deaf friends I could see when not in class. But as a kid being mainstreamed, trying to make friends and be in school activities that would have been very difficult.

Mainstreaming may not be the best choice for every deaf student, some might succeed and some fail, but as for me, I would prefer that every deaf student to be send to Deaf school. Why? Socialization. This is the major part of life that many mainstreamed students miss.

When mainstreaming deaf children in a regular school, it can be either for better or worse. It depends on what and how the school district provides for each deaf child. In big cities, the deaf may all be put in one public school where they can socialize with each other and the education may be good. In small or rural cities, due to lack of interpreters or the teacher's experience as a deaf educator, the deaf child may not receive good education. Not only that, the worst is the deaf child's lack of social life. It is possible the deaf child might be the only deaf person in the whole public school.

Most former mainstreamed students who are adults now that I know, have told me they regret or wish they had attended a Deaf school. For some that decision was made by their parents; in other cases the deaf person chose to be mainstreamed.

The mainstreamed students I know lack experiences in social life skills, athletics, and participation in organizations. At NSD, I was able to be part of all the activities. Most mainstreamed Deaf students can't accomplish this. Many hearing parents are not aware their deaf child has an inner desire to be part of Deaf culture, the Deaf community, and use ASL.

For example, at Gallaudet, during homecoming, we had a spirit week that included many activities. Students who had attended Deaf schools were aware of this, because that was something we did at Deaf school. During spirit week, many mainstreamed students were not aware of the activities and didn't understand why it's important to be part of such fun, because they had never experienced it.

In addition, the mainstreamed students often had not belonged to any organizations or clubs, so they did not understand the process of conducting a meeting or how to organize an event. The mainstreamed students usually never had a chance to experience what most Deaf students did like have a social life, act in a drama, play sports, or know ASL. Their "lost years" are regained by being a member of Deaf community in adult life.

There is a very strong chance that deaf students who are mainstreamed will be isolated from their peers at school. They are not as likely to be involved in sports or clubs because of the lack of communication. Mainstreamed deaf students are mostly on their own when classes end. Interpreters usually provide their service only during class, not at lunch, recess, or after school, so the deaf students have little chance to make friends and become involved socially. Mainstreamed deaf students usually just go home when school classes are finished.

Some deaf students who are mainstreamed are lucky because there are a large number of deaf students in their school, but this is not common. Unfortunately, most mainstreamed deaf students are the only deaf student in the entire school, so they feel very isolated and different.

Deaf children need socialization at home, as well as at school. It can be difficult for a deaf child, whether they are mainstreamed or attend residential school, if their family is not able to sign or communicate with them. If the deaf child has hearing parents, there may be a limited amount or a lack of communication skills within the family. If the parents of a deaf child make an effort to learn ASL that would be great, because the deaf child could be a part of the family.

There is a unique unconditional love in a deaf child's family, but that love may not be enough. As for me, I never had a desire to be mainstreamed. I enjoyed being at a residential school, because it gave me the chance to be part of everything, and especially to socialize with my peers through ASL. With my experience of being a main-streamed student in college, I cannot imagine myself like that for all of my school days; it would have been too difficult. I wouldn't be what I am today if I had been mainstreamed as a child, because my education and social skills would have suffered.

49

Deaf in the Hearing World

Amy

Many people wonder what it's like to be deaf. Are Deaf people hiding inside their homes to avoid hearing society? What can they do to make their life interesting and amusing? Perhaps hearing people think that deaf people can't really experience life or accomplish anything. They may wonder if Deaf people have real lives, something beyond Deafness.

YES! Some Deaf may hide in their homes, but that is not for me and most Deaf people. We are no different than people in the hearing society; some accomplish a lot, and others do very little. I have many accomplishments and experiences in my life beyond Deafness. I believe if you want to do something, you can just do it, no matter if you are Deaf or hearing. I have done many things in my life as a Deaf person in a hearing world.

As a teenager, for two summers, I worked as a corn detasseller, the only jobs available to fourteen- and fifteen-year-old kids, except for babysitting, which I never did. The work was hot and dirty, but I made money. Once in a while I worked at my father's grocery store. Both of these jobs were in the hearing society. Even though I interacted with the hearing people, I didn't really communicate with them much as my job was something I did as an individual. Both jobs gave me good experiences and added some delight in my life.

For six or seven hours a day I walked through miles of corn stalks snapping off the tassel, high on the top of the corn plant. If it rained that day or the day before, it was very dirty work slopping through the mud. One morning when I was going to work in the corn fields, I got on the wrong bus. My crew leader was working with another group, and I followed her onto the bus instead of going with my regular bus and crew. I was surprised to see all boys on the bus because boys and girls did not work in the same fields. My crew leader said to me, "What are you doing here?"

I said, "I don't know. I thought this was where I was supposed to be. I followed you."

While the crew I should have been with was already in the field working, I was riding a bus in another direction. The ride went on for a long time. I just sat back and relaxed. I did not know it but, the assistance crew leader had called my mother at work and asked, "Where is Amy? She is always here every day. Is she sick?"

"What?" My mother said. "I left her at the bus pick up point at 6:30 this morning. Where is she?"

Neither my mother nor the boss knew where I was. Later the supervisor called my mother and said, "Don't worry. I found Amy. She got on the wrong bus. We'll see she gets to where she belongs."

That night when Mother got home from work she asked me, "Were you worried or scared when you realized you were on the wrong bus?"

I said, "No, I thought I was getting a little vacation. I was glad I did not have to work!"

After earning my master's degree, I decided I wanted to live in the southwest, as I never had been there. I applied and got a job as a middle school teacher at the Deaf school in Santa Fe, New Mexico. I taught there one year, and for the next six years I was an ASL instructor for the Interpreter Program at Santa Fe Community College. Wow!

During my time in New Mexico, I directed a school play, obtained my scuba diving license, and was treasurer for the American Sign Language Teachers Association of New Mexico. On the weekends, to gain more experience and to see what I could accomplish in hearing society, I worked at the GAP store. My job was as a stock person. I put clothes on the shelves or unpacked the clothes that had just been shipped to the store. It was a much different experience than working the in the cornfield. At the GAP, I had to interact with hearing employees. I communicated through paper and pen. When they had a meeting, they hired an interpreter. I worked there for about four-and-a-half years. The best part of that job was I could buy clothes at half price. I did it with a big grin on my face!

During the six years I live in New Mexico, I traveled throughout the Land of Enchantment, which is rich with many cultures and old ruins. I even visited the bat cave, Carlsbad Cavern. I also took a cruise that I won to the Bahamas with my brother.

In 2001, I decided to reach a higher goal. I became an ASL coordinator and lecturer at the University of Nebraska in Lincoln (UNL), so I moved back to my home state after being away for fourteen years. For some people what I have accomplished would be enough, but not for me.

My work at the university is with hearing students and staff. So far I have received four awards. Twice the University of Nebraska Parent's Association has awarded me a Certificate of Recognition for Contributions to Students, and I have received five years and ten years of service awards from UNL. While working at the University of Nebraska–Lincoln, I have given numerous presentations and workshops, and was a sponsor of Friends of the Deaf Community, an undergraduate organization.

I have been involved in the American Sign Language Teacher Association, National Association of the Deaf, Gallaudet University Alumni Association, and Nebraska School for the Deaf Alumni Association of which I have been on the Board of Trustees for three terms. I was the program book chairperson for the NSD Alumni Association in 2009 and Chairperson for the NSDAA 2012 Conference.

Also, I am involved with a local Deaf club and have served on several event committees, such as banquet chairperson. From 2005 to 2010, I was a judge for the Nebraska oratory contest for Deaf and hard of hearing students.

Because of my love of cats, since the spring of 2007, I have been a volunteer at The Cat House, a nonprofit no-kill cat shelter. There I clean, feed, and play with the kitties. The cats don't care that I am Deaf. I adopted three beautiful white kittens who are deaf. Now I have five cats, two hearing and three deaf.

Amy swimming with the stingrays on our Eastern Caribbean cruise taken for John and Amy's fortieth birthday, November 2007.

Some people thought that when I moved back to Nebraska and took a higher level job that would be enough for me. That there was nothing else I could do to gain more experience. WRONG! I still go all-out to see something new, and I will never stop doing this until the day I die.

Since returning to Nebraska, I have visited more countries and taken several cruises. I can't name all countries I have visited but I went to North and South America, Honduras, Jamaica, Barbados, Antigua, Australia, China, Europe, and many other Caribbean islands. During my trip to Australia with a deaf friend in 2005, I went to the Deaf Olympics. It was great seeing an international gathering of Deaf people. In the fall of 2008, I went with three other the deaf friends on a tour with hearing people to China. I climbed the Great Wall, saw the Forbidden City, and other sights. It was an amazing trip! I have been excited to visit all these different places, because I enjoying sight-seeing and learning about different cultures, food, and history.

How could I afford all this travel? I have always worked since I was fifteen and saved my money. Before I went to college Mother paid for our trips, but we always had to earn our own spending money.

On vacation she would not buy us any souvenirs or extra treats; she expected us to earn money for that. I learned at a young age to save and plan for vacations. I had a bank that looked like a green mailbox with a red flag when I was a child. It had a small padlock and I always locked it to make sure John or Mother did not take my money. I did not take my green mailbox to NSD, as someone might have taken the money. Every week when I came home, I made sure to the last penny that all my money was there, even though Mother and John told me, "We would never take your money." But I had to be sure.

Many people, especially hearing, think that Deaf people can't do this and that, because they can't hear. That's not true, but of course there are communication barriers. Everyday our barriers are the same as for hearing people who travel at foreign lands and do not know the language. We are often unable to communicate or understand what is happening. To deal with this when traveling, I depend on information from books or brochures distributed at museums and historical places. If there is no interpreter or any text to read, I find a way to get the information by asking people questions, gesturing, or using writing. I do this because I want to see, experience, understand, and accomplish much in my life.

For me, this is what life is all about, to see and experience the world before you are no longer alive. So, for me, life beyond Deafness does not mean "I can't do this or that because I am living in hearing society," I just go for it. And that shows I can, I will, and I did.

Now you know life beyond Deafness in the hearing world does not have to be empty or boring. I have seen and done more in the hearing society than many hearing people have. A Deaf person's life can be filled with many amusing and exciting adventures. Deaf people must reach for it, just as I did.

Many people, Deaf or hearing, would be pleased with what I have accomplished, and relax, but not me. Shooting for the stars is not enough; I am going for the universe.

50

Deaf or deaf,
Does It Matter?

Amy

Through this book you might have noticed there are two different terms: Deaf and deaf. The big D and the small d. Is this a mistake? No. Does it matter if deaf is spelled Deaf or deaf? Yes, it does. A person is defined by being either Deaf or deaf. The basic definition of Deaf and deaf is this. Using a capital d, Deaf, describes a person who identifies themselves as culturally deaf. This person will use ASL and usually does not see deafness as a disability. A lowercase-d, deaf, is a person who has a slight hearing loss, little or no connection to deaf culture and ASL, and might consider deafness as a disability. Not all deaf people are Deaf.

Some people with a hearing loss will be Deaf—others will be deaf; it depends on the person's background. Some deaf adults started as deaf, and later in life became Deaf. For example, a person with a hearing loss might have been mainstreamed into a public school and used a different method of sign language and spoken language. Then, in adult life, that person became involved with the Deaf community and changed their language to ASL. Therefore that person with a little d became a big D and now considers themselves Deaf, a part of Deaf culture. People who consider themselves deaf usually are not found in the Deaf community and remain in the hearing society.

We Deaf have our own culture. What is it? Deaf culture defines who we are and how we live. Deaf culture describes many things such as social behaviors, art, literature, history, and values. Deaf people attend Deaf clubs and organizations that support Deaf issues and understand history related to our deafness. In Deaf environments, we use flashing lights instead of noise for fire alarms, door bells and warning devices. Lights alert us to telephone calls and that someone is at our door. Pounding the table is used to get someone's attention, and hand waving is used for that and to show appreciation. Deaf people also share common feelings or experiences or situations in the community, and our main communication is American Sign Language.

ASL is a very expressive language. Deaf people use facial expressions and nonmanual behaviors for ASL grammar. When using ASL, your eye brows, head movements, and eye gaze are clues to what you are signing. These are called nonmanual behaviors. Their main function is grammar, but they have some emotive purpose. Is it a question? Is it a rhetorical question? Is it an angry or happy comment? Hearing people do this with their tone of voice. For example, "Oh, wonderful!" can be sarcastic or a happy expression.

Deaf do not understand the tone of a spoken voice, or puns and idioms in the spoken language. ASL has its own idioms. For example, if hearing people are talking and someone joins them and asks, "Tell me what you are talking about?" instead of stopping and starting the conversation all over, they might say, "Sorry you missed it. I will tell you later." If this happened to Deaf people, they would sign, TRAIN-GONE, which means the same.

Another example, for Deaf people, is about asking a "wh" question. If the first two letters of the word begin with " wh"—why, when, where, etc.—this is called a wh-question. When signing wh-questions, a person lowers their eyebrows and leans forward to represent the grammar in ASL. If the person raises their eyebrows, that indicates the question only needs a "yes" or "no" answer. There are many different ways to use the eyebrows to define the meaning of ASL grammar. The same is true for head movements and eye gaze. The use and understanding of facial expression is part of Deaf culture, something hearing people may not understand.

As Deaf people, my friends and I sometimes wish there were more Deaf people in the world. Many hearing people do not understand us. If most of the people in the world were Deaf, the hearing people might understand what it is like to be Deaf. They would have to adjust, and use an interpreter or they would not understand what is going on around them. They would need to learn to adapt like the Deaf people have. Could they do it? Yes for some, no for others.

The Deaf have a good advocate with the National Association of the Deaf (NAD). This group works to make Deaf people equal with hearing people at jobs, in school, and in daily life. NAD works to pass laws beneficial to Deaf and investigates discrimination complaints they receive. You do not have to be a member of the NAD to report an incident to them.

If a parent of a deaf child is having difficulty with their school board, the NAD may become personally involved if it is an unusual case. In any event, they will explain to the family their deaf child's right to an interpreter and the right to attend school in their home community. Similar things happen if a Deaf worker complains that his employer does not supply an interpreter for meetings. NAD will advise the Deaf worker and the employer of the law and what is re-quired. I have never been discriminated at my jobs. I guess I am lucky.

Getting jobs is easier if Deaf people work with other Deaf people, because we can communicate with ease and understand each other. I would prefer to work in a Deaf world, with just Deaf people around me, but for most Deaf people that is not possible. It would be easier for me to communicate if everyone around me was Deaf, but I still adjust anyway.

Deaf people can accomplish much in our Deaf world. Our world is smaller than hearing world, but Deaf people still have many of the same opportunities. I am a proud capital-d Deaf person.

51

Adapting to Live in Two Worlds: Hearing and Deaf

Amy

Since the day I was born, I have always lived in two worlds: a hearing world and a Deaf world. What is that like? How do Deaf people function and survive in two worlds, especially the hearing world? Can they do it? Yes!

For a Deaf person living in the hearing world, each day is like navigating through an asteroid belt composed of hearing people. Every day in the hearing world, we Deaf have to pass through and cross the orbits of hearing people. There is no way to avoid it. Many hearing people do not understand what Deaf people are capable of doing, and fewer yet understand our language, ASL, or our Deaf culture.

Traveling through the hearing world means I must be careful; colliding with an asteroid (a hearing person) can be painful to my feelings. I am an adult, and yet sometimes I am treated as if I need help, as if I were not smart. Worse than this is when I can read a hearing person's mind by their actions, or see pity in their eyes. I know they are thinking, "Oh, I am sorry you can't hear," or "It's too bad that you are deaf." Sometimes I wish I could tell them, "I'm sorry you can hear."

What is the main difference between our worlds? The language. In the Deaf world, everyone is moving their hands; in the hearing world, everyone is moving their lips. For me, the easiest way to communicate is with my hands, but that will not work in the hearing world.

The communication barrier is the most enormous asteroid Deaf people navigate when living in two worlds. In my daily life, I encounter many hearing people in the mall, grocery store, and convenience shops. These situations are generally easy, and I do not need the services of an ASL interpreter, because I can make a gesture, point to what I want, or use a Deaf person's always handy items: a paper and pen.

Writing requests may confuse hearing people; they are not sure what to do. For example, at a restaurant, once food servers discover I am Deaf, often they talk louder. I can tell they are shouting by the way their mouth opens wide, but it does not change my inability to hear. On other occasions when I have gestured that I need a paper and pen, the restaurant server has stood there confused. I had to repeat the gesture of my fingers writing on my hand several times before the server brought me paper so I could write down what I wanted to order. This may be frustrating, but I don't need an interpreter when I dine out with friends or for normal shopping. Deaf people will always have a communication barrier with the hearing world, but in these circumstances, we can deal with it and easily solve it.

Sometimes when hearing people see a group of Deaf people signing, they make fun of us by making different gestures at us with their hands. My friends and I will then look at them, and make mouth movements, like "blah, blah, blah," then the hearing people stop making fun of us and leave us alone. One time a group would not stop. They made more gestures, so we made more mouth movements, after awhile we knew we were just teasing each other, so we did not get upset or hurt. We thought it was funny. It was like a competition. Guess what? We won!

The only time I require an ASL interpreter is for events or meetings where I must understand exactly what is being said, such as business workshops, a legal meeting, banking business, a doctor's appointment, or at a drama. The main advantage of having an interpreter in these circumstances is that I can express my comments and questions in my own language, ASL, through an interpreter, and receive answers in a language I understand. The interpreter makes the meeting easy for the hearing person also. Indeed, we save a lot of time, and of course, many trees do not need to be chopped down to make all that paper.

Another asteroid Deaf people must cope with is communications at their work sites. Many devices are available that allow the Deaf to communicate easily, but sometimes employers do not have the devices available. Employers are required to provide such devices, but until an agreement can be reached on obtaining them, the Deaf worker may be frustrated.

A serious problem for Deaf people is the lack of visual messages and warnings. Many TV stations are getting better about putting weather warnings as a visual, not just a spoken announcement, which is helpful, but more needs to be done. In public buildings, Deaf people have no way to know about fire or other hazards, unless we watch other people.

One of the worst places for me and other Deaf people is the airport. When a flight is changed or delayed, we don't know what is going on, because most airline announcements are said over a microphone. This has happened several times to me, and I figured out what had occurred by looking at the other passengers' body language and facial expression, which were angry, or reflected, "What the heck is happening?"

One time I was flying home from Minneapolis. I was very tired and in a rush to get home. The flight was changed, and I missed it. I was so pissed off that I had to spend the night at a hotel. Because of this, I usually ask the airline staff several times through paper and pen if I am at the right gate. I am sure these problems occur with other forms of transportation also. This problem could be eliminated if airports and other transportation centers used computer-generated signs, instead of just audio announcements, so Deaf people could see important messages.

Deaf people miss most commercial messages on TV because they are not captioned, which is okay sometimes, and of course we miss all the information that is on the radio. Once John told me that the price of gasoline would be cheaper the next day, and for that day only.

I asked, "How do you know that?"

And he replied, "I heard it on the radio when I was driving home."

Lucky for me he told me, as I saved money, but without him telling me, I would never have known. There are many other places and occasions where Deaf people have limited understanding, but I manage to survive, and so do most other Deaf people.

While I live in two worlds, Deaf and hearing, most hearing people have never experienced my Deaf world. A hearing person attending a Deaf function will feel very left out (as I often do at hearing events) if they do not know ASL or have an interpreter with them. In the Deaf world, ASL allows me to communicate with ease, have free expression, and not be misunderstood. All our hands are moving nonstop. Our conversations are very animated. We have slang and dialects, just as the hearing world does. We discuss friends, family, work, and sports. In a group of Deaf people, I feel calm and peaceful. I have no limitations to my conversations, who I can talk to, and what I can say.

Our Deaf events are very visual. At meetings, we use signs and bulletin boards for information and directions. Hearing people may think our world is silent, but they are wrong. Our world is noisy too. Deaf people make sounds, such as stomping on the floor or pounding on a table to get someone's attentions. Others use their voice to yell an action. If someone is telling a story about a car accident, when they get to the part about the cars bumping each other, they might yell to make a noise. The sound is silent to us, but very loud in our Deaf environment.

A topic of interest to Deaf people is new technological advances that will help us. In the past twenty-five years, many devices have been invented that are useful to the Deaf and other handicapped people. These devices let Deaf people understand television programs, shop online, communicate over the telephone, and thus be more independent. Deaf adults no longer have to rely on their hearing children to make doctor appointments or make travel arrangements.

When I was a child, there were no closed captions on TV. Of course, I watched TV, but I had to use my imagination to make up a story about what was happening. If I was at home, my brother or mother would sometimes tell me what the program was about, not every detail, but at least I knew something. At residential school, my friends and I discussed what the people on TV might be talking about. Then in 1980, when I was eleven, closed-caption devices came on the market and Mother bought one.

The first closed-caption devices were huge, ugly brown boxes manufactured by Sears. I did not care about the beauty of the device, because I was thrilled I could understand the TV shows. Many of the shows I watched when I was younger were now being shown as reruns. I discovered I had a huge imagination. The programs were not like I had imaged at all! In many cases, what I imagined was better.

Since the captioning devices were expensive, Deaf had to pay more than hearing people just to watch the news and other programs. At first, very few programs had captions, and I would get pissed off when the captions were garbled or scrambled. Soon more and more programs had captions. In the 1990s, the Federal Communications Commission ruled that all TVs manufactured must have the ability to receive closed captions. This was a real blessing to Deaf people. Now I could not live without closed captions. But what has happened to my imagination? I still have it, but use it for other things, not for watching TV.

Until 1960, Deaf had to ask a hearing person to make telephone calls for them. This was a slow process, and invaded the deaf person's privacy. Hearing children born to deaf parents often became interpreters for their parents as they got older, and made telephone calls for them, but now with all the technology available to the deaf this is not really necessary. After the invention of the teletypewriter (TTY) or telecommunications device for the Deaf, as it is also called, all this changed. The first TTY I saw was a huge, ugly green machine. Later the machines were much smaller. A TTY allows a deaf, hard of hearing, or a speech-impaired person to use the telephone. Callers type messages back and forth to one another. One disadvantage is that both people on the telephone call, even if one is hearing, must have a TTY. Also, both people cannot type messages at the same time, so the conversations are slow.

At one time, Mother, John, and I owned TTYs. It was a great way to communicate, even though it was slow because I had to wait until the other person stopped typing, even if I knew that they were telling me, before I could begin typing. I could not interrupt our typed conversation like a hearing person can on the telephone by saying, "I know what you are talking about." In addition, I could only call people who had a TTY, not any other places.

In the 1990s, as result of the Americans with Disabilities Act, telephone relay service was started. This service is supported by a small charge on everyone's telephone bill. Check your bill; you are probably paying four or five cents a month so Deaf people can have relay operators. The relay service allowed Deaf people to call hearing people who do not have a TTY and vice versa. An operator, who can hear, relays the message to the Deaf on the TTY, and then reads and speaks the message the Deaf person has typed to the hearing person. This method of communication is still used, but most Deaf people today prefer the video relay service (VRS) to call hearing people and Video Phone (VP) to call deaf people, which became available after the year 2000.

The VRS equipment is free, one per each Deaf household. All you need to do is contact a company that provides VRS equipment and have a high speed internet connection at home. The company will install the equipment for you. A VRS caller uses a television or a computer with a video camera to contact a VRS communication assistant (CA) who knows ASL. The CA places the telephone call. If the call is to a hearing person, the CA interprets between the Deaf person and hearing person. If the call is to another Deaf person, I don't contact the CA but call directly to a Deaf person.

VRS is in high demand by Deaf, because it allows us to express our conversations in our own language, ASL. For many Deaf people, ASL is their first and true language, so it is a much easier way to communicate than by typing messages. Since the Deaf watch the telephone conversation on a video monitor, VRS allows Deaf people to fully express themselves through facial expressions and body language, which we cannot do with text. Also, both parties can talk or sign at the same time, like hearing people do on a telephone conversation, so calls do not take as long as they do on a TTY.

Other devices Deaf people use to adapt to the hearing world are lighted, flashing doorbells and telephone alerts. There are baby crying alert devices for Deaf parents who have either a deaf or hearing baby.

A light alerts the mother or father that the baby is crying in the other room. That's another good way for Deaf people to be independent and raise their family without any assistance from hearing people. And in case you wonder, hearing children with Deaf parents usually have no problem learning to speak, because most of the time there are other family members who hear and speak, such as grandparents, uncles, friends, neighbors, or siblings. And of course they can hear voices on the TV and radio.

These are the most common devices used in the Deaf world. But there are many other devices Deaf people can purchase that will fit their lifestyle and needs at home or at work. Deaf alarm clocks are either a light that flashes or a device that vibrates under your pillow. I used to have a vibrating alarm clock, but it really shook and scared me when it vibrated, so I switched to a flashing lamp so I can dream in peace and not be scared when I wake up. These simple devices mean I don't have to rely on hearing people, and I can be responsible for my daily life.

All of these devices can be very costly or free. It depends on the assistance programs in each state. Some states will provide a deaf person a voucher with a limited amount of money, which Nebraska does. Even with the voucher, I still had to spend extra money from my pocket, because the voucher was limited to certain devices. I am not complaining, the voucher was at least some help to me and other Deaf people who used it.

Just like hearing people, deaf people drive. While we cannot hear sirens, we watch for them. Our insurance does not cost any more than for hearing drivers. In Louisiana where my mother lives, it is possible to get a license plate for your car that indicates you are deaf, but I do not want that, because dishonest people could follow me and know where I live. Then they could rob my house while I am sleeping since they know I am deaf. Some deaf people have information on their drivers' license about their deafness, but not on their license plate. This is safer.

Deaf people can be very independent and are able to do most things on their own without the help of hearing people. Compared to fifty years ago, many hearing people thought that Deaf people couldn't do anything. Not even drive a car, raise a family, or attend school to learn to read and write. Naturally, through the years Deaf people fought for their rights and wanted to be equal with hearing people. Deaf people want equal insurance rates on our cars, equal salaries, closed captions on TV, and telephone access. We are no difference than hearing people, only our ears are silent.

Deaf people will always have to live in two worlds, but thanks to new technologies, we can do more on our own than in the past. We are very independent and able to adapt in the hearing world. I wonder, could hearing people survive in my Deaf world?!?

52

My Eyes Are My Ears

Amy

The day I was born it was snowing outside. Not an inch or two but plenty of snow, a blizzard that turned the world into a winter wonderland. Naturally, I don't remember the day I was born, but Mother told me about it.

I was born with two perfect, cute little ears that should have heard the sounds around me, but my ears never heard any sounds from the day I was born. Mother said the doctor who delivered me had just come from the bowling alley and wore a navy blue bowling shirt. My eyes first saw the color royal blue. Later in life, blue became my favorite color. My first memories are sight, not hearing, after I was born. Therefore, my eyes are my ears.

I don't know when or how I discovered I was Deaf. I feel so natural not hearing any sounds, because I never have. My silent ears are very peaceful, content not having to hear anything.

I remember Mother telling me about taking me to an audiologist for a hearing test. I sat in a small room with padded walls. Mother told me if I heard anything to raise my arm so the audiologist could identify what sound levels I could hear. For a while, I just sat and stared, I wondered when the audiologist would turn up the sounds. Actually, he did, but I could not hear them.

Finally, I heard a funny buzzing sound and raised my arm. The testing ended fast after I raised my arm. The result: I was identified as "profoundly deaf." Therefore, I was fitted for hearing aids. I remember the smelly, pink gooey stuff with an "eew" feeling when it was put inside of my ears to create ear molds for my hearing aids. I can still remember what company manufactured my hearing aids: Zenith. The aids were a very shiny gold color and expensive. I wore two mini gold bars, but they were worth nothing to my ears.

I had a two-pocket harness for my hearing aids. Each had a cord that went from the aid to my ear piece. One for my right ear, another for my left ear. Did I hear any sounds? Yes, I did, but I never was able to identify what the sounds were. Most of the time, the sounds I heard were like static. I don't remember how long I kept the aids on during the day, but I'm quite sure I slept without them.

At age four, I was enrolled in Prep 1 at the Nebraska School for the Deaf in Omaha. The school used total communication, which meant the teachers used voice and signs at the same time. I always wore my hearing aids during school hours, as required. If I didn't, a teacher would ask me, "Where are your hearing aids, Amy?"

I would wear my aids, but seldom turned them on during class hours, because all I heard was noise or static, and I disliked that sound. Therefore, my teachers always checked my aids to make sure they were turned on, the batteries were good, and the volume set on high so I could hear what they were saying or if they called my name. Ironic isn't it? I don't think I ever responded to sound, but when I happened to turn my head, I'm sure the teachers praised me for doing that. My responses must have been just pure luck!

Sometimes the hearing aids were in my way, because the pockets for the hearing aids were on the outside of my clothing. When I was signing one day, I accidently caught one of the cords with my fingers, and my ear mold flew out of my ear. This did not happen ten times, but millions. Wearing body aids on top of my clothes did not suit me well, so the problem was solved by having me wear my two pockets inside of my clothes. That way, it wouldn't be in the way when I was signing, but it made more static.

Hearing aids for my ears didn't last long, because they didn't suit me well. I wore my hearing aids from when I was one year old until I was a third grader, about age nine. That was when I had my first deaf teacher, and I realized hearing aids were useless and worthless.

All I ever heard was NOISE and STATIC, such as my classmates yelling, or pounding their feet or hands to get somebody's attention. Or dragging a chair or desk across the floor instead of picking it up. Actually, it is very noisy at a deaf school, not quiet as many hearing people might imagine.

Were hearing aids worth it to me? I only wore my hearing aids during class hours at school. After school, I always took them off. I felt my ears were at a better place then. I used my eyes all the time, not my ears, because I watched others signing with my eyes. My ears did not benefit me much compared to my eyes.

My eyes are worth more to me than my ears because my eyes gave me an education, not my ears. My ears give me NOTHING, and hearing aids just gave me noise. I was so glad to give away my two mini gold bars at a young age. My ears are in a happy place because it's pure silence. I understand sounds through my eyes, not ears. My eyes gave me a language that I can use to communicate with others, not my ears. My eyes gave me laughter, not my ears. I see birds singing when they move their beaks. Or hear raindrops by watching them splash on the street. I even see music when colorful lights change through beating vibrations. My eyes are my music. My eyes are my life. Therefore, my eyes are my ears.

53

Concluding Thoughts

Amy and Rebecca

Sadly, there is no deaf school in Nebraska. NSD closed in 1998. All deaf children are placed in mainstream programs now. As I reflect on my education, I know that going to a residential school gave me the opportunity to be part of many activities compared to what I could have done if I were mainstreamed. Because of this, I would prefer that deaf students go to school that is just for the deaf, so they can socialize with their peers. The NSD campus was sold to a religious organization. An NSD museum is still there on the campus for now. Who knows what the future will bring to it.

I continue to travel. In 2011, I visited my fiftieth state, Alaska, with John, Mother, and Walt on a cruise. All I can say . . . Alaska is so beautiful in every corner. I had another first on this trip that I did with just my brother John: we flew in a seaplane. It was a fun experience to fly in an airplane and land on water instead of runaway.

In Alaska, Walt and I went zip lining. It was so much fun. Mother and John did not go because they do not like heights. I do have fear of heights but I can (try to) overcome. Mother and John were too chicken to go! On my first zip lining ride, I was very nervous and scared inside but did not show it. After the second and third, I loved it. I had a great time with Walt. He does not sign, but uses gestures or writes notes. We mostly do activities together.

We all rode on a helicopter and landed on a glacier. It was my second time to ride in a helicopter. Several years ago Mother, John, and I went to Hawaii again. Grandma Schmierer did not go with us this time as she had passed away. We went for my thirtieth birthday. Mother paid my way. John came along, but he had to pay his way. Ha! This time, I was on the big island of Hawaii and saw volcanoes flowing with lava while riding on a helicopter. That was my first helicopter ride. It was a thrilling sight to the lava slowing moving from the volcano into the sea! In the volcano park, we walked on dried lava rocks and through old lava tunnels that smelled of sulfur airs, which made me sick; I threw up. Not a very good memory.

One day we went to a beach to try boogie boards, which is like body surfing. While in the ocean, John heard something and told me to look where he pointed. I saw a humpback whale jumping out of the water twice. It was an amazing sight. It was a very far distance, but it looked pretty big. I can imagine if I it was right by me, it would be a very HUGE whale.

Soon I will have another trip to Hawaii. My high school class at NSD planned for a senior trip to Hawaii, but the school administration said no so my classmates are going there in May of 2012 for our twenty-fifth class reunion.

On almost every trip with my family, what I choose for us all to do was usually the best and the most fun. In the Virgin Islands, I chose to go on a Breathing Observation Submersible Scooter. Mother, Walt, and John were not sure about this, but they went anyway. We rode scooters under the water with a breathing tank attached. It was like SCUBA on a scooter. We had a fun time, because it was something different. I think my choices are better, because I choose something that will be more visual.

Mother, John, and I have taken many trips and cruises together. We still do this as adults and now Walt joins us. I also have traveled with my Deaf friends. I love to travel and see the world through my eyes.

You might wonder do I ever travel with my dad? I did, but only when John and I were preteens. My dad took my brother and me to Worlds of Fun and Oceans of Fun in Kansas City two different summers for a long weekend. I loved to ride on the roller coasters. Dad just let John and I do what we wanted. John and I rode on a double loop roller coaster. Dad refused to ride on it as he was little scared about the loops.

The water park was fun, since I love WATER. I rode on several waterslides. Basically, Dad just watched and waved. He joined us on simple water rides or rides that did not contain upside down loops or speed. At Oceans of Fun, we went on many waterslides together. We swam in the waves. It's less scary than the World of Fun's rides. So, Dad was able to do much more stuff at the Ocean of Fun. I don't remember if we communicated much, but I know I had a fun time doing things with Dad because he did not have to work.

My relationship with each member of my family is different. I see my brother most because he lives in Lincoln, not far from me. Mother comes to visit me every year, and sometimes Walt too. We take vacations together, and of course, I go to New Orleans some years for Mardi Gras or holidays.

As for my father, he does love me and my brother, but in a very different way. He treats me and my brother kindly, but does not talk or communicate with us much. Work was his life most of his years.

Father and his second wife, Linda, do not live near me. We only see each other a few times a year, mostly on holidays. Sometimes I go to their home, but more often they come to mine. I really don't have much of a relationship with my stepsister Brandi, who lives in Denver. I don't see her often, and didn't even when we were younger. She had a different life than I did, so we do not have a close friendship.

Do I have goals on where I want to travel and what I want to see next? Basically, I do want to see ALL, as I enjoy experiencing different environments and cultures. Plus, travel is a nice way to get out of the town and have fun. I choose my travel to be both fun as well as educational. I love to go to the beach to relax and catch some sunbathing, and spend few days with learning adventures. I would like to travel to more islands because they have the most beautiful beaches.

I will continue to travel until I no long can. I have been to all fifty states and five continents so far. And yes, I am going to finish all seven continents one day. I need only to visit Africa and Antarctica.

As of now, 2012, I am in my eleventh year working at the University of Nebraska–Lincoln. I enjoy teaching to hearing college students because I want them to be aware about deafness and American Sign Language. Everyone needs to understand being deaf is no difference than being hearing except being able to hear.

During my free time at home, I usually watch a lot of movies on any topic. From the worst to best movies! As you already know I love CATS! I play and spend time with my five spoiled rotten cats. They are REALLY spoiled by me! I want to save all cats, but I know I can't, so I volunteer at The Cat House, a no-kill shelter. I donate money annually to support their expenses. If I am rich, I would build the bigggggggest shelter for all cats. Basically, my life is like the state of Nebraska's motto: Nebraska, the good life! So is mine.

After John and Amy graduated from high school, I planned to indulge myself in adult relationships. The only problem with my plan: no one was beating a path to my door, so I became involved in Grand Island community theater, church activities, exercise programs, and night classes at our community college.

Several years into my employment with the federal government, I spent a week in Washington, D.C., to attend a conference. There I met coworkers from across the nation that I had talked to for years on conference calls. Among those I met was Walt Gernon, my cohort from the New Orleans office. We had an instant connection, perhaps because of our weird sense of humor. Like me, he was divorced and a single parent, raising his son alone, but with one difference: he was in a relationship. We became telephone and e-mail buddies.

In 1997, a pending reduction in force (RIF) had Walt and me on edge. The New Orleans Office survived the RIF, but my office in Grand Island was closed. My job took me to Denver. This was a good location for me. Amy was now teaching school in Santa Fe, so she was eight hours south of me on I-25, and John, who now owned

Walt and Amy in their penguin outfits taking in the sights of Mardi Gras 2009 in New Orleans.

a computer networking business in Lincoln, was eight hours east of me on I-80. Walt and I continued our email friendship.

Five years after we first met, Walt and I participated in a special government project in Miami. The sparks were still there, and this time he was footloose and fancy free. The airlines loved our long-distance relationship.

In January, shortly before Amy's thirty-first birthday, Walt and I drove from Denver to Santa Fe so he could meet her. Amy's deafness was no surprise, since we had talked about our children for years. Walt's son, Nick, was now in college.

Walt was slightly apprehensive about meeting Amy, not because of the language barrier, but because we planned to be married. He was seeking her approval.

"I can always write notes," Walt said.

"Absolutely," I replied.

"I'll figure out a way to connect with her," Walt said. "From all you've told me, she's adapted well to living in the hearing world. I'm sure we'll get along fine."

"So am I, but your moustache might be a problem." Walt frowned. "It's hard to read lips with a caterpillar on it."

Rebecca and Amy on the Alaskan cruise, July 2011.

"Too bad. I'm not shaving it off," he said. "I've had it for years."

The meeting went well, as did a visit with John the following month.

I had been divorced for twenty-five years when we married on July 4, 2000. John, Amy, and Nick were our only guests. I love fireworks and now I could enjoy them every year on our anniversary.

Marriage brought early retirement for me, which gave me the opportunity to pursue my love of writing. I moved from the mile-high dry air of Denver to the muggy, buggy South. Within a year of moving to New Orleans, I helped Amy move to Lincoln, Nebraska, which made visiting her, John, and two of my sisters easier since they all live in Nebraska.

Amy needed low-cost housing that would allow pets. Her best option was moving in with her brother in his home. She promised him it would be short term. Five years later, in 2006, she moved into a home she had built to her specifications. Living together gave John the opportunity to become fluent in sign. I was and still am jealous.

In 2007 for Thanksgiving, John, Amy, Walt, and I cruised through the islands of the Eastern Caribbean. Walt's son, Nick, was invited to join us, but being a New Orleans homicide detective means he is always busy. In Antigua, Amy played her "ultimate choice card" and forced us all to ride scooters under water. We swam with sting rays in St. Thomas, and at night Amy and I enjoyed the penny slots in the shipboard casino while Walt and John relaxed on the balcony with drinks.

I generally see John and Amy three or four times a year. They have attended Mardi Gras several times. Amy helped me make four penguin outfits one year, and Princess and the Frog costumes the following year. When here, she and Walt have played golf, attended a Hornets basketball game, and of course gone to parades. As I have always done, so Amy will feel included, our family events are activities where excellent communication is not needed to have a good time. Walt retires in December 2012, and we are planning to take a Mediterranean cruise in honor of John and Amy's forty-fifth birthdays and his retirement. I hope Nick and his wife Fran can join us, but solving crimes and prosecuting criminals consumes most of their time.

Where has the time gone? I'm only forty-seven (or at least I think I am); how can I have children this old?

My life is not as I imagined, but it is good. I have a loving husband; John, Amy, and Nick are all successful adults. Would I change things in my life? Yes, who wouldn't? I'd be tall like Julia Roberts and rich like Bill Gates, but I would not change the decisions I made for Amy. I love and embrace her as she is—an accomplished woman, my namesake, and my favorite daughter, who just happens to be Deaf.